Prince of Networks

Anamnesis

Anamnesis means remembrance or reminiscence, the collection and re-collection of what has been lost, forgotten, or effaced. It is therefore a matter of the very old, of what has made us who we are. But *anamnesis* is also a work that transforms its subject, always producing something new. To recollect the old, to produce the new: that is the task of *Anamnesis*.

a re.press series

Prince of Networks: Bruno Latour and Metaphysics

Graham Harman

re.press Melbourne 2009

re.press

PO Box 40, Prahran, 3181, Melbourne, Australia
http://www.re-press.org

British Library Cataloguing-in-Publication Data
A catalogue record for this book is available from the British Library

Library of Congress Cataloguing-in-Publication Data
A catalogue record for this book is available from the Library of Congress

National Library of Australia Cataloguing-in-Publication Data
A catalogue record for this book is available from the National Library of Australia

ISBN: 978-0-9805440-6-0 (paper)
ISBN: 978-0-9806665-2-6 (ebook)

Designed and Typeset by *A&R*

This book is produced sustainably using plantation timber, and printed in the destination market reducing wastage and excess transport.

Contents

Abbreviations

AR   *Aramis or the Love of Technology*, trans. Catherine Porter, Cambridge, Harvard University Press, 1996.

FD   *La Fabrique du Droit. Une ethnographie du Conseil d'Etat*, Paris, Découverte, 2002.

LL   *Laboratory Life. The Construction of Scientific Facts*, with Steve Woolgar, Princeton, Princeton University Press, 1986.

MB   'Can We Get Our Materialism Back, Please?', *Isis*, no. 98, 2007, pp. 138-142.

MP   'From Realpolitik to Dingpolitik, or How to Make Things Public,' in Bruno Latour and Peter Weibel (eds.), *Making Things Public: Atmospheres of Democracy*, Cambridge, MIT Press, 2005.

NM   *We Have Never Been Modern*, trans. Catherine Porter, Cambridge, Harvard University Press, 1993.

PE   'On the Partial Existence of Existing and Nonexisting Objects,' in Lorraine Daston (ed.), *Biographies of Scientific Objects*, Chicago, University of Chicago Press, 2006.

PH   *Pandora's Hope: Essays on the Reality of Science Studies*, Cambridge, Harvard University Press, 1999.

PF   *The Pasteurization of France*, trans. Alan Sheridan and John Law, Cambridge, Harvard University Press, 1988.

PN   *Politics of Nature: How to Bring the Sciences Into Democracy*, trans.
          Catherine Porter, Cambridge, Harvard University Press, 2004.

RS   *Reassembling the Social: An Introduction to Actor-Network-Theory*,
          Oxford, Oxford University Press, 2005.

SA   *Science in Action. How to Follow Scientists and Engineers Through
          Society*, Cambridge, Harvard University Press, 1987.

VI   *Paris ville invisible*, Paris, Editions la Découverte, 1998. Available
          in English at http://www.bruno-latour.fr/virtual/index.html#

introduction

The LSE Event

The initial manuscript of this book was discussed at the London School of Economics on 5 February, 2008 at a daylong symposium entitled 'The Harman Review: Bruno Latour's Empirical Metaphysics'. The host for the event was the Innovation Systems and Information Group in the LSE Department of Management, and warm support was provided by its Head, Professor Leslie Willcocks. Bruno Latour was in attendance to respond to the manuscript. The panel discussion was chaired by Edgar Whitley, with additional presentations by Lucas Introna, Noortje Marres, and the author of this book. Frances White provided critical help in organizing the event. The Symposium Organising Committee emphasised further the highly international flavor of the event, featuring Aleksi Altonen, Ofer Engel, Peter Erdélyi, and Wifak Houij Gueddana (all doctoral candidates) and Dr. Maha Shaikh. In addition, some forty-five specially invited participants were in the audience that day.

In the words of Erdélyi: 'It was such an unusual and unlikely event; even in retrospect it is difficult to believe it actually had taken place. What are the chances of hosting a metaphysical debate between a Heideggerian philosopher and a sociologist known for his dislike of Heidegger on the grounds of a management school, organised by PhD students of an information systems department?'[1] The chances are greatly increased when an energetic and visionary group like ANTHEM is involved. The acronym stands for 'Actor-Network Theory-Heidegger Meeting'. Thanks to Erdélyi and his friends in ANTHEM my intellectual life over the last two years

---

1. Peter Erdélyi, 'Remembering the Harman Review'. Blog post at http://www.anthem-group.net/tag/the-harman-review/

3

has been greatly enriched, and this book was able to become a public actor long before publication in its current, final format. Though I normally avoid 'acknowledgments' sections in books from fear of making my readers feel bored or excluded, Erdélyi's group is not boring and excludes nobody. It is worthwhile to join ANTHEM's mailing list and browse their website: http://www.anthem-group.net/

Another non-boring, non-exclusive person is Latour himself. At various stages of writing this book I received the warmest possible treatment from Bruno and Chantal Latour—in Cairo, Paris, and at the Latour 'hut' in Châtelperron dans l'Allier. Latour has responded graciously to my queries from as early as 1999, when I was just an obscure and unpublished fresh Ph.D. struggling in Chicago. But there are countless such stories of Latour's openness to the young and the unknown, and readers of this book may one day discover this for themselves.

Preface

This book is the first to consider Bruno Latour as a key figure in metaphysics—a title he has sought but rarely received. Latour has long been prominent in the fields of sociology and anthropology, yet the philosophical basis of his work remains little known. While his many admirers are seldom concerned with metaphysical questions, those hermits and outcasts who still pursue 'first philosophy' are generally unfamiliar with Latour. My aim is to bring these two groups into contact by expressing Latourian insights in terms bearing on the basic structure of reality itself. When the centaur of classical metaphysics is mated with the cheetah of actor-network theory, their offspring is not some hellish monstrosity, but a thoroughbred colt able to carry us for half a century and more. Though Latour's career has unfolded largely in the social sciences, his origins lie in a rigorous traditional education in philosophy marked by a strongly Jesuit flavour. His choice of topics, his wit, and his literary style are those of a contemporary, yet his works are a contribution to disputes over metaphysics traceable to ancient Greece.

As often happens with the most significant thinkers, Latour is attacked simultaneously for opposite reasons. For mainstream defenders of science, he is just another soft French relativist who denies the reality of the external world. But for disciples of Bloor and Bourdieu, his commerce with non-humans makes him a sellout to fossilized classical realism. In Latour's own works, however, this tiresome strife between objective physical matter and subjective social force gives way to a more fascinating theme: *objects*, which he generally calls 'actors' or 'actants'. Unlike Heidegger and others, Latour takes apples, vaccines, subway trains, and radio towers seriously as topics of philosophy. Such actors are not mere images hovering before the human mind, not just crusty aggregates atop an objective stratum of real microparticles, and not sterile abstractions imposed on a pre-individual flux or becoming. Instead, actors are autonomous forces to reckon with, unleashed in the world like leprechauns and wolves.

The first part of this book considers Latour's metaphysical position as developed in four key works: *Irreductions* (1984), *Science in Action* (1987), *We Have Never Been Modern* (1991), and *Pandora's Hope* (1999). Beginning in 1987, Latour also worked secretly on a mammoth alternate version of his system—which makes him surely the only philosopher in history to undergo his early and later phases simultaneously. The 'later Latour' is partly inspired by the forgotten French thinker Etienne Souriau (1892-1979), and Latour often describes his hidden system with Souriau's own catchphrase: 'the different modes of existence'. Latour's new philosophy was partly unveiled to participants in a June 2007 colloquium in Cerisy-la-salle, Normandy. But the manuscript discussed in Cerisy was merely a working draft, and at present there is no finalized later system or even a single later book that might be discussed here without pre-empting Latour's own rights as an author. For this reason, I confine myself to the Bruno Latour who can be known from the key works published through 1999. As I see it, this is also the best way to prepare oneself for whatever new works appear under Latour's name in the years to come.

The second part of the book considers the merits and drawbacks of Latourian metaphysics, which I hold to be the most underrated philosophy of our time. Given that Latour's strictly philosophical position is not widely known, I will present him as a largely *sui generis* figure, though this is only a half-truth. It would certainly be fruitful to consider Latour's similarities and differences with fellow non-analytic/non-continental (i.e., basically non-Kantian) thinkers such as Alfred North Whitehead, Henri Bergson, William James, Gilles Deleuze, Michel Serres, Gilbert Simondon, Gabriel Tarde, Etienne Souriau, and Latour's own friend Isabelle Stengers. But when this emerging 'School X' is promoted under such misleading titles as 'process philosophy' or 'philosophy of immanence', the result is a false sense of beatnik brotherhood. For in fact, there is a major family quarrel underway on this list over a highly classical problem: the isolation and interbleeding of individual things. On one side are figures like Bergson and Deleuze, for whom a generalized becoming precedes any crystallization into specific entities. On the other side we find authors such as Whitehead and Latour, for whom entities are so highly definite that they vanish instantly with the slightest change in their properties. For the first group, substance is too determinate to be real; for the second, it is too indeterminate to be real. But Latour's own standpoint deserves special illumination before it is lost amidst the turmoil of civil war.

the metaphysics of latour

Irreductions

Bruno Latour was born in 1947 in Beaune, in the Burgundy region of France. The town's cobbled ramparts and outdoor cafés make it a favourite of travelers, and its popular wines are enjoyed even by the fictional Sherlock Holmes. For generations, the philosopher's family has produced the famous Louis Latour label of wines; the family estate at Aloxe-Corton is easily visible on organized vineyard tours heading north from Beaune. Latour is a friendly and approachable figure, a tall man fond of good cigars and good jokes. He is married with two adult children, and resides in a comfortable flat on the rue Danton in the Latin Quarter of Paris. After working for many years at the Centre de Sociologie de l'Innovation at the Ecole des Mines in Paris, he recently moved to a senior administrative post at the Institut d'études politiques de Paris (or Sciences-Po, as it is commonly known). His greatest intellectual impact has probably been in the Anglophone world, where he is a frequent guest of our elite universities.

Latour's early schooling blended rigorous Jesuit classicism with a private fondness for Nietzsche. Following study at the University of Dijon, national service duties took him to the Ivory Coast. His increasing interest in fieldwork while in Africa set the stage for his long visit to Roger Guillemin's neuroendocrinology lab near San Diego, where Latour's famous program of the 'anthropology of the sciences' began. This period culminated in his first book, co-authored with the British sociologist Steve Woolgar, published in 1979 as *Laboratory Life*. This early work shows the influence of the so-called 'Strong Program' of the Edinburgh School of the sociology of science, with its infamous anti-realist tendencies. Nonetheless, even Latour's first book escapes the strict form of social constructionism, since real inanimate objects are responsible for constructing facts no less than are power-hungry humans. In later works, Latour moved even further from the constructivist vision of reality, and now occupies a strange middle ground misunderstood from all sides. On one flank, he is either praised by Rorty[1] or condemned by Sokal and Bricmont[2] as the latest in a long parade of French relativists who deny the objective reality of the world. On the other, he is banished from the constructivist fold by Bloor[3] as a tin man tainted by realism, a compromised if witty reactionary who pulls up short of explaining science by social factors. Latour's middle ground between these positions is not an eclectic compromise mixing elements of both, but marks a position of basically greater philosophical depth. The following chapters aim to present Latour's standpoint in accessible and memorable form.

'Any argument about my "philosophy,"' Latour writes, 'has to start with *Irreductions*, which is a totally orphan book'.[4] The orphan in question is really only half a book—a ninety-page appendix attached to the masterful study known in English as *The Pasteurization of France*. Latour has never written anything as compact and systematic as this small treatise, nor anything so unjustly ignored. Here I will take him at his word, and treat *Irreductions* as the gateway to the rest of his philosophy, despite his caveat that he is 'not sure how much [he] holds to these aphorisms'.[5] If Latour eventually abandons some of the claims in this treatise, we should first adopt them in order to share in their later abandonment. Written at a time when the phrase 'French philosophy' was merely a collective nickname in the Anglophone mind for Michel Foucault and Jacques Derrida, *Irreductions* belongs to what I regard as a more advanced stage of philosophy than either of these figures. Although the first principle of this early work is that 'nothing is, by itself, either reducible or irreducible to anything else' (PF, p. 158), the book is surely irreducible to either of the rival schools of analytic and continental philosophy. Latour's taste for clear academic prose no more qualifies him for the first group than his French passport admits him to the second.

A. THE BIRTH OF A PHILOSOPHY

Late in 1972, a remarkable young thinker was driving his Citroën van along the highways of Burgundy. Only twenty-five years old, already married, he was teaching at a village *lycée* and preparing for national service in Africa. In one respect the young philosopher was an outsider, emerging from remote

1. Richard Rorty, *Truth and Progress: Philosophical Papers, Volume 3*, Cambridge, Cambridge University Press, 1998, p. 8.

2. Alan Sokal and Jean-Luc Bricmont, *Fashionable Nonsense*, New York, Picador, 1998.

3. David Bloor, 'Anti-Latour', *Studies in the History of the Philosophy of Science*, vol. 30, no. 1, March 1999, pp. 81-112.

4. Personal Communication, Electronic mail to Graham Harman of 11 November, 2005.

5. Personal Communication, 11 November, 2005.

Dijon rather than the elite institutions of Paris. Yet this provincial outlier
had also ranked first nationally in the *Agrégation*, a stunning success that
must have felt like a license to speculate as freely as he wished. Too little
has been written about dramatic flashes of insight in the history of philosophy. We know of Descartes's dreams and his stove-heated room, Rousseau
weeping under a tree, and Avicenna saying prayers and giving money to the
poor after reading Farabi's commentary on Aristotle. But we are unfamiliar with the breakthrough moments of Heidegger, Kant, Leibniz, or Plato,
though we know these moments well for every Zen monk worth his salt.
In *Irreductions*, Latour joins the minority by publishing his own moment of
epiphany: 'I taught at Gray in the French provinces for a year. At the end
of the winter of 1972, on the road from Dijon to Gray, I was forced to stop,
brought to my senses after an overdose of reductionism' (PF, p. 162). There
follows a Homeric catalog of various humans who like to reduce the world
to some special reality that explains all the others: Christians, Catholics, astronomers, mathematicians, philosophers, Hegelians, Kantians, engineers,
administrators, intellectuals, bourgeoisie, Westerners, writers, painters, se-
mioticians, males, militants, and alchemists. All these reducers had finally
managed to repel the young Latour, who sat on the roadside dreaming of a
new principle of philosophy:

> I knew nothing, then, of what I am writing now but simply repeated to
> myself: 'Nothing can be reduced to anything else, nothing can be de-
> duced from anything else, everything may be allied to everything else'.
> This was like an exorcism that defeated demons one by one. It was a win-
> try sky, and a very blue. I no longer needed to prop it up with a cosmolo-
> gy, put it in a picture, render it in writing, measure it in a meteorological
> article, or place it on a Titan to prevent it falling on my head [...]. It and
> me, them and us, we mutually defined ourselves. And for the first time in
> my life I saw things unreduced and set free (PF, p. 163).

An entire philosophy is foreshadowed in this anecdote. Every human and
nonhuman object now stands by itself as a force to reckon with. No actor,
however trivial, will be dismissed as mere noise in comparison with its essence, its context, its physical body, or its conditions of possibility. Everything
will be absolutely concrete; all objects and all modes of dealing with objects
will now be on the same footing. In Latour's new and unreduced cosmos,
philosophy and physics both come to grips with forces in the world, but so
do generals, surgeons, nannies, writers, chefs, biologists, aeronautical engineers, and seducers (PF, pp. 154-6). And though all these examples of actors
are human, they are no different *in kind* from the forces that draw objects to
the center of the earth or repress desires in the unconscious. The world is
a series of negotiations between a motley armada of forces, humans among
them, and such a world cannot be divided cleanly between two pre-existent
poles called 'nature' and 'society'. As Latour puts it: 'we do not know what

forces there are, nor their balance. We do not want to reduce anything to anything else [...]. What happens when nothing is reduced to anything else? What happens when we suspend our knowledge of what a force is? What happens when we do not know how their way of relating to one another is forever changing?' (PF, pp. 156-7). What happens is the birth of an object-oriented philosophy.

Latour always insists that we cannot philosophize from raw first principles but must follow objects in action and describe what we see. Empirical studies are more important for him than for almost any other philosopher; later in his career, he will even speak of an 'experimental metaphysics' (PN, pp. 123, 241-2). Nonetheless, there are a small number of basic principles that guide his vast empirical labours. In *Irreductions*, Latour's first philosophical treatise, there seem to be four central ideas from which the others blossom.

First, the world is made up of *actors* or *actants* (which I will also call 'objects'). Atoms and molecules are actants, as are children, raindrops, bullet trains, politicians, and numerals. All entities are on exactly the same ontological footing. An atom is no more real than Deutsche Bank or the 1976 Winter Olympics, even if one is likely to endure much longer than the others. This principle ends the classical distinction between natural substance and artificial aggregate proposed most candidly by Leibniz. It also ends the tear-jerking modern rift between the thinking human subject and the unknowable outside world, since for Latour the isolated Kantian human is no more and no less an actor than are windmills, sunflowers, propane tanks, and Thailand. Finally, it shows the deep ambivalence of Latour's relationship with Aristotle. For in one sense, Latour joins Aristotle in insisting that what is real are only concrete entities. The billions of cats in the world are real individuals, not a single cat-form stamped in despicable clots of corrupt physical matter. But in another sense, Latour takes concreteness in a more radical direction than Aristotle would permit. For Aristotle, individuals are substances—and substances are deeper than their accidents and their relations to other things, and capable of enduring despite changes in these inessential features. For Latour, by contrast, an actant is not a privileged inner kernel encrusted with peripheral accidents and relations. After all, this would make a thing's surface derivative of its depth, thereby spoiling the principle of irreduction. There cannot be an essential Socrates hiding behind the Socrates who happens to be speaking and wearing white at this very moment. For Latour, a thing is so utterly concrete that none of its features can be scraped away like cobwebs or moss. All features belong to the actor itself: a force utterly deployed in the world at any given moment, entirely characterized by its full set of features.

Second, there is the principle of *irreduction* itself. No object is inherently reducible or irreducible to any other. In one sense we can never explain religion as the result of social factors, World War I as the result of rail timetables, or the complex motion of bodies as pure examples of Newtonian physics. Yet in another sense we can *always* attempt such explanations, and sometimes they are fairly convincing. It is always possible to explain anything in terms of anything else—as long as we do the work of showing how one can be transformed into the other, through a chain of equivalences that always has a price and always risks failure.

Third, the means of linking one thing with another is *translation*. When Stalin and Zhukov order the encircling movement at Stalingrad, this is not a pure dictate trumpeted through space and transparently obeyed by the participant actors. Instead, a massive work of mediation occurs. Staff officers draw up detailed plans with large-scale maps that are then translated into individual platoon orders at the local level; officers then relay the orders, each making use of his own rhetorical style and personal rapport with the soldiers; finally, each individual soldier has to move his arms and legs independently to give final translation to the orders from above. Surprising obstacles arise, and some orders need to be improvised—the enemy melts away at unexpected points but puts up stubborn resistance in equally startling places. Moving from war to logic, we find that even logical deductions do not move at the speed of light. Deductions too are transformed one step at a time through different layers of concepts, adjusting themselves to local conditions at each step, deciding at each step where the force of the deduction lies and where possible variations can be addressed or ignored. No layer of the world is a transparent intermediary, since each is a medium: or in Latour's preferred term, a *mediator*. A mediator is not some sycophantic eunuch fanning its masters with palm-leaves, but always does new work of its own to shape the translation of forces from one point of reality to the next. Here as elsewhere, Latour's guiding maxim is to grant dignity even to the least grain of reality. Nothing is mere rubble to be used up or trampled by mightier actors. Nothing is a mere intermediary. Mediators speak, and other mediators resist.

Fourth, actants are not stronger or weaker by virtue of some inherent strength or weakness harbored all along in their private essence. Instead, actants gain in strength only through their *alliances*. As long as no one reads Mendel's papers, his breakthroughs in genetics remain weak. An airplane crashes if a few hydraulic lines malfunction, but the resistance of these lines is weakened in turn if they are discovered and exiled to a garbage dump. For Latour, an object is neither a substance nor an essence, but an actor trying to adjust or inflict its forces, not unlike Nietzsche's cosmic vision of the will to power.

Although Latour generally opposes reducing multiplicities to simple explanatory structures, his four metaphysical axioms all stem from a deeper principle: absolute concreteness. Every actant simply is what it is. This entails that all actants are on the same footing: both large and small, both human and nonhuman. No actant is just fodder for others; each enhances and resists the others in highly specific ways. Since every actant is entirely concrete, we do not find its reality in some lonely essence or chaste substrate, but always in an absolutely specific place in the world, with completely specific alliances at any given moment. Everything is immanent in the world; nothing transcends actuality. In other words, Latour is proudly guilty of what Roy Bhaskar and Manuel DeLanda both call 'actualism'. For Latour the world is a field of objects or actants locked in trials of strength—some growing stronger through increased associations, others becoming weaker and lonelier as they are cut off from others.

Latour's difference from present-day analytic and continental thought should now be clear. Whereas Latour places all human, nonhuman, natural, and artificial objects on the same footing, the analytics and continentals both still dither over how to bridge, ignore, deny, or explain away a single gap between humans and world. While graduate students are usually drilled in a stale dispute between correspondence and coherence theories of truth, Latour locates truth in neither of these models, but in a series of translations between actors. And whereas mainstream philosophy worries about whether things exist independently of us or are constructed by the mind, Latour says they are 'socially' constructed not just by human minds, but also by bodies, atoms, cosmic rays, business lunches, rumors, physical force, propaganda, or God. There is no privileged force to which the others can be reduced, and certainly no ceaseless interplay between pure natural forces and pure social forces, each untainted by the other. Nothing exists but *actants*, and all of them are utterly concrete.

B. ACTANTS, IRREDUCTION, TRANSLATION, ALLIANCE

Having abandoned the Kantian landscape of the analytics and continentals, Latour enters exotic terrain. His philosophy unfolds not amidst the shifting fortunes of a bland human-world correlate, but in the company of all possible actants: pine trees, dogs, supersonic jets, living and dead kings, strawberries, grandmothers, propositions, and mathematical theorems. These long lists of random actors must continue until their plurality and autonomy is no longer suppressed. We still know nothing about these objects or what they entail. All that is clear is their metaphysical equality. The world is a stage filled with actors; philosophy is object-oriented philosophy.

But as already noted, this does not lead Latour to a philosophy of substance. Traditional substance can be defined by contrast with its qualities, accidents, and relations. A substance can easily be distinguished from its own qualities, such as warmth or villainy, since these traits may change over time without the thing becoming a different thing. In fact, one of Aristotle's best definitions of a substance is that which supports different qualities at different times. We can also distinguish a thing from its accidents, as when a person wears a particular fluorescent shirt, since this garment can be removed or replaced without the wearer changing identity. Finally, a substance is distinct from its relations, since it remains the same thing whether it is positioned three or fifty meters away from me. In this way traditional substance remains identical beneath all its trivial surface fluctuations, and this immediately suggests that the thing has an essence. But Latour emphatically rejects this rift between an inner substance and its trivial exterior. His 'actant' is a concrete individual, but not a nucleus of reality surrounded by shifting vapors of accidental and relational properties. There is another obvious difference between Latour and the substance-thinkers as well. Aristotle and his heirs grant the title of 'substance' only to certain privileged things in the world, usually those that exist by nature. A cat, a tree, or a soul would be substances, but not the nation of Egypt or vast machines with thousands of parts. But since Latour grants all actants an equal right to existence, regardless of size or complexity, all natural and artificial things must count as actants as long as they have some sort of effect on other things.

This brings us to a related point. For Latour an actant is always an *event*, and events are always completely specific: 'everything happens only once, and at once place' (PF, p. 162). An actant does not hedge its bets, lying behind its current involvements in the manner of a substance eluding its surface fluctuations. Instead, an actant is always completely deployed in the world, fully implicated in the sum of its dealings at any given moment. Unlike a substance, an actant is not distinct from its qualities, since for Latour this would imply an indefensible featureless lump lying beneath its tangible properties. Also unlike a substance, actants do not differ from their accidents, since this would create a hierarchy in which some parts of the world were mere detritus floating on a deeper sea, and Latour's principle of democracy between actants would thereby be violated. And unlike a substance, actants are not different from their relations. Indeed, Latour's central thesis is that an actor is its relations. All features of an object belong to it; everything happens only once, at one time, in one place. But this means that Latour rejects another well-known feature of traditional substance: its durability. We generally speak of the same dog existing on different days over many years, but for Latour this would ultimately be no more than a figure of speech. It would entail that we abstract an enduring dog-substance or dog-essence from an entire network of relations or trials of strength in which the dog is involved at each moment of its life. Ultimately the unified 'dog' is a sequence of closely related heirs, not an enduring unit encrusted with shifting accidents over time.

Since an actant cannot be split into durable substance and transient accident, it follows that *nothing* can be reduced to anything else. Each thing simply is what it is, in utter concreteness. We cannot reduce a thing to some privileged inner core by stripping away its inessential features. But at the same time, *anything* can be reduced to anything else, provided the proper labour is done. This two-faced principle of irreduction is less paradoxical than it seems, since both faces stem from the same basic insight. To reduce one thing to another is to see it as an effect explainable in terms of a more fundamental layer of reality. Can we reduce the frenzy of flagellant nuns to sexual frustration? Yes and no. On Latourian principles, this flagellation is a concrete event in the world, just as real as any other, and cannot be explained away as a hypocritical symptom masking the sole underlying reality of the sex drive. Yet Latour is also not some postmodern champion of disjointed simulacra, as if nothing could ever be derived from anything else. The behavior of the nuns certainly might have an explanation that differs from their own accounts of it. Yet to establish this connection involves theoretical labour: studying the nuns, carefully observing the exact nature and rhythm of their punishment, its connection or lack thereof with other rituals or symptoms, and perhaps interviews by trained psychiatric observers. It also requires a willingness to modify our approach if reality resists it in any way. Finally, a successful reading of the nuns in terms of drives will pay a price even when successful: namely, it will suppress all additional features of their actions, leading inevitably to distortion and oversimplification. In this sense, a theorist is no different from an engineer digging a tunnel through the mountains near Barcelona. One studies the rock, carefully assessing its weak and solid points, the cost of selecting one path over another, the safety concerns of workers, the availability of drill bits needed for specific tunneling methods, and other such factors. The engineer is not a free-floating mastermind of stockpile and calculation, as Heidegger imagines. Instead, the engineer must *negotiate* with the mountain at each stage of the project, testing to see where the rock resists and where it yields, and is quite often surprised by the behavior of the rock. The same is true of a historian studying the nuns, a lover deciding when to show vulnerability and when unyielding strength, a food taster detecting the faint signals of poison, and an artillery officer gauging the proper angle of a gun. All are engaged in the same exercise, however different their materials may be.

Nothing is pure calculation, nothing follows directly from anything else, nothing is a transparent intermediary. Everything is a mediator, demanding its share of reality as we pass through it toward our goal. Every medium must be negotiated, just as air and water strike back at the vehicles that traverse them. Since every actant is only itself, and always a totally concrete event, it is impossible to derive one thing instantly from another without the needed labour. In other words, the link between actors always requires *translation*. In the case of the nuns, only the most arrogant critical debunker would smirk while unmasking the erotic roots of their frenzy in a matter of seconds. Note that Freud himself never does this: his dream interpretations involve painstaking translations from one image or symbol to the next, often requiring so many intermediate stages that his opponents mock their unlikely complexity. For this reason, truth for Latour is never a simple correspondence between the world and statements that resemble it, since we can only link a statement to the world through the most difficult set of displacements. But neither is truth a kind of 'unveiling', as in Heidegger's model, since this still implies that we approach truth asymptotically. For Latour, one thing never resembles another in the least, and for this reason correspondence and unveiling are equally fruitless models of truth.

This brings us to the last of Latour's four major concepts: alliance. Since actants are utterly concrete, they do not have an inner kernel or essence encrusted with trivial additional properties. Actants are always completely deployed in their relations with the world, and the more they are cut off from these relations, the less real they become. Pasteur initially stands alone in his fight with Liebig over the cause of fermentation, or with Pouchet over spontaneous generation (PH, Chap. 4). Gradually, Pasteur amasses a formidable army of allies. But notice that not all of these allies are human. Despite the word 'Prince' in my title, Latour is no Machiavellian reducing truth to human power games. Instead, Pasteur's motley allies include mighty politicians who grant him funding, pieces of glassy or metallic equipment, and even bacilli themselves. Actors become more real by making larger portions of the cosmos vibrate in harmony with their goals, or by taking detours in their goals to capitalize on the force of nearby actants. For Latour, the words 'winner' and 'loser' are not inscribed in advance in the essence of a thing, since there is no essence in the first place. Any actant has a chance to win or lose, though some have more weaponry at their disposal. Winners and losers are inherently equal and must be treated symmetrically. The loser is the one who failed to assemble enough human, natural, artificial, logical, and inanimate allies to stake a claim to victory. The more connected an actant is, the more real; the less connected, the less real.

One of the most vigorous schools of contemporary philosophy is the small Slovenian circle associated with Slavoj Žižek. But Žižek himself speaks with embarrassment of his situation: 'Many of my friends think that if there is a Slovenian Lacanian School and we publish so much abroad, then what must happen in the center? The answer is nothing, absolutely nothing [...]. It is almost as if we are caught with our pants down when somebody comes to Ljubljana and then we just have to tell him that nothing is happening here'.[6] Though Žižek reads this predicament in terms of Lacan's 'void' or 'lack' at the center, a Latourian interpretation of Ljubljana is more convincing. Namely, Žižek's group is not a powerful essence housed in some mighty fortress of the Slovenian capital, but merely a network that mobilizes

---

6. Slavoj Žižek and Glyn Daly, *Conversations with Žižek*, Cambridge, Polity, 2003, p. 37.

disciples, publishers, and other allies throughout the globe. The supposed center is as frail and vulnerable as any other point in the network, just as Allied Supreme Headquarters could have been ruined on D-Day by an exploding water pipe or a sudden invasion of mice. In similar fashion, Bruno Latour as a thinker is found in the bookstores that carry his works, the admirers who recommend them to others, and the careers that are altered by contact with his writings. If we meet Latour in the Latin Quarter we will surely have a good conversation, but we may learn just as much from taking one of his books to Peru and discussing it with a random stranger. When we encounter Latour in person, trumpet blasts do not sound; trains of devotees do not follow him shaking tambourines in the street as we approach a glittering interior compound at Sciences-Po, from which new philosophy would emanate like radiation from Chernobyl. There is no central point in the network where we encounter the very heart of Latour and his philosophy. There is no inner Latour-essence wrapped in transient wool or chaff, but only a network of allies mobilized by his philosophy. Most of this network lies outside Latour's personal control, and much of it even remains unknown to him.

To repeat, actants do not draw their power from some pristine inner hearth, but only through assembling allies. This always entails risks, since 'forces are always rebellious [...] the concrete in the power station that cracks, the acryllic blues that consume other pigments, the lion that does not follow the predictions of the oracle [...]. The moment we turn our back, our closest friends enroll themselves under other banners' (PF, p. 198). The force of an actant remains in doubt, and hinges on a decision: 'As it associates elements together, every actor has a choice: to extend further, risking dissidence and dissociation, or to reinforce consistency and durability, but not go too far' (PF, p. 198). Further extension has only one method at its disposal:

> in order to spread far [...] an actant needs faithful allies who accept what they are told, identify itself with its cause, carry out all the functions that are defined for them, and come to its aid without hesitation when they are summoned. The search for these ideal allies occupies the space and time of those who wish to be stronger than others. As soon as an actor has found a *somewhat more faithful ally*, it can force another ally to become *more faithful* in its turn (PF, p. 199)

It is never the actant in naked purity that possesses force, but only the actant involved in its ramshackle associations with others, which collapse if these associations are not lovingly or brutally maintained: 'In order to extend itself, an actant must program other actants so that they are unable to betray it, despite the fact that they are bound to do so [...]. *We always misunderstand the strength of the strong*. Though people attribute it to the purity of an actant, it is invariably due to a tiered array of weaknesses' (PF, p. 201). Anticipating his later full-blown rejection of modernism, Latour scoffs at the notion that the imperialist West succeeded by purifying objective truth from the naïve superstition of gullible Indians. The Spaniards triumphed over the Aztecs not through the power of nature liberated from fetish, but instead through a mixed assemblage of priests, soldiers, merchants, princes, scientists, police, slavers (PF, pp. 202-3). Call them legion, for they are many. Imperialism is not an almighty center, but a chain of raggedy forces in equal parts spiritual, intellectual, and economic. The same sort of motley-coloured force is unleashed by politicians, and hence Latour is among the few present-day philosophers who admires politicians rather than sneering at their venal compromises: 'It takes something like courage to admit that we will *never do better* than a politician [... Others] simply have somewhere to hide when they have made their mistakes. They can go back and try again. Only the politician is limited to a single shot and has to shoot in public' (PF, p. 210). And again: 'What we despise as political "mediocrity" is simply the collection of compromises that we force politicians to make on our behalf' (PF, p. 210). The politician forever balances information, funding, threats, kindness, politeness, loyalty, disloyalty, and the perpetual search for ways and means. In this respect the politician is the model for every sort of actor. To declare oneself untainted by strife between conflicting forces is to deny that one is an actant.

Yet there are only actants, forever lost in friendships and duels. Any attempt to see actants as the reducible puppets of deeper structures is doomed to fail. The balance of force makes some actants stronger than others, but miniature trickster objects turn the tide without warning: a pebble can destroy an empire if the Emperor chokes at dinner. Forces are real, and real tigers are stronger than paper ones, but everything is negotiable (PF, p. 163). There is no pre-established harmony among the actants in the world, but only a *post*-established harmony (PF, p. 164). The current order of things is the result of a long history of negotiations and midnight raids of one actant against the weak points of others. It takes work to subordinate serfs to the Czar or equations to a theory. The world could have been otherwise. But neither is there merely a random play of chance, since the Tartar hordes do not vanish from the Middle East with a wave of the hand. Harmony is a result, not a guiding principle.

Even *power*, that favourite occult quality of radical political critics, is a result rather than a substance (PF, p. 191). The supposed 'panopticon' of modern society stands at the mercy of the technicians and bureaucrats who must install and maintain it, and who may go on strike or do a sloppy job because of bad moods. The police are outwitted by seven-year-olds in the slums. The mighty CIA, with its budget of billions, loses track of *mujahideen* riding donkeys and exchanging notes in milk bottles. A lovely Chinese double agent corrodes the moral fiber of Scotland Yard true believers. Actants must constantly be kept in line; none are servile puppets who do our bidding,

whether human or nonhuman. The world resists our efforts even as it welcomes them. Even a system of metaphysics is the lengthy result of negotiations with the world, not a triumphant deductive overlord who tramples the
details of the world to dust. The labour of fitting one concept to another ob-
sesses a Kant or Husserl for decades, and even then the polished final product will be riddled with errors detectible by a novice. The same is true for
our prisons, our gas and water infrastructure, the sale of potato chips, international law, nuclear test bans, and enrollment in universities. Systems are
assembled at great pains, one actant at a time, and loopholes always remain.
We are not the pawns of sleek power-machines grinding us beneath their
heels like pathetic *Nibelungen*. We may be fragile, but so are the powerful.

More controversially, Latour holds that even truth itself is a result, not
a starting point. 'A sentence does not hold together because it is true, but *because it holds together* we say that it is "true." What does it hold onto? Many
things. Why? Because it has tied its fate to anything at hand that is more
solid than itself. As a result, no one can shake it loose without shaking everything else' (PF, pp. 185-6). We call 'true' whatever has attached itself to
something more durable, less vulnerable to the resistance of other actants.
As Latour puts it with his typical irreverent wit, this is equally so for 'a problem in geometry, a genealogy, an underground network, a fight between
husband and wife, or the varnish painted on a canoe' (PF, p. 185). And further, 'this is why "logic" is a branch of public works. We can no more drive a
car on the subway than we can doubt the laws of Newton. *The reasons are the
same in each case*: distant points have been linked by paths that were narrow at
first and then were broadened and properly paved' (PF, p. 185). This may of-
fend hard-core scientific realists, but they should remember that the inability to drive a car on the subway is also real. It can certainly be done, but only
at the high cost of arrest or the expensive refitting of your car. Newton's laws
also *can* be doubted: but only at the cost of rejection by your professors and a
life sentence as an obscure Swiss patent officer if your equations contain errors or Eddington's observations rebut your theory. We are now amused to
think that there used to be two kinds of physics, one for the earth and one
for the sky. But it is equally absurd that we still recognize two different kinds
of reality: one for hard scientific fact and another for arbitrary social power.
What exists is only actants: cars, subways, canoe-varnish, quarreling spous-
es, celestial bodies, and scientists, all on the same metaphysical footing.

Despite certain frequent criticisms of Latour, this does not turn the world
into a matter of human perspective. For the world *does* resist human fabrication, just as human innovation resists polio deaths and the annual flooding of
the Nile. 'Anything does not go. Discourses and associations are not equivalent, because allies and arguments are enlisted precisely so that one association will be stronger than another. If all discourse appears to be equivalent,
if there seem to be "language games" and nothing more, then someone has

been unconvincing. This is the weak point of the relativists [...]. By repeating "anything goes," they miss the work that generates inequivalence and asymmetry' (PF, pp. 168-9).[7] Yet in another sense everything does go, as long as the price is paid and the work is successful. Perhaps we can travel to Pluto or even travel through time once centuries of research are expended on these projects. Perhaps we can use a telephone in Cairo to speak immediately with a friend in Honolulu—indeed, this is already possible, but only as a result of the most prolonged negotiations between chemists, copper cable, and leaders of business and state. Perhaps we can show that Lamarck was right and Darwin was wrong, but there will be a high cost in theoretical labour and initial public ridicule, and the efforts may ultimately fail. 'Nothing is by itself either logical or illogical, but not everything is equally convincing. There is only one rule: "anything goes;" say anything as long as those being talked to are convinced' (PF, p. 182). But never forget that 'those being talked to' and 'those to be convinced' include inanimate objects. A charlatan might convince a roomful of dupes that they can walk on hot coals without being harmed, but the coals remain unconvinced—leading the charlatan into lawsuits or beatings from his angry mob of victims. If you succeed in your dealings with humans, equations, or car engines, then 'those you sought to convince have acquiesced. For them, there is no more "anything goes." That will have to do, *for you will never do any better* [...]. We can say anything we please, and yet we cannot. As soon as we have spoken and rallied words, other alliances become easier or more difficult' (PF, p. 182).

The world is not made of stable, rock-solid forms, but only of front lines in a battle or love story between actants. Stable states are the result of numerous forces (PF, p. 198), just as the apparently timeless shapes of ducks or butterflies actually reflect a history of ancestral struggles. 'There is no *natural end* to [controversies...] In the end, interpretations are always stabilized by an array of *forces*' (PF, p. 197). The world is not packed with so-called natural kinds, but only with mutant objects that have struck a hard bargain with reality to become and remain as they are. 'We end up distinguishing shapes that can be classified, at least in peacetime. But these classifications never last for long before they are pillaged by other actors who lay things out quite differently' (PF, p. 195). But once again, the existing shapes and forms are never broken up in effortless fashion. They are real, and are invaded or transformed only by those who pay close attention to their real contours: 'despite everything, networks reinforce one another and resist destruction. Solid yet fragile, isolated yet interwoven, smooth yet twisted together, [they] form strange fabrics' (PF, p. 199).

Latour's rejection of natural kinds, isolated substances, and rock-hard billiard balls should never be confused with the triumph of relativist language

---

7. Punctuation modified slightly for ease of reading.

games. For he insists that things in themselves are real even when humans do not see them: 'if you missed the galloping freedom of the zebras in the savannah this morning, then so much the worse for you; the zebras will not be sorry that you were not there, and in any case you would have tamed, killed, photographed, or studied them. Things in themselves lack nothing [...]' (PF, p. 193). The same could be said not only of zebras, but of plastic and stars as well. Things themselves are actants—not signifieds, phenomena, or tools for human praxis. Latour makes the point with wicked mockery: 'Once things are reduced to nothing, they beg you to be conscious of them and ask you to colonize them. Their life hangs by nothing more than a thread, the thread of your attention [...]. Without you "the world," as you put it, would be reduced to nothing. You are the Zorros, the Tarzans, the Kants [...]' (PF, p. 193). Referring obviously to Heidegger, Latour taunts aloud: 'Who told you that man was the shepherd of being? Many forces would like to be shepherd and guide the others as they flock to their folds to be sheared and clipped. In any case there is no shepherd' (PF, p. 194). He closes with a final deserved slap at the wearisome 'linguistic turn' in philosophy: 'Recently there has been a tendency to privilege language [...]. Language was so privileged that its critique became the only worthy task for a generation of Kants and Wittgensteins [...]. What a fuss! Everything that is said of the signifier is right, but it must also be said of every other kind of [actant]. There is nothing special about language that allows it to be distinguished from the rest for any length of time' (PF, pp. 184-5).

Despite his rejection of language as the basis for all philosophy, Latour's focus on the concreteness of actants leads him to a surprising Derridean moment. Since actants are always fully deployed in the universe, with no true reality lying in reserve, Latour dismisses any distinction between literal and metaphorical meanings of words. As Latour himself puts it, in a manner reminiscent of Derrida's 'White Mythology': [8]

> Because there is no literal or figurative meaning, no single use of a metaphor can dominate the other uses. Without propriety there is no impropriety. Each word is accurate and designates exactly the networks that it traces, digs, and travels over. Since no word reigns over the others, we are free to use all metaphors. We do not have to fear that one meaning is 'true' and another 'metaphorical'. There is democracy, too, among words (PF, p. 189).

The agreement here between Latour and Derrida (a normally unthinkable alliance) stems from their shared impatience with Aristotle's theory of substance. There cannot be some true reality of a flower or sun lying beneath

---

8. Jacques Derrida, 'White Mythology', in *Margins of Philosophy*, trans. Alan Bass, Chicago, University of Chicago Press, 1985. I have criticized Derrida's argument in *Guerrilla Metaphysics: Phenomenology and the Carpentry of Things*, Chicago, Open Court, 2005, pp. 110-6.

their interactions with other elements of the world. Hence, any name for anything at all is democratically confined to this layer of interrelations. No name can refer more directly than another to some non-existent underworld where a veritable sun-essence or tree-essence would be housed. While this is admirably consistent with Latour's notion of actants, there are good reasons to maintain a sense of the proper reality of objects apart from all their alliances. I leave this disagreement to the later portions of this book.

Like the works of Whitehead, Nietzsche, or Leibniz, *Irreductions* views objects as individual perspectives on the rest. 'Every actant makes a whole world for itself. Who are we? What can we know? What can we hope for? The answers to these pompous questions define and modify their shapes and boundaries' (PF, p. 192). Needless to say, for Latour these questions are asked by coal and tar no less than by enlightened humans. Stated more poetically:

> I don't know how things stand. I know neither who I am nor what I want, but *others* say they know on my behalf, others, who define me, link me up, make me speak, interpret what I say, and enroll me. Whether I am a storm, a rat, a rock, a lake, a lion, a child, a worker, a gene, a slave, the unconscious, or a virus, they whisper to me, they suggest, they impose an interpretation of what I am and what I could be (PF, p. 192).

No Copernican philosopher, whether analytic or continental, could write such a paragraph. This brief passage runs counter to all that is assumed by Husserl, Heidegger, Derrida, Russell, or Quine. The absence of rats, lions, and lakes from mainstream philosophical debate speaks not against Bruno Latour, but against the bland default metaphysics that reduces objects to our human access to them.

C. SOME COROLLARIES

The central themes of Latour's early masterpiece are now on the table. We need only consider a few additional corollaries. First, all relations in the world are of only one kind: trials of strength. This is not a reduction of reality to power plays and social constructions, since this would imply that human social forces are superior to those of comets and atoms themselves. But if all actors are on the same footing, then all forces come in only one variety, however numerous its sub-brands may be. Our habitual need to wall off objective natural forces from contamination by arbitrary human forces is the symptom of a modernist purification that Latour will attack in a later book. He is neither Machiavelli nor Thrasymachus, since for him tyrants and demagogues must negotiate with the same animate and inanimate forces as do moralists and priests. To say that all reality involves trials of strength is to say that no actant eclipses another *a priori* and without further effort; all objects must jostle in the arena of the world, and none ever enjoys final victory. The losers may come back to haunt the winners, as when Rome grows both Christian and barbarized, or when buried ideas arise resurgent from their graves. 'To force I will add *nothing*', as the young Latour brashly puts it (PF, p. 213). 'A force establishes a pathway by making other forces passive. It can then move to places that do not belong to it and treat them as if they were its own. I am willing to talk about "logic," but only if it seen as a branch of public works or civil engineering' (PF, p. 171). Logic is a logistics in which some translations are better supplied with food and ammunition than others, and thereby prevail for a time. Latour's position has nothing to do with old-fashioned realism, since it places physical mass on the same level as puppet shows and courtroom hearings. It has nothing to do with social constructionism, for it is not limited to human society, which is pounded by the demands of nonhuman actants as if by waves of the ocean. It is not deconstruction, because even those who falsely sneer at 'those who claim that Derrida reduces the world to a text' must still admit that inanimate objects have no place in Derrida. It is not phenomenology, because an electric drill or vein of silver are not appearances for human consciousness, but actants that undermine whatever humans encounter of them. It is not like Heidegger, because there is not a unified rumble of being that surprises us with a multiplicity of somber moods and broken hammers, but only a single immanent plane where anxious Dasein is no better or worse than wineries, snakes, oil wells, and moons. Copernican philosophy has no concept of trials of strength, because it situates every trial on the home turf of human being, which is anointed as sole arbiter of every trial.

Furthermore, Latour defines reality as *resistance*. While the same had been done in the early twentieth century by Max Scheler and José Ortega y Gasset (and a century earlier by Maine de Biran in France), the thesis has a special role in Latour's system. Every actant is fully deployed in the networks of the world, with nothing hidden beneath all the surface-plays of alliance. It is fair enough to call the world a site of immanence, as long as we reject any notion that immanence means 'inside of human awareness'. For Latour, two atoms in collision are immanent even if no human ever sees them, since both expend themselves fully in the labour of creating networks with other actants. 'Since whatever resists is real, there can be no "symbolic" to add to the "real" [...]. I am prepared to accept that fish may be gods, stars, or food, that fish may make me ill and play different roles in origin myths [...]. Those who wish to *separate* the "symbolic" fish from its "real" counterpart should themselves be separated and confined' (PF, p. 188). What is shared in common by marine biologists, the fishing industry, and tribal elders telling myths about icthyian deities is this: none of them really *knows* what a fish is. [...]ust negotiate with the fish's reality, remaining alert to its hideouts, mi-[...]al patterns, and sacral or nutritional properties. [...] cannot begin by denouncing tribal elders as naïve dupes who project their primitive superstitions onto an objective underlying biological fish-animal. The fish resists all efforts to reduce it to a known set of traits. 'The real is not one thing among others, but rather gradients of resistance' (PF, p. 151). This leads Latour to a pair of more dubious statements that he would presumably no longer maintain: 'The principle of reality is other people. The interpretation of the real cannot be distinguished from the real itself because the real are gradients of resistance' (PF, p. 166). The reader will be forgiven for viewing the first sentence as sheer social constructionism. That is certainly what it sounds like, and there are no caveats anywhere in the vicinity to prevent such an interpretation. But recall that the principle of irreduction forbids raising 'people' to a loftier pinnacle of reality than anything else, and hence we can view this sentence as a rhetorical anomaly, spoken in the same provocative spirit as Latour's phrase 'like God, capitalism does not exist' (PF, p. 173), a statement not meant literally by this devout Catholic. As for the second part of the statement, 'the interpretation of the real cannot be distinguished from the real itself', the apparent social constructionism disappears if we consider the broad sense Latour gives to 'interpretation'. For this is not the lonely act of a privileged human entity: 'For a long time it has been agreed that the relationship between one text and another is always a matter for interpretation. Why not accept that this is also true between so-called texts and so-called objects, and even between so-called objects themselves?' (PF, p. 166). To say that the real is no different from its interpretation is not to say that objects are socially constructed, but only that they are constructed by all manner of networks and alliances, including inanimate ones.

This brings us to an even more provocative statement: 'We cannot distinguish between those moments when we have might and those when we are right' (PF, p. 183). Once again, the sophists and tyrants might seem to be entering Latour's house through the side door. If might and right cannot be distinguished, then the more powerful scientists will crush the superior experiments of unknown outsiders through their mighty political influence, thereby 'socially constructing' their discipline. Rational argument will be reduced to oratorical gimmicks, to power plays by those holding the strongest positions. But the problem with this criticism of Latour is that he never interprets 'might' as identical with the sphere of arbitrary human action. Gravity is also might; bird flu is might; quarks are might; a tsunami is might. Once we accept a world made of nothing but actants, we can accept that the world is a translation of forces without cynically reclining on couches, knowing better than all the gullible, moralized sheep that there is really nothing in the world but power. In fact, to explain anything in terms of 'power' is an act of intellectual laziness. 'The philosophers and sociologists of power flatter the masters they claim to criticize. They explain the masters' actions in terms of power, though this power is efficacious only as a result of complicities, connivances, compromises, and mixtures' (PF, p. 175). Once an actant succeeds in lining up other actants to do its bidding, through numerous forms of complicity and connivance, we will later say that it did so by virtue of 'power'. Yet this explains nothing, and is really just another example of the *vis dormitiva* that presupposes what it was supposed to explain.

While rejecting power as an explanatory concept, Latour also dismisses the related notion of potency or potentiality, so central to the history of metaphysics. Since Latour is committed to a model of actants fully deployed in alliances with nothing held in reserve, he cannot concede any slumbering potency lying in the things that is currently unexpressed. To view a thing in terms of potential is to grant it something beyond its current status as a fully specific event. To defend potency is to claim that an entity here and now contains others *in potentia*: this acorn may not have tree-like features now, but they are already lying there in germ. And Latour holds that 'with potency injustice also begins, because apart from a happy few—princes, principles, origins, bankers, and directors—other [actants], that is, all the remainder, become details, consequences, applications, followers, servants, agents—in short, the rank and file' (PF, p. 174). Put somewhat differently, 'talk of possibilities is the illusion of actors that move while forgetting the cost of transport. Producing possibilities is as costly, local, and down to earth as making special steels or lasers. Possibilities are bought and sold like anything else. They are not different by nature. They are not, for example, "unreal"' (PF, p. 174). The claim to have potential is the claim to be more than what one currently is, without admitting that one must haggle and borrow to change one's current state. As Latour expresses it, with all due irony, 'if an actor contains many others in potentia, it is impressive because, even when alone, it is a crowd. That is why it is able to enroll other actors and borrow their support more easily' (PF, p. 174). But this is merely a shell game, and 'although it starts out as a bluff by claiming to own what has only been borrowed, it becomes real [...]. Power is never *possessed*. We either have it *in potentia*, but then we do not *have* it, or we have it *in actu*, but then our allies are the ones that go into action' (PF, pp. 174-5).[9]

In this respect, Latour's position is reminiscent of the ancient Megarians, who saw no room for potentiality lying outside the current state of the world. They were vehemently opposed by Aristotle, who in *Metaphysics* IX.3 is vexed in particular by the following consequence of their views: 'for instance someone who is not building a house is not capable of building a house, but only the one who is building a house, when he is building [it], is capable of it, and similarly in other cases. The absurd consequences of this opinion are not difficult to see'.[10] Aristotle wonders: if the house-builder at rest does not have the art of house building, how does he acquire the art when it is time

---

9. Punctuation modified slightly.

10. Aristotle, *Metaphysics*, trans. Joe Sachs, Santa Fe, Green Lion Pres, 1999, p. 170.

to return to work? Latour's response would probably be that the idle house-builder is capable, not *in potentia*, but only through a series of mediations be-tween the builder and other actors, which vanish when the builder is at rest. Aristotle would remain unsatisfied, since he has deeper metaphysical objec-tions to a world without potency. For one thing, it would entail that nothing is hot or sweet when it is not being touched or tasted, which Aristotle calls 'the Protagorean claim',[11] though it is now better known from Locke's dis-tinction between primary and secondary qualities. But Latour would surely endorse the doctrine of Protagoras and Locke that nothing is hot or sweet when it is not perceived. Nor would he be swayed by Aristotle's objection that 'these assertions abolish both motion and becoming. For [according to them] what is standing will always be standing and what is sitting always sitting [...] since what does not have the potency of standing up will be in-capable of standing up'.[12] The position assaulted by Aristotle is defended by Latour's ancestral ally Whitehead, who objects to the notion of substance as an enduring entity undergoing adventures in space and time. Since Latour has already stated that every actant is an event, and that every event hap-pens only once, in a single time and place, he is committed to entities with only a momentary existence.

As described earlier, Latour's rejection of potency also leads him to abandon the model of logical deduction as a transparent channel that auto-matically leads from one thought to another. As he puts it, in one of his bold-est stabs at Kant:

> There has never been such a thing as deduction. One sentence *follows* an-other, and then a third affirms that the second was already implicitly or potentially already *in* the first. Those who talk of synthetic a priori judg-ments deride the faithful who bathe at Lourdes. However, it is no less bi-zarre to claim that a conclusion lies *in* its premises than to believe that there is holiness *in* the water (PF, p. 176).[13]

Arguments are not linked together like dominoes or a house of cards, each toppling the next automatically: 'Arguments form a system or structure only if we forget to test them. What? If I were to attack *one* element, would *all* the others come crowding round me without a moment's hesitation? This is so unlikely! Every collection of actants includes the lazy, the cowardly, the dou-ble agents, the indifferent, and the dissidents' (PF, p. 177). For this reason it is wrong to seek truth in the *foundations* of what lies before us: 'All research on foundations and origins is superficial, since it hopes to identify some [ac-tants] which potentially contain the others. This is impossible [...]. Those who look for foundations are reductionists by definition and proud of it' (PF,

---

11. Aristotle, *Metaphysics*, p. 170.

12. Aristotle, *Metaphysics*, p. 170.

13. Punctuation modified slightly.

p. 188). Thinkers do not deduce, critique, or build reality out of first principles or foundations. Instead, they simply *work*, negotiating with actants in
the same way as butchers, engineers, technicians, carpenters, and clowns.

More generally, this leads us to a reality made up of different *levels*. If
one statement does not follow with automatic logical force from another, if
one actant never contains another *in potentia*, then it is impossible to call one
actant matter and another form, or one of them part and another the whole.
'There are neither wholes nor parts. Neither is there harmony, composition, integration, or system. How something holds together is determined on
the field of battle [...]' (PF, p. 164). Every actant can serve any of these roles
(matter or form, whole or part) in different situations. Using a Leibnizian
image to undercut Leibniz, Latour states that 'no matter how far we go,
there are always forms; within each fish there are ponds full of fish. Some
believe themselves to be the molds while others are the raw material, but this
is a form of elitism. In order to enroll a force we must conspire with it. It can
never be punched out like sheet metal or poured as in a cast' (PF, p. 161).

This leads to another striking feature of Latour's metaphysics. We have
seen that his entire cosmos is made of nothing but individual actors, events
fully deployed at each instant, free of potency or other hidden dimensions lying outside their sum of alliances in any given moment. For this very reason
there can be no independent reality known as 'time', as if actants were driv-
en forward by some temporal *élan* or *durée*, some flux of becoming distinct
from their total reality here and now. This lack of interest in flux and flow
apart from specific entities separates Latour from such figures as Bergson
and Deleuze, who do regard becoming as something different from a series
of concrete states of actors. Although Latour does not stress the point, he
basically defends a cinematic universe of individual instants of precisely the
sort that Bergson abhors.[14] Latour is, in fact, the Anti-Bergson. Just as with
power, logic, and truth, Latour holds that time is merely the result of negotiations among entities, not what makes these negotiations possible. As he
puts it: 'Time is the distant consequences of actors as they each seek to create a fait accompli on their own behalf that cannot be reversed. In this way
time passes' (PF, p. 165). Or rather, 'Time does not pass. Times are what is at
stake between forces' (PF, p. 165). Certain negotiations between actants lead
to something asymmetrical or irreversible, and this is what we call time: 'Act
as you wish, so long as this cannot be easily undone. As a result of the actants' work, certain things do not return to their original state [...]. There are
winners and losers, there are directions, and some are made stronger than

---

14. Elsewhere I have argued that, despite all appearances to the contrary, the philosophy of Heidegger is also more consistent with a cinematic model of isolated temporal
instants than with Bergson's temporality. Here we find one of the few hidden points in
common between Latour and Heidegger. See also my book *Tool-Being: Heidegger and the
Metaphysics of Objects*, Chicago, Open Court, 2002, pp. 63-66.

others' (PF, p. 160). And 'to create an asymmetry, an actant need only lean on a force slightly more durable than itself' (PF, p. 160). Finally, '"time" arises at the end of this game, a game in which most lose what they have staked' (PF, p. 165). In Latour's universe no external force, not even 'time', exceeds the full concrete deployment of actants.

These conclusions push Latour to a grand finale in which numerous bridges and ships are set aflame. For one thing, there is no special activity that deserves to be called 'thinking', as if there were a sort of privileged transcendent critique that intellectuals alone could accomplish. 'When we talk of "thought," even the most skeptical lose their critical faculties. Like vulgar sorcerers, they let "thought" travel at high speed over great distances' (PF, p. 218). For similar reasons, Latour denies that anything like 'science' exists. While this might strike some observers as just another case of trendy French relativism, it follows directly from Latour's model of the world as a network of actants. 'So you believe that the application of mathematics to the physical world is a miracle? If so, then I invite you to admire another miracle; I can travel around the world with my American Express card' (PF, p. 221). A few pages earlier, there was a more emphatic version of the same insight:

> If the most obscure Popperian zealot talks of 'falsification', people are ready to see a profound mystery. But if a window cleaner moves his head to see whether the smear he wants to clean is on the inside or the outside, no one marvels. If a young couple move a piece of furniture in their living room and conclude, little by little, that it does not look right and that all the furniture will have to be moved for everything to fit again, who finds this worthy of note? But if 'theories' rather than tables are moved, then people talk excitedly of a Kuhnian 'paradigm shift'. I am vulgar, but this is essential in a domain where injustice is so profound. They laugh at those who believe in levitation but claim, without being contradicted, that theories can raise the world (PF, p. 217).

The power of science comes from a motley armada of the most various actants, yet the results of science are attributed to a special form of transcendent critique that is strangely denied to bakers and musicians.

If all of these networks are obscured by present-day philosophy, this will turn out to be the result of a modernist drive to purify subjects from objects and nature from society. We must bring a halt to the attempted cleansing that puts naïve praxis on one side and critical-intellectual transcendence on the other. For Latour, modernity is the impossible attempt to create a radical split between objective natural fact and arbitrary human perspective. Moreover, the modernist tries to purify objects by assigning them solely to one side or the other of this artificial divide, denying the existence of anything lying in the middle. Admirers and critics of the modern world are at least united in agreement that the modern world *exists*. But in fact we have never been modern, as Latour will demonstrate in his classic work of the same title. In yet another slap at Heidegger, Latour writes that 'they say this "modern world" is *different* from all the others, absolutely and radically different [...]. This poor world is absolutely devoid of soul, and the tawdriest hand-carved clog has more being than a tin can' (PF, p. 208). Latour can aptly be described as the philosopher who grants a full dose of being even to tin cans.

In this opening chapter, I have tried to convey the power and precision of *Irreductions*, which has been available to readers since 1984. In that year, Chernenko led the Soviet Union, Reagan was only half-finished in Washington, and ten nations of today's European Union were either single-party police states or did not yet exist. 1984! More than two decades, and not a single new object-oriented philosophy.

2

Science in Action

Though Latour is better known for his philosophy of science than for his metaphysics, the 1987 book *Science in Action* provides plenty of both. While Latour sometimes takes a distance from certain aspects of this work, it remains as fresh today as when it was published. In a helpful pair of appendices (SA, pp. 258-9), he recounts the key ideas of the book, divided into seven rules of method and six principles. Here I will take the liberty of reorganizing these rules and principles into two basic concepts: (1) black boxes, and (2) action at a distance. Both themes resonate in some form throughout Latour's career. Respectively, they display his novel approach to two of the pivotal concepts in the history of philosophy: (1) substance, and (2) relation. He adopts a radical position on both of these traditional themes, replacing durable substances with black boxes, and direct relations with indirect links between separate actants. To read *Science in Action* in this way reinforces the view of Latour as belonging to venerable currents in the history of metaphysics.

While the term 'black box' is not of Latour's own invention, he deserves much of the credit for importing it into philosophy. A black box is any actant so firmly established that we are able to take its interior for granted. The internal properties of a black box do not count as long as we are concerned only with its input and output. I am typing these words on a Macintosh PowerBook G4 laptop computer. There is a long history behind this particular machine, and numerous technical and marketing struggles were needed to establish personal computers as a familiar everyday product. The internal engineering of this device would be a complete mystery to me if I were to reflect on it, which happens only rarely. Yet it was just eight months ago that my previous computer (a black one, incidentally) began to erase my data

33

without warning. In that case the former black box became a mysterious instrument of panic, like some evil demon of myth, ruining weeks or months of life as I slowly assessed which files had not survived the disaster. In similar fashion, we all know the brief horror of unexpected popping or buzzing sounds in an airplane. In such moments, the black box of air travel breaks open and reminds us that we are located 35,000 feet above the surface of the earth, without wings of our own, and with no means of independent breath at such a height. For Latour, the black box replaces traditional substance. The world is not made of natural units or integers that endure through all surface fluctuation. Instead, each actant is the result of numerous prior forces that were lovingly or violently assembled. While traditional substances are one, black boxes are many—we simply *treat* them as one, as long as they remain solid in our midst. Like Heidegger's tools, a black box allows us to forget the massive network of alliances of which it is composed, as long as it functions smoothly. Actants are born amidst strife and controversy, yet they eventually congeal into a stable configuration. But simply reawaken the controversy, reopen the black box, and you will see once more that the actant has no sleek unified essence. Call it legion, for it is many.

Instead of a privileged layer of pampered natural substances, we now have a world made up of manifold layers, none more unified or natural than any other. Every actant can be viewed either as a black box or as a multitudinous network, depending on the situation. Actants can be either matter or form in different respects: matter for the larger assemblies that make use of them, form for the tinier components they unite beneath their umbrella. Is my laptop computer matter or form? That depends on whether you ask me as I write ('matter'), or ask the numerous components from which it is built ('form'). To say that the world is made of black boxes is to say that it consists of numerous democratic levels—that there is no uniquely solid, durable substance lying in the basement of the world. Even a chaotic or multifarious actant can appear solid under the right circumstances; by the same token, any supposed black box can be unpacked, and its components rearranged or challenged.

This leads us directly to the second metaphysical concept of *Science in Action*, action at a distance. We have seen that Latour insists on an absolute democracy of objects: a mosquito is just as real as Napoleon, and plastic in a garbage dump is no less an actant than a nuclear warhead. We cannot reduce these objects to their appearance in consciousness or to their attributes as defined by language. Furthermore, no actant contains any other actants in germ, just as parents do not 'implicitly' contain their children. The democracy of objects means that *all objects are mutually external*. This is what Latour means by action at a distance. Since no object contains another, all certain distance from one another; even a whole is distant from its arts. But action also means nearness, since to act on something means to affect, touch, or interfere with it in some way. In other words, action at a distance means nothing less than 'nearness at a distance'. And this is the central paradox not only of Latour's philosophy, but of philosophy as a whole.

The theme of action at a distance has long been a major problem of metaphysics. Beginning in the Western tradition with Descartes, the problem of *communication* came to be of decisive importance. If mind and body are entirely different, then their means of communication becomes a difficulty, and God is needed to mediate between the two kinds of substances. This brand of philosophy, widely known as 'occasionalism', was as acceptable in the seventeenth century as it is ridiculed today. But the problem never really disappeared—it simply took on a new and less interesting form. Whereas Descartes saw a problem in the communication between souls and bodies, and between souls and souls, his model of the physical universe allowed him to ignore the problem of communication *between bodies*. This deeper question had already been posed in the Islamic world by such earlier figures as al-Ash'ari and al-Ghazali, and was revived by Nicolas Malebranche once he and Géraud de Cordemoy adopted an atomic model of the physical world in the post-Cartesian context. For our purposes, all that matters is that the problem of communication never really disappeared, and was simply transformed into more innocuous form by Hume and Kant. From its high-water mark as a thrilling perplexity lying between all animate and inanimate entities, the communication problem was reduced to a dreary provincial riddle positioned solely between humans and the world. Any relation not containing a human being as one of its terms is now largely seen as lying outside the scope of philosophy altogether, fit only for the natural sciences just as hay is reserved for donkeys.

One of Latour's virtues is his refusal to focus on a single magical gap between thinking, practical, moody humans on the one hand and stupefied inanimate clods of matter on the other. The problem of communication is raised anew by Latour as soon as he grants full democratic rights to all actants in the cosmos, denying that any of them contain the others. His actors are all mutually external. His own answer as to how actants communicate is through *translation*. Things do not touch one another if left just as we found them. They need interfaces in order to touch, and to build an interface requires labour. Ultimately, this requires the appearance of a new entity through which the two communicating terms are joined, however briefly. This problem entails the same model of human thought encountered in the previous chapter: namely, there is no such thing as 'thinking' as a special critical transcendence that leaps beyond the world and reflexively sees things 'as' they are. Instead, the relation between my mind and the room is metaphysically no different from the relation between the computer and the desk within that room. In both cases, there is a problem of communication between two actants vested with full autonomous rights.

A. BLACK BOXES

The title *Science in Action* suggests a specific and limited topic: science, as opposed to history, literature, cooking, or sports. For the same reason, Latour is often called a 'philosopher of science', as though his subject matter were limited to a single domain of human activity. And true enough, the book contains numerous examples drawn from scientific practice. But recall that Latour has already denied the existence of a special type of reality called 'science' that magically transcends all other sorts of dealings with actants. In fact, his book could just as easily be called *Objects in Action*, or *Actants in Action*. Latour might have written comparable works about seducers, mechanics, thieves, or chefs—and *has* written one about judges (*La fabrique du droit*). Latour is not so much a 'philosopher of science' as a metaphysician working in a philosophy-of-science idiom. What actants do is *act*, as the words themselves immediately suggest. In negative terms, this means that actants are not ready-made essences that happen to stumble into relations every now and then. An actant is always born from crisis and controversy; only when it succeeds in establishing a foothold in the world do we forget the tribulations of its birth and eventually treat it as a seamless black box. The reason for focusing on science in particular is simply that science generates its objects through more explicit controversies than most other ways of dealing with actants. It is easy to view a pebble on the beach as a black box to be collected or thrown, until a geologist teaches us the stress of volcanoes or sediments through which the pebble was slowly assembled. It is only natural to take the decline of the Roman Empire as a dull unit remembered from schoolhouse days, until we read Gibbon and are lost in reverie over decadent personae and the sadness of what might have been. To speak of objects in action is to convert objects from black boxes into withering trials of strength, re-enacting the torrid events that gave birth to the most obvious facts in the world. Thank God we do not do this for all actants at every moment; thank God we are ignorant of the turbulent details and razor-thin margin of victory in the love story of our parents.

No brief summary can replace the wealth of examples given in Latour's book, which shows in detail how black boxes in science and industry arise from controversy. Some of his best examples include diesel engines, vaccines, and the chemical element polonium. But let's consider his example of DNA, which since 1953 has been described as having the shape of a double helix. Opening an encyclopedia, we read the following sentence: 'DNA has the structure of a double helix'. No one questions this anymore, except a few cranks or fringe dissidents. It is now the central dogma of genetics. You are free to fight against it, as long as you are willing to be mocked by the entire profession of chemistry and large segments of the educated public. The double helix has become a black box, serving as the unshakeable basis for more uncertain theories, and has already been taught to several generations of children. But if we wish to open this particular black box, we need only read the classic account by James Watson[1] of how it was born. When Crick and Watson began to collaborate at Cambridge in 1951, it was not even clear whether DNA was the medium of genetic activity at all, since many still held that proteins were the vehicle of heredity. Beyond this, the shape of the DNA molecule was entirely unknown; photographs taken by crystallographers were inconclusive. For the two young dark horses to unlock the DNA structure, they had to fend off numerous difficulties and assemble numerous allies. While racing Linus Pauling for the prize, they had to endure the teasing of rivals and the warnings of their lab director. To assemble the final model, they had to bring numerous elements into harmony, including Chargaff's laws and metallic pieces from the Cambridge machine shop. Eventually their model became strong enough to resist doubts, and was approved by their most serious colleagues; their landmark article was published in *Nature*, the most respected journal in their field. But even this did not end the controversy forever, since alternative triple-helix models for DNA were still proposed by serious scientists for years to come. Here we have a progression of statements that become increasingly more solid: from 'we believe it's a double helix', to 'Crick and Watson claim it's a double helix, but certain doubts may be raised', to 'Crick and Watson have shown that it's a double helix', to the simple final stage of 'DNA is a double helix'. We have a true black box when a statement is simply presented as a raw fact without any reference to its genesis or even its author. As Latour asks, 'who refers to Lavoisier's paper when writing the formula H_2O for water?' (SA, p. 43) Truckers who use diesel engines have never heard of the embarrassing early failures of these engines, which led to controversy over their real inventor and ultimately to the suicide of Diesel himself.

In a sense, all human activity aims to create black boxes. Boeing engineers labour to create a new model of jet, which will never reach the market if its various parts break down during test flights. In forming a friendship, settling a marriage, or composing a manuscript, our hope is to establish something durable that does not constantly fray or break down. A job in which our roles are reassigned each week, or with the constant danger of being sacked by an emotionally unstable superior, is more of a headache than anyone can endure. Earning a doctoral degree would not be worth the trouble if our transcript and thesis were scrutinized monthly by a panel of experts for the rest of our lives, or if long-time professors had to retake their comprehensive exams every summer. In everyday language we now refer to certain cars and people with the wonderful phrase 'high-maintenance'. By definition, a black box is *low-maintenance*. It is something we rely on as a given

---

1. James Watson, *The Double Helix*, New York, Norton, 1983.

in order to take further steps, never worrying about how it came into being. The reason it can be either so refreshing or so annoying to speak of one's work with outside amateurs is that they lack awareness of the black boxes widely recognized in our respective professions. Beginners in philosophy often make wild assaults on the positions of Plato and Kant, and this opens up new vistas when done sincerely, just as it causes frustration when it takes the form of contrarian taunting by troublemaking insiders.

Black boxes face two primary and opposite dangers: too much attention from other actants, or too little. When a black box receives too little attention, it is simply ignored. And this is the fate of most of the objects in the world. We are surrounded by trillions of actants at any given moment, and overlook the vast majority of useless flies, beetles, and electrons that swarm amidst our more treasured objects. Most patents are for inventions that never catch on in the market, or are never built at all. Most novels and scholarly articles go entirely unread: not *criticized*, but simply overlooked. Black boxes go nowhere if they fail to become obligatory points of passage for other entities. The second danger for black boxes is the opposite one—that of gaining too much interest in the form of skepticism and scrutiny. The work of the fraudulent South Korean clone doctor was not overlooked, and neither was that of Utah's failed cold fusion researchers. Instead, their black boxes were torn open and laid waste by sophisticated doubters. We do not want our love letters to arrive unnoticed, but neither do we wish them to be challenged or critiqued, their grammar marked with red ink.

In the case of a scientific article, let's assume that it succeeds in gaining the attention of a certain number of readers. As Latour observes (SA, p. 60), there are now three possible responses by the reader: giving up, going along, or re-enacting. In an amusing twist, he offers rough estimates of the percentage of frequency for each type of response. In perhaps 90% of all cases, the reader of a scientific or scholarly text loses interest or is overwhelmed by technical language, and simply gives up trying to follow or challenge whatever is written. Such readers may contribute to the prestige of the text anyway, whether through being vaguely impressed, or by passing the word along that 'the article looked pretty good, but it was too deep for me to follow'. But such readers are not the primary support for the article. This comes from the estimated 9% [*laughing*-g.h.] who go along with the article, basically convinced by the arguments of Crick and Watson, or Pasteur, or Heidegger, or Latour, or Edward Said, and use it as a black box for additional claims of their own. This leaves a mere 1% of the pie for the re-enactors, those skeptics or enthusiasts who repeat an experiment or trace the exact steps of a philosophical argument—leading to verification, modification, or outright rejection. We are in dangerous terrain when this daring 1% puts on the gloves and opens our black boxes, since the boxes may end up destroyed or drastically altered.[2]

As an extreme case of such behavior, Latour invents a marvelous person called 'The Dissenter', a contrarian cynic who challenges every least detail he observes in a laboratory. Latour imagines that the Dissenter reads the following sentence in a scientific article: 'Fig. 1 shows a typical pattern. Biological activity of endorphin was found essentially in two zones with the activity of zone 2 being totally reversible, or statistically so, by naloxone' (SA, p. 64) As one of the estimated 1% of readers who actively doubt this claim, the Dissenter appears at the laboratory to speak with the Professor in person. Aware of the questions surrounding his article, the Professor says 'let me show you', and points to a device making an even inscription of peaks and valleys on a roll of graph paper. 'OK', the Professor continues, 'this is the base line; now, I am going to inject endorphin, what is going to happen? See?!' The peaks on the graph paper immediately decrease in size, eventually flattening altogether. 'Immediately the line drops dramatically. And now watch naloxone. See?! Back to base line levels. It is fully reversible' (SA, p. 65).

This recording device is an *instrument*, which Latour defines as the final link in a long chain of transformations that allow us to see something 'directly' for ourselves. The instrument normally remains invisible until it is challenged: usually we accept images from cameras and telescopes as unquestionable data, until some dissident begins to pick apart flaws in the distortion of their lenses. Viewed in this way, any object can function as an instrument under the right circumstances, working to mediate forces reliably as they pass from one location to another. But perhaps our Dissenter is not satisfied with inscriptions on graph paper. For this reason, the professor takes him to see the actual experimental device, the physiograph, in which 'a massive piece of electronic hardware records, calibrates, amplifies and regulates signals coming from another instrument, an array of glassware' (SA, p. 65). We now see a bubbling glass chamber with something inside that looks like elastic. 'It is indeed elastic, the Professor intones. It is a piece of gut, guinea pig gut [...]. This gut has the property of contracting regularly if maintained alive' (SA, p. 65). This elastic remnant of a dead animal is what reacts to chemical injections and makes inscriptions on the graph paper. If we merely look at the twitching piece of gut, it is hard to make visual sense of what is going on; hence the use of graph paper, which gives legible form to a wildly throbbing muscle. After a time the Professor grows dissatisfied with the experiment, 'swearing at the gut, saying it is a "bad gut"' (SA, p. 66). He blames the technician who dissected the first guinea pig, and now

---

2. Then again, this 1% also includes the Aristotles who modify the Platos and the Einsteins who modify the Newtons, as opposed to the trusty 9% who simply strengthen the black box by using it without significant improvement. Which kind of student would you rather have? Who did Husserl more good in the long run: the Husserlians who mimicked him, or Heidegger who transformed him?

orders the slaughter of a second doomed animal. Latour describes the scene grimly: 'A guinea pig is placed on a table, under surgical floodlights, then anaesthetized, crucified, and sliced open [...]. Suddenly, we are much further from the paper world of the article. We are now in a puddle of blood and viscera, slightly nauseated by the extraction of the ileum from this furry little creature' (SA, p. 66).

When reading the original article it was possible, though difficult, for the Dissenter to doubt what was written. But now it is vastly more difficult. In order to doubt the Professor, he needs to find some way to undermine the graph paper and the various recording devices. Eventually, he may even need to master the gruesome techniques of dissecting live animals. As Latour puts it, '"Showing" and "seeing" are not simple flashes of intuition. Once in the lab we are not presented outright with the real endorphin whose existence we doubted. We are presented with another world in which it is necessary to prepare, focus, fix and rehearse the vision of the real endorphin. We came to the laboratory in order to settle our doubts about the paper, but we have been led into a labyrinth' (SA, p. 67). Nowhere in the Professor's demonstration do we confront the thing itself as angels play harps and lightning flashes in the distance. To see something 'directly' means to follow a lengthy chain of transformations from one medium into another and on into another. Behind the graph paper with its regular patterns there lies a massive series of objects, each translating its message into a different level of the world. Initially, we might have thought we could argue with the Professor simply by consulting further articles in a library. But now that we have 'seen for ourselves', under the Professor's direction, further dissent will incur painful costs in time, energy, and money.

> At this present point, in order to go on, we need guinea pigs, surgical lamps and tables, physiographs, electronic hardware, technicians and morphine, not to mention the scarce flasks of purified endorphin; we also need the skills to use all these elements and to turn them into a pertinent objection to the Professor's claim [...]. Longer and longer detours will be necessary to find a laboratory, buy the equipment, hire the technicians and become acquainted with the ileum assay (SA, p. 67).

In other words, we cannot object to the Professor's article with any sort of direct appeal to 'nature', but must intervene in a full range of intermediate layers. Yes, we *could* still make objections, but the price will be high in the form of isolation and ostracism. Yes, there have been lone scientists and lone artists who have stood fast amidst poverty and ridicule—but such heroes can never just trumpet their insights aloud and blame the ignorance and corruption of the populace when their ideas fail to catch on. To succeed, these loners first need to displace an entire network of black boxes that are stacked against them, some of them especially sleek and heavy. "'See for yourself,'" the scientist says with a subdued and maybe ironic smile. "Are you convinced now?" Faced with the thing itself that the technical paper was alluding to, the dissenters now have a choice between either accepting the fact or doubting their own sanity—the latter is much more painful' (SA, p. 70).

Yet even now our Dissenter remains unconvinced, and is cocky enough not to doubt his own sanity. The Professor behaves as if he were the official spokesman for the graph paper and other pieces of technical apparatus. But perhaps the Professor is not letting the things themselves speak through this experiment as transparently as he claims. It may be that the graph proves nothing: 'It may be that all sorts of chemicals give the same shape in this particular assay. Or maybe the Professor so dearly wishes his substance to be morphine that he unwittingly confused two syringes and injected the same morphine twice, thus producing two shapes that indeed look identical' (SA, p. 73) When the Dissenter continues to express doubt, the Professor calmly offers to let him do the injections himself. The Dissenter now checks the labels on the two vials, and using first morphine and then endorphin, he finds that the same result is obtained in the same amount of time. The Professor seems to be vindicated once more; he 'cannot be dissociated from his claims' (SA, p. 74). The Professor is not isolated, but has all the black boxes in the experiment on his side, while the Dissenter is gradually stripped of possible allies.

But imagine that our Dissenter is so skeptical that he now becomes openly rude. How can we be so sure that the vials labeled 'morphine' and 'endorphin' are not the subject of a mix-up, or even an act of deliberate fraud? The Professor remains calm, and shows the Dissenter the protocol book filled with numbers, showing a correlation between code numbers and specific vials of chemicals. This is still not enough to satisfy our anti-hero, the pompous skeptic. 'By now, we have to imagine a dissenter boorish enough to behave like a police inspector suspecting everyone and believing no one and finally wanting to see the real endorphin with his own eyes' (SA, p. 76). In this spirit of boorishness, the Dissenter openly disbelieves that the numbers in the book actually correlate with the vials of chemicals. For the first time, the Professor begins to show signs of anger. He leads the Dissenter into a room filled with glass columns in which a liquid slowly percolates through a white substance. The desired chemical eventually filters down into a row of tiny flasks, sorted on the basis of how long it took to pass through the substance. 'Here it is, says the guide, here is your endorphin' (SA, p. 76). When the Dissenter continues to express skepticism, the Professor gives an annoyed technical explanation of how the apparatus works, concluding huffily that the vial of endorphin used by the Dissenter came from this same rack two days earlier. Even now the Dissenter remains stubborn, challenging the principle that the different chemicals will all filter through the apparatus at different rates, thereby denying outright that the Professor can be sure of which chemical is which in the first place. 'The pressure is mounting. Everyone in the lab is expecting an outburst of rage, but the Professor politely leads the visitor towards another part of the laboratory' (SA, p. 76). Here, the Professor explains that the chemicals can also be identified by their optical spectra, thereby definitively proving their identity. When this demonstration is met with silence from the Dissenter, Latour gives a fine display of his rare dramaturgical talents, as the Professor launches an over-whelming pre-emptive strike against any further waste of his time:

> Oh, I know! Maybe you are uncertain that I did the experiment with *your* vial of endorphin? Look here in the HPLC book. Same code, same time. Maybe you claim that I asked this gentleman here to fake the books, and obtain this peak for me with another substance? Or maybe you doubt the measurement of optical spectra. Maybe you think it is an obsolete piece of physics. No such luck, my dear colleague. Newton described this phenomenon quite accurately—but maybe he's not good enough for you (SA, p. 77).

All of Latour's books are peppered with delicious imagined speeches of this kind. And like all good comedians, he sends the audience home with a final laugh even after the climax has apparently passed. The Professor's voice is now quivering with rage, and the Dissenter has a decision to make. Is he really prepared to insult everyone in the laboratory by doubting the HPLC code book or the fraction collector into which the liquids percolate? 'He *could* in principle, but he *cannot* in practice since time is running out and he is sensitive to the exasperation in everyone's voice. And who is he any-way to mount a dispute with Water Associates, the company who devised this HPLC prototype? Is he ready to cast doubt on a result [Newton's laws for optical spectra] that has been accepted unquestioningly for 300 years, one that has been embedded in thousands of contemporary instruments?' (SA, p. 77). The Dissenter tries one last flick of the wrist, wondering aloud whether the pure substance reflected on the graph is actually endorphin. The Professor responds with a withering analysis marked by great techni-cal precision. He then asks whether his adversary can drum up any other possible doubts. 'No, I must admit, whispers the believer, I am very im-pressed. This really looks like genuine endorphin. Thank you so much for the visit. Don't trouble yourselves, I will find my own way out... (exit the dissenter)...' (SA, p. 77).

Although Latour ends the story here, the aftermath for the Dissenter would probably be much worse than an embarrassed exit. Within a few minutes of his departure, the Professor's rage turns to mirth, as he chuckles aloud over the Dissenter's behavior. His assistants join in energetically, roll-ing their eyes, some of them cussing over 'that bastard' and wondering 'what his problem is'. After work the technicians all meet for drinks, and as each new friend drifts into the pub, the Professor has a fresh chance to vent his ridicule: 'Hey Alex, you're not going to *believe* what happened in the lab to-day!' By nightfall, the story has been retold in dozens of e-mails to colleagues around the world. The Dissenter is now a scientific laughingstock. At future conference presentations, smirks and knowing glances are exchanged among those who bother to attend his papers at all. Some of the Dissenter's grant proposals now mysteriously fail, and his once friendly co-workers seem to turn the other way down the hall as he approaches. Maybe he's just being paranoid? No, he's not. The Dissenter's scientific isolation has permanently increased. His former allies have deserted him in droves, and his career will take years to recover even after an abject letter of apology to the Professor, who ruthlessly circulates the letter with his own sarcastic marginal notes.

I have retold this scenario in such detail partly for entertainment's sake; there have always been too many boring philosophers, and we are fortunate that Latour is not among them. But it was also important to do some justice to the meticulous detail of Latour's empirical accounts of laboratory life, which must otherwise be excluded from a metaphysical book like this one. What the story shows is that the Dissenter can continue to dispute *ad infinitum*, but only at the cost of growing isolation and perhaps even mental illness (and here I do not jest). The Professor has countless allies: the guinea pig gut, the recording device, Sir Isaac Newton, armies of technicians, a research budget, and powerful friends to whom the Dissenter can be ridiculed afterward. By contrast, the Dissenter has no one and nothing to back up his doubts. The Professor is surrounded by numerous black boxes that *can* be opened, but that in practical terms are extremely difficult to open. He stacks up so many black boxes that the Dissenter is overwhelmed by their combined force, and has no idea how to escape (SA, p. 59). Each black box that falls on our side, whether it be an experiment, a respected authority, a strong institutional position, or a compelling idea, makes us stronger and our opponents weaker (SA, p. 93). Every time we link ourselves to a black box, our opponents will have a hard time separating us from it.

This is the moment when Alan Sokal and other scientific realists will begin to nod knowingly. They have caught Bruno Latour in the act: he reduces all of science to the sophistry of human power politics. According to Latour, powerful lab directors strong-arm their weaker subordinates into obedience. Knowledge is power, nothing else. But I find it hard to see how this reading of Latour could even occur to a fair-minded reader. In the first place, he never makes any sort of clean split between nature on one side and political power on the other. As we saw in *Irreductions*, all actants are on the same footing. In the preceding example, Latour never even tells us that the Professor *is* more politically powerful than the Dissenter. We only know that by the end the Dissenter has made a public fool of himself. Yet it could just as easily be the case that the Professor is a poorly funded maverick biologist and the Dissenter an aggressive captain of the Academy or an arrogant Nobel Laureate. Rewritten in this way, the story is no longer about the 'power' of distinguished professors to bully greenhorn skeptics, but rather about the victory of bold experiment over mediocre establishment science. Furthermore, even if the Professor really were a 'more powerful' figure than the Dissenter in purely social terms, his victory is not yet guaranteed. All we know is that the Dissenter has just left the lab in disgrace, utterly demoralized. But what if the Dissenter goes to work more diligently than ever before? Perhaps he has a brainstorm leading to a new *annus mirabilis* of science, and two years later has shocked the world with an ingenious refutation of Newton's optics. It is now the Dissenter who has the last laugh. Flash forward to the close of his dramatic Nobel Prize Address in Stockholm: 'Fifteen years ago I was ridiculed in one famous laboratory by a leading scientist of the day. His name is now forgotten, and I will spare his surviving colleagues any further embarrassment. The important thing is that a new age in the interpretation of optical spectra has begun. Experimental work is only now reaping the harvests that were sown at our darkest hour of ridicule and isolation. The lesson taught by the courage of Giordano Bruno in the dungeon of the Inquisition is verified once more, and for all time: lonely seeker of the truth, never fear the scorn of the powerful! [followed by a standing ovation]'. Latour's point is not that social power trumps objective proof. Instead, the point is that whether the scientific prize goes to the swaggering aristocrats of the major labs or falls instead to the stunning dark horses, both must follow the same path to glory: assembling as many black boxes as possible to force one's opponents to give way.

What the laboratory fable shows is that we never see truth directly in the flesh. The Dissenter may be a loathsome pest, but he does have a point: anything *can* be challenged. There is never a red light flashing in our head once we hit the right answer, no genie or magic fairy to whisper in our ear that we now have the truth. (Crick and Watson felt just as sure of their embarrassing first solution as of their correct second one.) Instead, we assemble the truth as painstakingly as a symphony or an electrical grid, and any of these things can collapse beneath the weight of unexpected resistance. Powerful superiors and reigning paradigms are no more and no less black boxes than anything else. The brilliance of *The Double Helix* lies in the way that it places hard science, flirtation, gossip, and the lust for honor all on the same footing. All of these are events; all involve actants. It is hard to imagine a more Latourian book than Watson's masterpiece. Whatever else you may wish to call Bruno Latour, do not call him a relativist, a power politician, or a social constructionist. The world is constructed at each moment out of many actants, and most of these actants are not 'social' in the narrow sense, since they can just as easily be made of cement or geometric solids as of human conspiracies.

But if Latour's actants are not just illusions generated by human power plays, they are also not objective rock-hard substances. An object is not a substance, but a *performance*. 'Some in fairy tales defeat the ugliest seven-headed dragons or against all odds they save the king's daughter; others inside laboratories resist precipitation or they triumph over bismuth' (SA, p. 89). He is referring here to the work of Marie and Pierre Curie in identifying the new chemical element called polonium, which some dissenters initially claimed was just a well-known element in disguise:

> What are these famous things which are said to be behind the tests made of? They are made of a list of victories: ['polonium'] defeated uranium and thorium at the sulphurated hydrogen game; it defeated antimony and arsenic at the ammonium sulphur game; and then it forced lead and copper to throw in the [towel], only bismuth went all the way to the semi-final, but it too got beaten down during the final game of heat and cold! At the beginning of its definition the thing is a *score list* for a series of trials (SA, p. 89).

In this way Latour holds to the notion of a thing as a list of attributes or definite properties, making him no more an anti-realist than Frege or Russell. The difference is that for Latour attributes are not inert qualities, but performances or active victories over their rivals. One can certainly argue against this view by means of various metaphysical objections—but *not* by claiming that Latour is just another French relativist peddling fashionable nonsense about the unreality of the world.

Instead of inert substances or essences that circle in the void, forever just being what they are, Latour gives us black boxes. These boxes are forces to reckon with, and they resist trials of strength. Even so, the box does not continue in the world by inertia alone: 'in the most favourable cases, even when it is a routine piece of equipment, the black box requires an active customer and needs to be accompanied by other people if it is to be maintained in existence' (SA, p. 137). If black boxes are to endure, there must always be citadels of Thomist or Darwinian orthodoxy beating down deviant heretics. Every school needs its brutal enforcers as bulwarks against chaos. Yet a black box is never fully closed, and never safe from all challenge. Cracks eventually appear even in seemingly unshakeable black boxes: Newtonian gravity, the Roman Empire. The same thing can happen with any intellectual orthodoxy. Indeed, one of the goals of the present book is to open the black box of the stale analytic/continental dual monarchy, exposing its interior to the blows of sunlight, eagles, and dogs. A black box is low-maintenance, but never maintenance-free.

Just as he will later say of machines, Latour notes that a black box assembles various elements in a single package: 'when many elements are made to act as one, this is what I will now call a black box' (SA, p. 131). Initially an object is an object *in action*, identified by its great victories and its trials of strength against other actants. But over time, we forget about this drama, and the black box turns into something like a substance: 'New objects become *things*: somostatin, polonium, anaerobic microbes, transfinite numbers, double helix, or *Eagle* computers, things isolated from the laboratory conditions that shaped them, things with a name that now seem independent from the trials in which they proved their mettle' (SA, p. 91).[3] These things are retroactively endowed with a competence or potential, and in this way they are mistaken for a solid essence: 'each performance [seems to presuppose] a *competence* which retrospectively explains why the hero withstood all the ordeals. The hero is no longer a score list of actions; he, she or it is an essence slowly unveiled through each of his, her or its manifestations' (SA, p. 89). Only scholarly specialists remember the contemporary opponents of Aristotle, Maxwell, Cantor, or Bohr, figures who now seem kissed by the gods from the moment of their birth, though it never felt this way to any of them at the time. Latour does not praise this process, which always veers toward so-called 'Whig history': the Allies defeated the Nazis *because* they were better and stronger; Pasteur defeated Pouchet *because* he saw more clearly; the fire burned the paper *because* it was endowed with burning force; the pill makes us sleep *because* it contains sleeping-force. The word 'nature' should never be used to explain something that ought to be explained instead by the concrete drama of translations between specific actors.

Before moving on, we should review once more what is accomplished by the notion of black boxes. *First*, unlike substances, they exist at every possible level of the universe, since Disneyland is a black box no less than each of its costumed characters, the cars that circulate inside the park, the tyres on the cars, the rubber from which the tyres are made, and the molecules and atoms inside the rubber. There is no special plane of reality on which we find substances as opposed to mere conglomerates of parts. This puts Latour at odds with both the Aristotelian and materialist traditions.

Second, black boxes are different from their accidents or relations only in a relative sense. We might be able to distinguish Russia as an actor from the details of its current political and cultural situation. But in practice this requires a labour of abstraction, since what now exists is only Russia as a total concrete event, containing all its details. To abstract anything from its environment requires that it no longer silently function as a black box, but instead become noticed as such a box, available for possible opening.

Third, Latour's black boxes do not automatically endure through time, unlike most traditional versions of substance. Since they are events, they include all of their relations as parts of themselves. But since these relations shift from moment to moment, the black boxes do not endure for more than an instant, unless we consider them as 'trajectories' crossing time across a series of minute transformations. They must also be constantly maintained. This makes Latour an ally of the doctrine of continuous creation, which is also a frequent feature of occasionalist philosophy. There is no connection

---

3.Punctuation simplified.

between instants, since each is an absolutely unique event, with nothing enduring automatically from one moment to the next. But occasionalism has an even more powerful implication already mentioned above: the inability of any two actors to touch one another directly. Before ruling on whether Latour also adheres to this feature of occasionalism, we should consider his model of relation as a kind of action at a distance.

B. ACTION AT A DISTANCE

For Latour there are no cryptic essences lying behind whatever lies inscribed in reality here and now. There are only actants of all possible varieties, and actants are fully expressed in each moment with nothing held in reserve. It is true that new features of objects appear through the unfolding of successive events, but these new features cannot be ascribed to 'potentials' or 'capacities', except perhaps in retroactive fashion. Actors are *events*, and events are always fully deployed. They are the sum total of reality rather than an incidental surface-effect of the movement of dormant substrata. In this respect, there is only one world for Latour; all actants are here and nowhere else. But notice that this does not make him a holist: everything *does not* affect everything else. A character in Latour's book *Aramis* demonstrates this point with brute physical force: 'the violent blow he struck with his fist on his desk had no visible influence on the chapter of Aristotle's *Metaphysics* that was filed under the letter *A* at the top of his bookshelf. 'You see: not everything comes together, not everything is connected' (AR, p. 152). A philosophy of networks does not require that the network be devoid of separate parts. If everything were already linked, translation would not be such a pressing issue for Latour.

The traditional notion of substance is dropped in his philosophy altogether, replaced by endless layers of black boxes that resist various trials of strength. Latour's theory of relations has yet to be determined, but it will need to reflect his conclusion that all objects lie on the same plane of reality, even if there are separate zones not entirely commensurate with the others. Objects can be linked together, but are mostly *not yet* linked. But the sheer fact that objects have any hope at all of being linked tells us that even if actants are separate from each other, it must be possible to link them through their *qualities*. Two actors will be able to link up only in partial fashion: no two things have completely identical attributes, since even two highly similar entities will occupy different footholds in the cosmos and hence will have different relations to other things. We cannot fuse Austria, Sweden, and Portugal into the same union without effort, and it takes great energy to melt a car's engine into its windows in a homogeneous mass. Nonetheless, these actants must share certain features in common if we are able to link them at all. Whenever one actant has some effect on another, this can be described as 'action at a distance'—all actants, by the mere fact of being themselves, are distant from each other, split off from others by unknown firewalls.

Anytime we have an alliance, we have action at a distance, and without this there would be no reality of any kind: 'reality has many hues [...] and entirely depends on the number of elements tied to [a] claim' (SA, p. 105). Such elements cross any supposed gap between humans and nonhumans, so that there is no pristine objective science tainted now and then by 'social factors' such as 'wicked generals, devious multinationals, eager consumers, exploited women, hungry kids and distorted ideologies' (SA, p. 175). But along with this morally impeccable roster of the greedy and the victimized, we must not forget about 'microbes, radioactive substances, fuels cells and drugs' (SA, p. 175). While these may lack the academic pathos of all the oppressors and oppressed, they are actants nonetheless.

In every situation the only question to ask, whether of theories, armies, policies, restaurants, or machines, is whether they are able to link enough actants to flourish. If not, then our theory collapses, our platoon flees under fire, and our business folds up within months. We will find ourselves isolated, confined to an inner fantasy life while all the actants pass through other points, leaving us behind as dusty ghost towns. For scientific purposes, this leads Latour to the following conclusion: 'The adjective "scientific" is not attributed to *isolated* texts that are able to oppose the opinion of the multitude by virtue of some mysterious faculty. A document becomes scientific when its claims stop being isolated and when the number of people engaged in publishing it are many and explicitly indicated in the text' (SA, p. 33). We could easily change Latour's topic and write as follows: 'The name "restaurant" is not attributed to *isolated* storefronts that draw multitudes by means of some mysterious faculty. A restaurant becomes real when it stops being isolated and when the number of people engaged in eating there are many and explicitly engaged in passing the word along'. Both statements are equally interesting, and equally vulnerable to the same critique. Was Mendel's work in genetics really less scientific before it came to general notice, or was he not rather an *unknown great scientist*? Was China House really less of a restaurant when it struggled for three weeks than when a blistering ad campaign made it suddenly fashionable, or was it not rather an undiscovered gem? Was Cézanne less a painter, Hölderlin less a poet, or Latour less a philosopher before they were recognized by others to be so? This is one of the more troubling consequences of Latour's hostility to lonely, isolated essence. He seems to realize this, responding to a personal query that '*Science in Action* is terribly biased toward the winners and does an injustice to the losers [...] the underdogs get short shrift'.[4] But in a sense the difference between winners and losers is not the most problematic rift, since Latour at least offers

---

4. Personal Communication, Electronic mail to Graham Harman of 14 January, 2006.

a criterion for distinguishing them: the winner has stronger alliances. The more interesting distinction is between the deserving and the undeserving among both winners and losers. Not all losers are equal, just as all winners are not. This question is not just interesting for the purposes of historical work, since it also bears on Latour's rejection of substance. For substance is the ultimate underdog: if it exists, it will always remain obscured behind the networks that deploy it. But we saw that substance is excluded from Latour's philosophy from the very outset of *Irreductions*. It remains doubtful whether anyone but 'the winners' can prevail or even *exist* in a metaphysics that grants such primacy to concrete events over concealed objects or essences.

Leaving this question aside for now, the goal of the various assemblies Latour describes is to fuse numerous allies into an apparent single whole, forbidding them any quarrelsome independent action. A black box is a kind of machine, which 'as its name implies, is [...] a machination, a stratagem, a kind of cunning, where borrowed forces keep one another in check so that none can fly apart from the group' (SA, p. 129). Ideally, a machine should be so well designed that there is almost no chance of its parts rebelling against the streamlined whole: a box put together so effectively that it seems *unthinkable* to change it (SA, p. 122). It is true that a new black box must mark some kind of innovation or improvement, or no one would bother to use it. Yet when an innovation requires us to change too many things, its fate is normally not a happy one. Some experimental novels enjoy great success. But imagine an ambitious avant-garde novel that tried to combine experimental content (talking mushrooms as the only characters), *and* experimental form (printing the novel on playing cards to be shuffled in random order), *and* an experimental message (preaching the tenets of Scientology), *and* experimental distribution (advertising on television and inviting people to subscribe to the cards), *and* experimental language (clipped slang borrowed from the Southern working classes and organized into limericks), *and* an experimental audience (tailoring the message to recent immigrants). This grotesque example suggests the grim consequences of trying to open too many black boxes at once. Marshall McLuhan informs us that a publisher told him that for a book to succeed, only ten percent of its content should be new. Latour himself draws the same lesson from the failure of Aramis, the proposed automated metro system in Paris: 'Don't innovate in every respect at once' (AR, p. 298). Or as we read in *Science in Action*, 'if you are too timid, your [scientific] paper will be lost, as it will if you are too audacious' (SA, p. 51).

But by far the greatest danger for a black box lies in simply being ignored. Even the most brutal criticism of our labours is less damaging than sheer indifference; any published author knows it is better to receive vicious reviews than no reviews at all. 'This is the point that people who never close to the fabrication of science have the greatest difficulty in gra They imagine that all scientific articles are equal and arrayed in lin soldiers, to be carefully inspected one by one. *However, most papers are never read at all* (SA, p. 40, emphasis added). The observation lends powerful support to Latour's metaphysics of alliances:

> No matter what a paper did to the former literature, if no one else does anything with it, then it is as if it never existed at all. You may have written a paper that settles a fierce controversy once and for all, but if readers ignore it, it cannot be turned into a fact; it simply *cannot*. You may protest against the injustice; you may treasure the certitude of being right in your inner heart, but it will never go further than your inner heart; you will never go further in certitude without the help of others. Fact construction is so much a collective process that an isolated person builds only dreams, claims and feelings, not facts (SA, pp. 40-41).

As is usually the case with Latour, the statement remains equally powerful if we shift it away from the human realm. He could just as easily have written: 'No matter what an object is, if it affects no other objects, then it is as if it never existed at all [...]. Reality is so much a collective process that an isolated object is merely a dream, claim, or feeling, not a fact'.

To build a new black box, we need to enroll other animate and inanimate objects. We must control their behavior as much as possible, or they may act as 'high-maintenance' elements and tamper with the smooth workings of our box. Our goal is to make the box so sleek and foolproof that no one even *thinks* of opening it. In a long and fascinating passage, Latour reflects on different possible strategies for enrolling the assistance of other actants (SA, pp. 108-121). (1) We can cater to their interests by giving them what they need, as Pentagon contractors usually do. (2) We can persuade them that what they want is not feasible, and that they should be interested in something else instead. (3) We can tell them that they only need to make a short detour through what *we* are doing to get to where *they* want to go. (4) In a more complicated strategy, we can displace the goals of our allies, invent new goals to inspire them, invent entirely new groups that want the same things we want, and even try to hide the fact that we are leading anyone along detours in the first place. (5) Finally, we can try to make ourselves so indispensable that no one can do without us, creating a monopoly over a certain type of force. If we succeed in this final strategy, we become an 'obligatory passage point', a mandatory port of entry where everyone else is forced to trade (SA, p. 132).

Along with assembling allies for ourselves, it is a good idea to cut our opponents off from their own allies. As Latour puts it, 'the most sudden reversal in the trial of strength between authors and dissenters may be obtained simply by cutting the links tying them to their supporters' (SA, p. 85). In the previous example, the Dissenter tried to sever the links that tied the Professor to every piece of his equipment. In each case, the Dissenter failed. But consider what might have happened if the code books had contained obvious errors, there were problems with the wiring in the physiograph, the needle were found to be stuck in a groove on the graph paper, if the Professor had misunderstood Newton's laws for optical spectra, or if outright fraud had been detected. The Professor would have been grievously weakened, and the Dissenter would have emerged triumphant. For two centuries, Immanuel Kant's Copernican Revolution has been the obligatory point of passage for any philosophy that does not wish to look antiquated. Anyone coming forth with old-style rationalist *proofs* for the existence of God or the infinity of the universe will have a hard time being taken seriously by mainstream philosophy, as will anyone who claims the ability to speak of the things-in-themselves apart from human experience. Alfred North Whitehead, clearly no fool, makes a bold attempt to sever Kant from his central ally: the notion that the gap between human and world is more philosophically important than the gaps between any other sorts of entities. Once Whitehead makes this single incision in Kant's chain of allies, he is able to move with ease amidst the supposed junkyard of seventeenth century philosophy, taking Leibniz and Berkeley as seriously as most professors now take Davidson and Quine. But Whitehead pays a heavy price for this gamble: he remains an isolated hero for a small minority, unable to stack enough black boxes to move the philosophical mainstream back toward speculative metaphysics. Perhaps a posthumous triumph is coming, but for most of the profession Whitehead remains at best an ingenious oddball with a clever imagination and an obscure prose style. His list of allies remains far weaker than Kant's.

Severing an actor from its allies is easier than it sounds, since allies are never as submissive to a black box as we think. As Latour puts it: 'Even colleagues who had been "unalterably" convinced by a laboratory demonstration can change their minds a month later. Established facts are turned into artifacts, and puzzled people ask, "How could we have believed such an absurdity?" Established industries that looked as if they were to last forever suddenly become obsolete and start falling apart, displaced by newer ones' (SA, p. 121). This process can be accelerated if we actively force our opponents' allies to change camp. Surprisingly enough, the easiest way to undermine our opponent's network of allies often lies in attacking our opponent's *strengths,* not weaknesses. If Odysseus stabs the foot or hand of the Cyclops, he merely causes rage. But go straight for the head, for the single ominous eye, and the Cyclops has been neutralized.

In recent politics, we have the example of Karl Rove, political advisor to the former American President George W. Bush. Whether accurately or not, it is often said that Rove makes expert use of this method of frontal attacks against the apparent strong suit of an opponent. If your opponent is a crusader for children's rights, spread the rumor that he is a pedophile.[5] If

5. I make no claims as to the accuracy of these charges against Rove, and use them only as a well-known popular example.

Senator Kerry is a Vietnam War hero, then attack this strength by lining up military veterans who question his war stories. But whatever one may think of Rove, it need not be lies and smears that we use to cut the links between allies. Let's imagine that, in our efforts to counter the dominance of Kant's Copernican Revolution in philosophy, we hire Karl Rove as a consultant. Since Kant has the reputation of a quiet, ascetic seeker after truth, Rove might begin by spreading rumors of Kant's secret moral turpitude. To simplify the tale, let's imagine that the rumors are actually *true*. In a surprising discovery, Rove's research team uncovers previously suppressed correspondence between Kant and the jailed Marquis de Sade, along with a shocking diary that records midnight deflowerings and Baudelairean hymns to triple-great Satan. When the discovery is announced, the defenders of Kant's legacy are initially skeptical. They respond by pointing to Rove's long history of dirty manoeuvres and bemoan the invasion of philosophy by 'the crass politics of sleaze'; some even picket Rove's home demanding a retraction. But let's assume that the authenticity of the Kantian documents is verified by unimpeachable forensic experts. Rove was telling the truth, and in fact was just as surprised as we are by news of Kant's dark double life. It is easy to imagine what would happen in this case. There would be a brief *furore* in the educated press, followed by several years of tedious printed debate over whether a bad person can still be a great thinker. ('Although the new revelations show that Kant was far from an admirable human being, the fact remains that...') But even with Kant unmasked as a shocking hypocrite, no one's philosophical positions will change very much. The biography of the man is newly distasteful, yet it somehow seems irrelevant, and his Copernican philosophy will remain the dominant paradigm. In short, Kant's reputation for personal rectitude has turned out *not* to be one of his most important allies. Rove senses that the battle is lost, and resumes his investigation into Kant's literary remains.

A few months later, Rove is delighted to uncover something far more threatening than immoral diaries. In a withered manuscript buried in a crate of old papers, Rove's team makes another stunning discovery: Kant seems to have written his entire philosophy as nothing but a hoax! It turns out that Kant never believed a word of his own writings, making him a more sinister, systematic forerunner of Alan Sokal. The key passage runs as follows: 'Fools! For they take me at my word... Such is their ignorance that, with only the slightest nudge, one convinces them that black is white, that cold is hot, or that a "Revolution" has turned philosophy inside-out like an old sock'. There follows a diabolical survey of his embittered motives for the hoax, along with descriptions of the deep pleasure he took in executing each step of his sham argument. The Kantian legacy is now in a much ᵉ embarrassing position than in the case of mere immorality. Let's as- ᵉ here once more that initial doubts about Rove's trickery give way to

irrefutable proof that the document was composed by Kant himself, probably at some point during the early 1790's. The ensuing controversy would
be both enjoyable and confusing. There would be months or years of embarrassment for Kant scholars, with a handful even claiming that they sensed
the irony all along. But once the dust had settled, we would probably find
that nothing much had changed in the philosophical world. The followers
of Whitehead, Latour, Hume, and Aquinas might feel newly emboldened by
this weakening of their rival. But in the end, most observers would probably
conclude that it is not so important whether Kant *meant* what he said. Kant's
arguments would still be taken seriously insofar as they have 'genuine merit independent of Kant's barely relevant sardonic intent'. Back in suburban
Virginia, Karl Rove now finds himself in a difficult position. Even his bomb-
shell revelations are failing to dislodge Kant from the central stronghold of
modern philosophy. Facing the greatest failure of his career, he has now become obsessed with defeating Immanuel Kant.

While reading press accounts of the controversy, Rove learns for the
first time of the criticisms of Kant made by a few isolated dissenters. He
is intrigued by their claim that the relation between human and world is
just a special case of any relation whatsoever, and that this makes it illegitimate to root all philosophical questions in the transcendental standpoint.
Spending long nights in the library, Rove begins to discover additional useful passages in Leibniz and other thinkers. Within a few years, he prepares
his first plausible *philosophical* case against Kantian philosophy, and labours
tirelessly to recruit other key figures in the academic world, showing them
how it is possible to rewrite their philosophies of language and mind even
more effectively using pre-Kantian theories of relation. After another two
decades of research, the elderly Rove is now a philosophical juggernaut,
hailed in many quarters as the most original metaphysician of the century. Rove has learned an important lesson. Though he was able to win some
tight American elections by shifting a few groups of key swing voters with
personal innuendo, he cannot dethrone Kant in this way even when the
gossip is grounded in stone-cold truth. The philosophical world turns out
to be relatively unimpressed by the kind of personal dirt that ruined Gary
Hart and tarnished Bill Clinton. Kant's central strength lies not in his moral
character nor even in his sincerity, but in the force of the critical model itself.
For Rove or for anyone else, there is no way to topple this model without becoming a full-blown philosopher oneself, fighting the philosopher with philosophical weapons. To assemble the black boxes needed to defeat the great
philosopher Kant, Karl Rove *had to become a great philosopher himself,* or at least
a skilled spokesman for some unknown great thinker who does the work but
languishes in obscurity while Rove takes the credit. In other words, Rove's
attempt to 'socially construct' the reputation of Immanuel Kant has failed.
Instead, the ideas of Kant have constructed the new life of Karl Rove, just as

the double helix constructed the lives of Crick and Watson.

An actant is always a strength, and a strength is a central point that gath-ers other actants around it. Summing up his detailed account of a French navigational voyage, Latour reminds us that such a voyage does not belong to any familiar category. We cannot really call it 'knowledge', since 'becom-ing familiar with distant events requires [...] kings, offices, sailors, timber, lateen rigs, spice trades' (SA, p. 223). But it would be just as ridiculous to say that the voyage can be explained in terms of 'power'. After all, 'the reckon-ing of lands, the filling-in of log books, the tarring of the careen, the rigging of a mast, cannot without absurdity be put under the heading of this word ["power"]' (SA, p. 223). More generally:

> we need to get rid of all categories like those of power, knowledge, profit or capital, because they divide up a cloth that we want seamless in or-der to study it as we choose [...]. The question is rather simple: how to act at a distance on unfamiliar events, places, and people? Answer: by *somehow* bringing home these events, places, and people. How can this be achieved, since they are distant? By inventing [methods] that (a) render them *mobile* so that they can be brought back; (b) keep them *stable* so that they can be moved back and forth without additional distortion, corrup-tion, or decay, and (c) are *combinable* so that whatever stuff they are made of, they can be cumulated aggregated, or shuffled like a pack of cards. If those conditions are met, then a small provincial town, or an obscure laboratory, or a puny little company in a garage, that were at first as weak as any other place will become centers dominating at a distance many other places (SA, p. 223).

Actants can be linked to a center by being rendered mobile, stable, and com-binable with others. And here is a key moment in Latour's philosophy, since by definition his actants normally *do not* have mobility, stability, or combin-ability. Since every actant is utterly concrete (and according to *Irreductions* happens only once and in one time and one place) to make an actant mobile, stable, and combinable demands some sort of *abstraction* from that one time and one place. Yet Latour's form of abstraction can be performed by any ob-ject, not just a transcendent knowing human.

Abstraction does not occur by rising above the gullible beliefs of a pre-theoretical actor, but by enabling another actant's energies to be siphoned away at a distance. In this sense, any relation is an abstraction. It is not only Kant and Einstein who behave 'abstractly': an astrologer abstracts by linking all those born with the moon in Libra through their shared vanity and sense of fair play; an eagle abstracts by diving at any rabbit regardless of its unknown specific history; an equation abstracts by linking all diverse turbulent fluids that have the same Reynolds factor; the earth abstracts by drawing all masses regardless of their colour; a windmill abstracts by spin-ning in any breeze regardless of its odour, and by unifying all its wooden parts regardless of their exact granular pattern. Abstraction is not a unique human faculty that magically outstrips the world, but the very stuff of relation itself. Since all actants are utterly concrete, confined to a single time and place, in the strict sense they cannot communicate with each other at all. They interact only by way of abstracting from each other. Wood is *mobilized* by being moved from a lumber yard to a construction site. It is also *stabilized*, by being selected only for features that remain durable between one place and another. And the wood is made *combinable* by selecting it for features compatible with the other entities to which it must be linked. 'If by "abstraction" is meant the process by which each stage extracts elements out of the stage below so as to gather in one place as many resources as possible, very well, we have studied [...] the process of abstraction, exactly as we would examine a refinery in which raw oil is cracked into purer and purer oils' (SA, p. 241). Unfortunately, the usual view of abstraction is rather different: 'the meaning of the word "abstraction" has shifted from the *product* [...] to not only the *process* but also to the *producer's mind* [...]. Lapérouse will be said to operate more abstractly than the Chinese when he handles latitudes and longitudes, and Mendeleev to think more abstractly than the empirical chemists when he shuffles his cards around' (SA, p. 241). For Latour this is impossible. Abstraction is not a feature of the human mind, but of any relation whatever, since two events are so utterly concrete that they make contact at all only at the price of abstracting from one another, dealing with a small portion of each other rather than the totality. In other words, Latour gives us a metaphysical concept of abstraction rather than an epistemological one.

What we have learned in this chapter can be summarized as follows. Instead of substances, there are black boxes that are not permanent, natural, or durable, and are always at risk of being reopened during future controversies. And instead of harmless relations that affect nothing, relations are always violent abstractions made from actants that would otherwise be trapped in a single time and place. Black boxes and action at a distance will provide Latour's answer to the central problem of modern philosophy.

3

We Have Never Been Modern

We Have Never Been Modern was first published in French in 1991. It is the best introduction to Latour, and possibly his finest work: if a more original piece of philosophy has appeared in the past twenty years, it is unknown to me. This book cuts new paths through the reader's brain, and remains impossible to classify among the more familiar orientations of contemporary philosophy. Indeed, a sense of continued astonishment from rereading it was the original motivation for writing the present book. *We Have Never Been Modern* is witty, hard-hitting, and balanced. It is also surprisingly comprehensive for a book short enough that one or two sittings in a café are enough to consume its contents.

For all the richness of this compact *magnum opus*, its major themes are simple. First, Latour advances the most powerful definition of modernism of which I am aware. Modernity tries to *purify* the world by dissecting it into two utterly opposed realms. On one side we have the human sphere, composed of transparent freedom and ruled by arbitrary and incommensurable perspectives. On the other side we have nature or the external world, made up of hard matters of fact and acting with objective, mechanical precision. As Latour puts it later in his *Politics of Nature*, a pluralistic *multiculturalism* is always opposed to a homogeneous *mononaturalism*. We are told that nature is one, but that humans have numerous diverse perspectives on it. Not surprisingly, Latour rejects this modernist vision. There are not two mutually isolated zones called 'world' and 'human' that need to be bridged by some sort of magical leap. Instead, there are only actants, and in most cases it is impossible to identify the precise sphere ('nature, or culture?') to which any given actant belongs. The division of the world into two zones is a pointless fiction, since we have never managed to purify the world. We have never been modern. We are unable to separate between the natural and cultural realms—not because they are hopelessly intertwined, but because the dualism of nature and culture is groundless in the first place. The world is not made of slavish members of two rival fraternities, two mournful districts resembling East and West Germany. Purification of one from another is impossible, since there were never two opposed zones in the first place. Instead, there is nothing but a cosmic hailstorm of individual actants, none of them inherently natural or cultural. In fact, precisely *because* of its attempts to purify the two districts of the world from one another, the so-called modern age has created a greater number of hybrid objects than have ever been known before.

A. MODERNITY

'We pass from a limited problem [...] to a broader and more general problem: what does it mean to be modern?' (NM, p. 8). Latour is no modern, since he defines his own philosophy against any effort to purify two zones of the world from each other. Nor is he among the anti-moderns, since this sect oddly accepts modernism's claim to have transformed everything that came before, and merely adds the minus sign of pessimism instead of basking in happiness over modern revolutions. And he is also no postmodern, since this group severs itself from the *reality* of actants to float pretentiously amidst collage and simulacrum, leaving no room in philosophy for real atomic nuclei, hurricanes, or explosions, except perhaps as clever literary tropes drawn from Jabès and Mallarmé. Instead, Latour is a *nonmodern*. There has never been a radical break with what came before. For we ourselves, just like Neanderthals, sparrows, mushrooms, and dirt, have never done anything else than act amidst the bustle of other actants, compressing and resisting them, or giving way beneath their blows.

The moderns 'have cut the Gordian knot with a well-honed sword. The shaft is broken: on the left, they have put knowledge of things; on the right, power and human politics' (NM, p. 3). Modernity is the attempt to cleanse each half of any residue of the other, freeing facts from any contamination with personal value judgments, while liberating values and perspectives from the test of hard reality. This familiar split now seems so obvious that we seldom remember its inherent strangeness. Why carve reality into precisely *these* two sectors? Why not the old celestial and terrestrial spheres, as in ancient physics? Why not call everything either male or female, as in the structure of primitive grammar? Why not distinguish between things that burn and things that melt? Or between matter and antimatter? The reason is that human knowledge is now viewed as a unique site where one type of entity magically transcends the world and forms more or less cloudy representations of it. The gap between human and mountain is now seen as different *in kind* from that between lightning and mountain. This bequest of special transcendent powers to humans forms one side of a great divide, while the other side is packed with stupid robotic objects acting with clockwork mechanical torpor. The first side is seen as sensitive and poetic, but essentially vague and unfalsifiable; the second is viewed as usefully exact, but rigid and merciless in its crushing unity. Yet both sides of the great divide belong to the same package: 'Modernity is often defined in terms of humanism, either as a way of saluting the birth of "man" or as a way of announcing his death. But this habit itself is modern, because it remains asymmetrical. It overlooks the simultaneous birth of "nonhumanity"—things, or objects, or beasts— and the equally strange being of a crossed-out God, relegated to the sidelines' (NM, p. 13). We are now left with nothing but

> the meeting point of the two extremes of Nature and Society in which resides the whole of reality. With this single line, realists and constructivists will be able to quarrel [...] for centuries: the former will declare that no one has fabricated this real fact; the latter that our hands alone fashioned this social fact [...].

> [Yet] the great masses of Nature and Society can be compared to the cooled-down continents of plate tectonics. If we want to understand their movement, we have to go down into those searing rifts where the magma erupts and on the basis of this eruption are produced [...] the two continental plates on which our feet are firmly planted (NM, p. 87).

If Kant's Copernican Revolution placed humans at the center of philosophy while reducing the rest of the world to an unknowable set of objects, what Latour recommends is a Counter-Revolution. Nature and culture are not 'inextricably linked', because they are not two distinct zones at all. He mockingly notes that 'the moderns have imposed an ontological difference as radical as the sixteenth-century differentiation between the supralunar world that knew neither change nor uncertainty [and the sublunar world of decay]. The same physicists had a good laugh with Galileo at that ontological distinction—but then they rushed to reestablish it in order to protect the laws of physics from social corruption!' (NM, p. 121, punctuation modified). In this respect, Latour is the Galileo of metaphysics, ridiculing the split between the supralunar world of hard scientific fact and the sublunar world of human power games. But unlike the social constructionists, he does not destabilize this split in order to create a new, inverted one where power games hold the upper hand. There is no 'upper hand' in this sense for Latour: there are only actants, nothing else, and they come in countless varieties rather than two. In dialogue with his quasi-allies Steven Shapin and Simon Schaffer, Latour gives a marvelous account of the nature/culture divide through a long account of the controversy over an air pump between Boyle and Hobbes (NM, pp. 15-43). When these historians conclude that

'Hobbes was right' to grant victory to the power of society over the reality of nature, Latour counters bluntly: 'No, Hobbes was wrong' (NM, p. 26). Demolishing in advance the view that his philosophy equals social constructionism, Latour writes that

> [Shapin and Schaffer] offer a masterful deconstruction of the evolution, diffusion and popularization of the air pump. Why, then, do they not deconstruct the evolution, diffusion and popularization of 'power' or 'force'? Is 'force' less problematic than the air's spring? If nature and epistemology are not made up of transhistoric entities, then neither are history and sociology—unless one adopts some authors' asymmetrical posture and agrees to be simultaneously constructivist where nature is concerned and realist where society is concerned [...]! But it is not very probable that the air's spring has a more political basis than English society itself [...] (NM, p. 27).

This radical split between the mechanical lethargy of objects and the transcendent dignity of human subjects is the typical feature of the West during the modern period. But in fact, there is no radical break between premoderns and moderns—only a difference in scale.

> It is not only out of arrogance that Westerners think they are radically different from others, it is also out of despair, and by way of self-punishment. They like to frighten themselves with their own destiny. Their voices quaver when they contrast Barbarians to Greeks, or the Center to the Periphery, or when they celebrate the Death of God, or the Death of Man, the European *Krisis*, imperialism, anomie, or the end of the civilizations that we know are mortal. Why do we get so much pleasure out of being so different not only from others but from our own past? What psychologist will be subtle enough to explain our morose delight in being in perpetual crisis [...]? Why do we like to transform small differences in scale among collectives into huge dramas? (NM, p. 114).

Any supposed difference between the cutting-edge West and archaic traditional societies emerges not from some radical transcendence that replaces gullible belief with critical freedom, but only from the vaster number of actants that are mobilized by the various Western networks. And 'when we see them as networks, Western innovations remain recognizable and important, but they no longer suffice as the stuff of saga, a vast saga of radical rupture, fatal destiny, irreversible good or bad fortune' (NM, p. 48). Once we view the world as a set of shifting networks involving trials of strength between actants, rather than a radical self-reflexive break with the naiveté of peasants and shamans, we begin to see the West as no more or less bizarre than any other assemblage of actants: 'is Boyle's air pump any less strange than the Arapesh spirit houses [...]?' (NM, p. 115). This rhetorical question asks that we stop debunking our enemies by displaying their ignorance from our lofty critical tower. As the Edinburgh School had already insisted, we need to give *symmetrical* explanations that treat winners and losers with equal fairness: 'if you want to account for the belief in flying saucers, make sure your explanations can be used, symmetrically, for black holes [...]. If you claim to debunk parapsychology, can you use the same factors for psychology [...]? If you analyze Pasteur's successes, do the same terms allow you to account for his failures [...]?' (NM, p. 93).

If the moderns are bad, this is not to say that the reactionary antimoderns or the flippant postmoderns offer anything better. All three groups are united in accepting modernity's claim of a radical schism between humans and things. 'Except for the plus or minus signs, moderns and antimoderns share all the same convictions. The postmoderns, always perverse, accept the idea that the situation is indeed catastrophic, but they maintain that it is to be acclaimed rather than bemoaned!' (NM, p. 123). Antimoderns, horrified by the wasteland of modernity, try to save whatever can still be saved: 'souls, minds, emotions, interpersonal relations, the symbolic dimension, human warmth, local specificities [...]' (NM, p. 123). As pale and lifeless as these residues may be, they are often preferable to the comical pose of the postmoderns and their fixation on the margins, subversion, and all that is oppressed. Such authors forge entire academic careers from 'fuzzy areas [such as] madness, children, animals, popular culture and women's bodies' (NM, p. 100), all due to their needless concession that modernity has already conquered everything else. Latour often describes this concession as 'an intellectual Munich', referring to Neville Chamberlain's surrender of the Czech frontier without a struggle. As he bitingly puts it: 'The defense of marginality presupposes the existence of a totalitarian center. But if the center and its totality are illusions, acclaim for the margins is somewhat ridiculous'. For example, 'it is admirable to demonstrate that the strength of the spirit transcends the laws of mechanical nature, but this program is idiotic if matter is not at all material and machines are not at all mechanical' (NM, p. 124). In a stirring appeal, Latour asks his readers: 'are you not fed up with language games, and with the eternal skepticism of the deconstruction of meaning?' If not, then you should be, since 'discourse is not a world unto itself but a population of actants that mix with things as well as with societies, uphold the former and the latter alike, and hold on to them both' (NM, p. 90).

The modern split actually makes the world *less* interesting, carving up the cosmos into human subjects and mechanical objects, divided by a Berlin Wall made porous only by a handful of fuzzy or 'problematic' checkpoints. In the eyes of the moderns, the critical, transcendent Westerner is no longer a normal entity, but instead a kind of 'Spock-like mutant' (NM, p. 115) freed from the normal relations between actors of every kind. Against this dismal caricature of human thought, Latour unleashes a deserved barrage of rotten eggs and tomatoes:

Haven't we shed enough tears over the disenchantment of the world? Haven't we frightened ourselves enough with the poor European who is thrust into a cold soulless cosmos, wandering on an inert planet in a world devoid of meaning? Haven't we shivered enough before the spectacle of the mechanized proletarian who is subject to the absolute domination of a mechanized capitalism and a Kafkaesque bureaucracy, abandoned smack in the middle of language games, lost in cement and formica? Haven't we felt sorry enough for the consumer who leaves the driver's seat of his car only to move to the sofa in the TV room where he is manipulated by the powers of the media and the postindustrialized society?! (NM, p. 115).

And in an equally devastating passage:

Take some small business-owner hesitatingly going after a few market shares, some conqueror trembling with fever, some poor scientist tinkering in his lab, a lowly engineer piecing together a few more or less favorable relationships of force, some stuttering and fearful politician; turn the critics loose on them, and what do you get? Capitalism, imperialism, science, technology, domination—all equally absolute, systematic, totalitarian. In the first scenario the actors were trembling; in the second, they are not (NM, pp. 125-6).

Latour is the prophet of trembling actants, as well as the satirist of all supposed hegemonies and totalitarian codings. In this respect, he is the long-awaited destroyer of the academic sanctimony that more or less ruined my youth. The postmodern divas have good reason to worry when Latour enters the house. Skipping ahead to a passage from *Pandora's Hope*: 'Yes, we have lost the world. Yes, we are forever prisoners of language. No, we will never regain certainty. No, we will never get beyond our biases. Yes, we will forever be stuck within our own selfish standpoint. Bravo! Encore!' (PH, p. 8). Here we encounter the vigorous attitude of a genuine philosopher, as opposed to the tedious professional enforcers of insights already won.

B. QUASI-OBJECTS

The shaky status of the modern settlement is seen most clearly in the multiplication of what Latour calls *hybrids*, or (following Michel Serres) *quasi-objects*. When reading a typical newspaper article, it becomes virtually impossible to distinguish supposed hard facts from supposed social constructions or projections of value. In Latour's daily newspaper, 'on page eleven, there are whales wearing collars fitted with radio tracking devices; also on page eleven, there is a slag heap in northern France, a symbol of the exploitation of workers, that has just been classified as an ecological preserve because of e flora it has been fostering! On page twelve, the Pope, French bish-onsanto, the Fallopian tubes, and Texas fundamentalists gather in a strange cohort around a single contraceptive' (NM, p. 2). There may be a few pages in *Le Monde* that deal with politics alone, along with 'the literary supplement in which novelists delight in the adventures of a few narcissistic egos ("I love you... you don't")' (NM, p. 2). But the number of obvious hybrids is overwhelming: 'frozen embryos, expert systems, digital machines, sensor-equipped robots, hybrid corn, data banks, psychotropic drugs, whales outfitted with radar sounding devices, gene synthesizers, audience analyzers [...]' (NM, pp. 49-50). These hybrids are a nightmare for any attempt to slice the world cleanly into two purified districts. For this reason, the modern position will deliberately misread them 'as a mixture of two pure forms' (NM, p. 78, punctuation modified). But such a mixture is impossible if the two pure forms do not exist in the first place. Latour's hybrids are not just another set of fuzzy grey areas suitable as campsites for those who are fond of the transgressive borderlands. For our world contains *nothing but* hybrids, and even the word 'hybrid' misleads us with its false overtones of a mixture of two pristine ingredients. If we call them quasi-objects, the work done by the 'quasi-' is to remove any lingering hint of solid natural objects approached through a colourful diversity of equally valid cultural standpoints. There are only actants: all actants are constructed through numerous trials of strength with others, and all have an intimate integrity that partially resists any effort to disassemble them.

While the moderns cut the Gordian knot in half, the goal of Latour and his friends in science studies is to retie the knot (NM, p. 3). He even gives names: Donald MacKenzie, Michel Callon, Thomas Hughes (NM, p. 3), and numerous others found in countless passages of his books. This listing of allies by name is not meant as a show of force, as when rappers assemble hundreds of acknowledgments on the jacket of a compact disc. Latour's hunger for collaboration is the only attitude consistent with his vision of how actants operate. Of all recent philosophers, Latour is the most difficult to imagine without friends and associates. Whereas Heidegger's Black Forest hut was the symbol of monastic communion between one man and Being itself, Latour's own hut in central France is simply a pleasant work space near a pond and a castle, surrounded by village neighbors, and open in principle to talkative guests. Whereas Heidegger sneered at the emptiness of conferences, Latour seems most at home in large academic gatherings. Through the work of Latour and his allies, 'science studies have forced everyone to rethink anew the role of objects in the construction of collectives, thus challenging philosophy' (NM, p. 55). If philosophy has not taken up the challenge, this tells us more about the current state of our field than about the merits of Latour's position.

We recall the paradox of the modern world that, even while claiming to purify the human and natural zones from each other, even while holding them in chaste isolation, it has produced a record number of hybrids. Indeed, the work of purification seems to be the very precondition for generating the greatest possible number of hybrids, whereas 'by devoting themselves to conceiving of hybrids, the other [premodern] cultures have excluded their proliferation' (NM, p. 12). Although we cannot discuss Latour's recent political writing here, one of its central points is that modern political forms are entirely built on the basis of an antiseptic split between nature and society. Against this split, he suggests 'that we are going to have to slow down, reorient and regulate the proliferation of monsters by representing their existence officially. Will a different democracy become necessary? A democracy extended to things?' (NM, p. 12).[1] But the reign of hybrids or quasi-objects is unavoidable: 'underneath the opposition between objects and subjects, there is the whirlwind of the mediators' (NM, p. 46).

Postmodern philosophy, with its antirealist excesses, can tell us nothing about quasi-objects. While scientific realists drop the 'quasi-' and wish to speak only of objects, the postmoderns celebrate the 'quasi-' alone. Attend any lecture by Bruno Latour, and ask yourself if his postmodern forerunners could honestly say anything interesting about the same topics: Derrida about the price of apricots in Paris, Foucault about soil samples in the Amazon, or Lyotard about brake failures on a new metro car prototype.

> When we are dealing with science and technology it is hard to imagine for long that we are a text that is writing itself, a discourse that is speaking all by itself, a play of signifiers without signifieds. It is hard to reduce the entire cosmos to a grand narrative, the physics of subatomic particles to a text, subway systems to rhetorical devices, all social structures to discourse. The Empire of Signs lasted no longer than Alexander's, and like Alexander's it was carved up and parceled out to its generals (NM, p. 64).

Hybrids cannot be grasped either by scientific realists, the power-gamers of sociology, or deconstructionists, because 'as soon as we are on the trail of some quasi-object, it appears to us sometimes as a thing, sometimes as a narrative, sometimes as a social bond, without ever being reduced to a mere being' (NM, p. 89). But here as in the related twofold split, there are not three distinct zones entitled 'thing', 'narrative', and 'society'. At best, these are concepts roughly useful in practical terms for carving up a vast terrain of heterogeneous actants. All that matters are actants and the networks that link them. To follow a quasi-object is to trace a network (NM, p. 89). There is nothing rarefied about this notion, since the best procedure is 'to look at networks of facts and laws rather as one looks at gas lines or sewage pipes' (NM, p. 117).

Latour now reminds us of the point from his earlier writings that entities are *events*, inconceivable in isolation from networks (NM, p. 81). They are

---

1. See also Latour's *Politics of Nature.*

not isolated points of essence that endure through space and time, but more like *trajectories* (NM, p. 87). Here we find a tension between events and trajectories that Latour's metaphysics never fully resolves. An event happens in a single time and place and is fully concrete, since it cannot be analyzed into essential and inessential elements. This entails that even the tiniest shift in a thing's interactions, as always occurs in every moment, suffices to transform an event into something altogether new. Whether I jump, unbutton my shirt, or lose the least hair from my head, my existence in each case will become an entirely different event, since Latour leaves no room to speak of 'accidental' variation in the same enduring thing. For this reason, events are effectively frozen into their own absolutely specific location and set of relationships, and cannot possibly endure outside them. By contrast, the (derivative) notion of trajectories teaches the opposite lesson. When considering a trajectory, we never find a thing in a single time and place, but get to know it only by following its becomings, watching the details of its *curriculum vita*. We learn of the successive trials from which it emerges either victorious or stalemated. And here is the paradox: in one sense, Latour's objects are utterly imprisoned in a single instant; in another sense, they burst all boundaries of space and time and take off on lines of flight toward ever new adventures.

But notice that in either case, there is no room for any model of *essence*. If we are speaking of instantaneous events, then there is no essential inner core that lies beneath the shifting accidents of the moment. And if we are speaking of trajectories or transformations, then there is still no cryptic domestic essence on the interior of a thing that could endure across time— here a thing is still found on the surface of the world, but it is now a surface unfolding through a succession of various shapes rather than a cinematic frame of absolute specificity. A merely apparent essence will gradually condense from this grand drama of instantaneous points and flying trajectories; even once it crystallizes, the essence will have only a pragmatic value in helping us identify certain things as the same. On the whole, this brilliant assault on essence and substance is my least favourite aspect of Latour's metaphysics, and will form the primary target of criticism in Part Two. Yet there is another side to Latour's concept of essence that I am happy to salute: namely, however limited the role of essence in his philosophy, he at least grants it to *all* entities. Instead of viewing inanimate objects either as invincible machine-like liquidators or as empty receptacles for human categories, Latour turns them into active mediators: 'actors endowed with the capacity to translate what they transport, to redefine it, redeploy it, and also to betray it. The serfs have become free citizens once more' (NM, p. 81). By contrast, the Heideggers and Derridas grow fat on a serf economy that leaves science with the dirty work of dealing with all the bumbling rocks, diamonds, and trees that may be out there somewhere. For Latour's part, he wants nothing to do with serfdom: 'history is no longer simply the history of people, it becomes the history of natural things as well' (NM, p. 82). Put differently, 'what Sartre said of humans—that their existence precedes their essence—has to be said of all the actants: of the air's spring as well as society, of matter as well as consciousness' (NM, p. 86). What Latour means is that the essence of a thing results only from its public performance in the world, and in this respect he does agree with certain postmodernist currents. Yet one can hardly imagine the Judith Butlers acknowledging the 'performativity' of *inanimate* objects as well as of human actors. In this way, Latour strikes a tacit below against every version of speech-act theory: what he gives us is not speech-act theory, but *actor-act* theory.

Countless stale dualisms now fall by the wayside. For instance, in a world made up of networks of actants, does anything remain of the distinction between global and local? 'If we wander about inside IBM, if we follow the chains of command of the Red Army, if we enquire in the corridors of the Ministry of Education, if we study the process of selling and buying a bar of soap, we never leave the local level. We are always in interaction with four or five people [...] the directors' conversations sound just like those of the employees...' (NM, p. 121). Gone is the Red Army commander who issues orders flawlessly applied by the lowly human masses who serve his whims. Also gone is the classical distinction between simple substance and complex aggregate: 'the aggregates are not made from some substance different from what they are aggregating' (NM, p. 122). Leibniz's mockery of a pair of diamonds and his courtly respect for a single diamond, his laughter at the Dutch East India Company as a pseudo-substance combined with his great assurance that the human soul is a substance, melt away in Latour's hands into an utter democracy of levels. There is not some magic natural stratum of the universe where all accidents and combinations fall aside to reveal pure natural unities known as substances. Any black box can be opened, and inside we will find nothing but more black boxes. For the same reason, there is no particular level where humans might stand so as to transcend the world and critically observe it, stripped of all naïve belief: 'by traversing [...] networks, we do not come to rest in anything particularly homogeneous. We remain, rather, within an *infra-physics*' (NM, p. 128, emphasis added). Making use of Leibnizian terminology, Latour says that 'we start from the *vinculum* [chain] itself, from passages and relations, not accepting as a starting point any being that does not emerge from this relation that is at once collective, real, and discursive. We do not start from human beings, those latecomers, nor from language, a more recent arrival still' (NM, p. 129). Instead, we explore the non-modern world with all its 'nuncios, mediators, delegates, fetishes, machines, figurines, instruments, representatives, angels, lieutenants, spokespersons and cherubim' (NM, p. 129), a sentence one would never find in the collected works of Heidegger. We have nothing but our turbulent of world of quasi-objects, which also means *quasi-subjects* (NM, p. 139).

According to the modern view, 'we may glorify the sciences, play power games or make fun of the belief in a reality, but we must not mix these
three caustic acids' (NM, p. 6). In a beautiful image, Latour counters that
the networks traced by quasi-objects are 'torn apart like the Kurds between the Iranians, the Iraqis and the Turks; once night has fallen, they
slip across borders to get married, and they dream of a common homeland
that would be carved out of the three countries which have divided them
up' (NM, pp. 6-7). Above all it is Kant who ruined Kurdistan, by cement-
ing the unjustified split between humans and nature: 'What was a mere distinction [between nature and humans] is sharpened into a total separation,
a Copernican Revolution. Things-in-themselves become inaccessible while,
symmetrically, the transcendental subject becomes infinitely remote from
the world' (NM, p. 56). No matter what variations we play on this theme,
whether through absorbing the supposed things-in-themselves back into the
human subject, or denying that the question makes any sense in the first
place, the gap between humans and world always remains privileged over
the gaps between tree and wind, or fire and cotton. 'To be sure, the Sun
King around which objects revolve will be overturned in favour of many
other pretenders—Society, epistemes, mental structures, cultural categories,
intersubjectivity, language; but these palace revolutions will not alter the fo-
cal point, which I have called, for that reason, Subject/Society' (NM, pp.
56-7). Opposed to all forms of critical philosophy, Latour also shuns any
form of debunking or unmasking. He refuses to pack everything into the
theater of the human subject, as in René Girard's denial of any real stakes
in human conflict (NM, p. 45), or the absorption of reality by society in the
'Strong Program' of the Edinburgh school (NM, p. 55).

We already know of Latour's distaste for the postmoderns: 'I have not
found words ugly enough to designate this intellectual movement [...] this
intellectual immobility through which humans and nonhumans are left to
drift' (NM, p. 61). The postmoderns 'accept the total [modern] division between the material and technological world on the one hand and the linguistic play of speaking subjects on the other' (NM, p. 61). As they see it, 'nothing has value; everything is a reflection, a simulacrum, a floating sign [...].
The empty world in which the postmoderns evolve is one they themselves,
and they alone, have emptied, because they have taken the moderns at their
word' (NM, p. 131). Latour extends his attack to a weightier target when he
takes aim at Heidegger, who is clearly guilty of the same sort of modern split
between Dasein and world, despite claims to the contrary by his loyal man-
servants. One should never forget the following litmus test: ignore all rhetoric about realism and idealism, and ask of any philosophy whether it places inanimate relations on the same footing as the relations between human
and world. If not, then we are still amidst the Copernicans, full stop. By this
criterion, Heidegger surely belongs in their ranks. For 'he and his epigones

do not expect to find Being except along the Black Forest *Holzwege*. Being cannot reside in ordinary beings. Everywhere, there is desert' (NM, p. 65). Although in my view (but not Latour's) Heidegger is the greatest philosopher of the past century, there are certainly moments when he deserves to have his tyres slashed. Who does not grow weary of his grave pomposity of tone, his insufferable claim to the mantle of his Teutonized pre-Socratics? Latour treats Heidegger with an appropriate degree of satire: 'here too the gods are present: in a hydroelectric plant on the banks of the Rhine, in subatomic particles, in Adidas shoes as well as in the old wooden clogs hollowed out by hand, in agribusiness as well as in timeworn landscapes, in shopkeepers' calculations as well as in Hölderlin's heartrending verse' (NM, p. 66, punctuation altered).

Modernity judges its progress according to a specific theory of time that Latour rejects. 'The past was the confusion of things and men; the future is what will no longer confuse them' (NM, p. 71, emphasis added). If we reject from the start any hope of purifying two nonexistent realms, our theory of time will also need to change. In a style reminiscent of his teacher Michel Serres, Latour observes that 'instead of a fine laminary flow, we will most often get a turbulent flow of whirlpools and rapids. Time becomes reversible instead of irreversible' (NM, p. 73). This can easily be seen from a quick glance at the present world: 'no one knows any longer whether the reintroduction of the bear in the Pyrenees, kolkhozes, aerosols, the Green Revolution, the anti-smallpox vaccine, Star Wars, the Muslim religion, partridge hunting, the French Revolution, service industries, labour unions, cold fusion, Bolshevism, relativity, Slovak nationalism, commercial sailboats, and so on, are outmoded, up to date, futuristic, atemporal, nonexistent, or permanent' (NM, p. 74). Time is made of spirals and reversals, not a forward march. All countries are 'lands of contrast', mixing different elements from different periods of history. The same is true even of our own bodies and genetic codes: 'I may use an electric drill, but I also use a hammer. The former is thirty-five years old, the latter hundreds of thousands [...]. Some of my genes are 500 million years old, others 3 million, others 100,000 years, and my habits range in age from a few days to several thousand years. As Péguy's Clio said, and as Michel Serres repeats, 'we are exchangers and brewers of time', [...]. It is this exchange that defines us, not the calendar that the moderns had constructed for us' (NM, p. 75). When properly unwrapped, the title *We Have Never Been Modern* contains the whole of Latour's philosophy. We have never been modern because we have never really made a purifying split between humans and world. For this reason, we cannot say that time passes in terms of irreversible revolutions, but only that it whirls and eddies according to shifts in the networks of actants. An actant is an instantaneous event, but also a trajectory that outstrips any given instant. On this paradoxical note, we can proceed to *Pandora's Hope*, Latour's outstanding book of 1999.

4

Pandora's Hope

The chapters contained in *Pandora's Hope* are partly new material, partly reworked articles dating from as early as 1993. As if writing from Las
Vegas rather than Paris, Latour sings a brash medley spanning his entire
career, retracing the various steps through which he had passed by century's end. The reader listens in: from the construction of scientific facts
in the jungle, through the ballad of Pasteur and the microbes, to the anti-
Copernican rhythms of his nonmodernist style, on to the closing strains of
a democratic politics of things. Yet the book is a unified work animated by
a powerful central theme. It also shows Latour in furious combat with his
enemies, conducted with bursts of sardonic wit. Kant's philosophy is nick-
named 'the Königsberg broadcast' (PH, p. 5) and his things-in-themselves
are dismissed as saying no more than 'we are here, what you eat is not dust'
(PH, p. 6). Even while speaking of 'a slow descent from Kant to hell' (PH,
p. 21). Latour offers backhanded praise, since 'for Kant there was [at least]
still something that revolved around this crippled despot [the human sub-
ject], a green planet around this pathetic sun' (PH, p. 6). The postmoderns
fare much worse, flattered with the acidic 'Bravo! Encore!' and described
as 'gloating prisoners' (PH, p. 8). Their verb 'deconstruct' is defined as 'to
destroy in slow motion' (PH, p. 8).

The book is best understood by simple reflection on its title and subtitle.
The title employs Pandora's fabled box as a symbol for the 'black box' of the
sciences, which Latour has now opened:

> [The box] was tightly sealed as long as it remained in the two-culture no-
> man's-land [...] blissfully ignored by the humanists trying to avoid all the
> dangers of objectification and by the epistemologists trying to fend off
> the unruly mob. Now that it has been opened, with plagues and curses,

sins and ills whirling around, there is only one thing to do, and that is
to go even deeper, all the way down into the almost-empty box, in order
to retrieve what, according to the venerable legend, has been left at the
bottom—yes, *hope* (PH, p. 23).

Equally instructive is the subtitle of the book, 'Essays on the Reality of
Science Studies'. The word 'reality' here is a frank call for *realism* in philosophy. And therein lies the surprise, since Latour is often held to believe
that reality is constructed by human society. He is aware of this reputation,
as shown by the sarcastic title of his opening chapter: 'Do You Believe in
Reality?' Reflecting jointly on the title and subtitle, Latour aims at a new
realism of interlocked black boxes. But his form of realism differs from the
familiar kind in at least three ways, none of them surprising after our survey
of his earlier books.

Point 1: Traditional realism usually accepts some ultimate substance,
whether it be otherwordly exemplars (Plato), concrete individual things
(Aristotle), God (Augustine, Spinoza), mirror-like monads (Leibniz), in-
destructible physical matter (Democritus, Marx), or some variant of
these. But these substances are merely treated as the terminal black
box—a final stratum of reality that can never be opened and examined.
Latour's realism denies any ultimate stratum on which everything else is
built. There are no black boxes that cannot be opened, no final layer of
substance from which all else is derived.

Point 2: Along with substance, traditional realism often defends the parallel notion of essence, since a substance ought to have essential properties opposed to its accidental traits or its relations. By contrast, Latour
recognizes no inner sanctum of the thing in which the essence could possibly reside. His actants are always public, not hermetic.

Point 3: Traditional realism also puts great stock in the difference between things and how they are perceived. For Latour, this split merely
leads to a Copernican rift between things-in-themselves and phenomena. His escape route is to insist that we are always in contact with reality, even though it resists us in some manner. Reality does not play hide-
and-seek behind a veil. Things relate to one another, translate into one
another, and are never out of mutual contact.

The metaphysics of Pandora's box gives us a democratic universe of actors.
Whether an actor is physical or purely delusional, it engages in trials of
strength with the others. Every actor can be opened to reveal its components, as long as we perform the necessary labour. There is no final infrastructure of reality that reduces the rest to mere ideological superstructure.
An actor has no essential inner core separated by a colossal gap from its trivial encrustations, or from its relations with other things. This list of principles will already be enough for some observers to deny Latour's claim to be

a realist. For my own part I am inclined to grant him the title, with a single reservation that will become important during the second half of this book.

A. CIRCULATING REFERENCE

Latour's phrase 'circulating reference' captures the whole of his metaphysical position, which replaces the tragic gap of subject and object with a single plane of countless dueling actors. We have seen the absolute equality of these actors, which cannot be segregated into genuine solid atoms on one side and mere figments of human beings on the other. Latour provides a fine example in his lengthy case history of Frédéric Joliot, son-in-law of the Curies, and in his day one of the world's leading authorities on radioactive chemistry (PH, pp. 80-92). Joliot and his colleagues grapple with uranium fission in their laboratory, trying to calculate the average number of neutrons released when uranium is bombarded. But uranium is not their only concern. Their studies lead them toward so-called 'heavy water', which is produced in sufficient quantities only by the firm Norsk Hydro Eletrisk; when its factory later falls under Nazi occupation, we will find that 'someone who wanted nothing but a Nobel Prize [sets] about organizing a commando operation in Norway' (PH, p. 89). At the same time, the Joliot team enters tricky negotiations with a mining company in the Belgian Congo, which will supply the uranium for their experiments. Simultaneously, they are urged by the physicist Leo Szilard to suppress their findings for fear that Nazi or Soviet scientists may be among their readers. Joliot must seek the financial support of cabinet minister Raoul Dautry, and must also do without his foreign assistants Halban and Kowarski, who as aliens are briefly excluded from the lab as potential spies.

Traditional history of science, like traditional realism in general, would split this story cleanly in two: 'purely political or economic factors would be added to purely scientific ones' (PH, p. 90). But Joliot's story is one, not two. It is true that uranium is a real actor outside Joliot's control: it will not yield its secrets without exactly the right point of attack, and even then it will startle him with endless surprises. Yet the same is true for the Belgian and Norwegian industrial firms, Leo Szilard, the French minister, and the German sentries guarding the heavy water plant. There is not some 'parallelogram of forces' in which pure states of affairs in nature are then filtered or shaped by social factors (PH, p. 133). There is not some 'regrettable intermixing of two pure registers' (PH, p. 90). Since neutrons, deuterium, and paraffin are no more or less real than ministers and spies, the first step should be to *refuse* to distinguish between these things. Latour's position 'rejects [...] the entire research program that would try to divide the story of Joliot into two parts [...]' (PH, p. 84).

Latour views his position as an enriched version of realism. But

traditional realists would call it an unrepentant form of social constructionism. The reasons for this disparity are interesting. For Latour, we cannot
begin with a naturalistic standpoint that assumes the world is built of tiny
physical particles with all else reducing ultimately to material interaction. At
the outset, the philosopher has no idea what is real and what is unreal. To
remove this perplexity by separating a privileged caste of real material entities from a horde of human-made figments amounts, for Latour, to a form of
idealism. It replaces the puzzling nature of an actor, so carefully unlocked
through diverse trials of strength, with an *a priori* dogma about the nature
of the real. This is why a general metaphysics of actors looks to Latour like
the only genuine form of realism. A theory that does not treat Frédéric Joliot
and Norsk Hydro Eletrisk in the same way as paraffin might be *materialism*,
but it cannot possibly be *realism*. Though materialism is usually viewed as the
realist philosophy par excellence, it is in fact a covert idealism that replaces
the mystery of actors with the dogmatic *idea* of an extended physical stuff lying at the root of everything.

But Latour strikes a far larger target than materialism. Even Leibniz,
who was no materialist, makes a similar distinction between natural monads
and artificial aggregates. In the Leibnizian system Joliot and Dautry would
be granted monads like all other humans, but the same would not be true
of uranium atoms (mere 'chains' of monads), let alone factories and uranium mines (mere 'aggregates'). Rifts of this kind exist in numerous philosophical realists besides Leibniz. Their main criterion for reality always
seems to be the natural as opposed to the artificial. But the weakness of this
standard is clearly displayed in the case of plutonium: although artificially created by humans and never found in nature, it is a chemical element
every bit as real as lead or gold. The fact that something is created by human artifice does not deprive it of reality, as Doctor Frankenstein quickly
learned. On this point Latour's argument is compelling, and does not suffice
to earn him the label of an 'antirealist'. Good realism actually requires that
we not reduce the number of actors by means of some dogmatic prelimi-
nary standard. For this reason we should not hesitate in endorsing Latour's
wry formulation that 'Golden Mountains, phlogiston, unicorns, bald kings
of France, chimeras, spontaneous generation, black holes, cats on mats, and
other black swans and white ravens will all occupy the same space-time as
Hamlet, Popeye, and Ramses II' (PH, p. 161).

Yet there is another point on which the unease of traditional realists
strikes closer to the heart of Latour's system. For such realists, reality is not
just taken to be natural or physical, but is also taken to exist 'whether we
like it or not'. Reality is independent of human perception, not created by it,
and will survive the extermination of all humans and all other animals. And
in principle, though traditional realists never seem to care much about this
point, reality should be independent even of its effect on other surrounding

inanimate things. This is the *only* point where Latour might seem to head off in an antirealist direction, since what he offers is a realism of relations, not of non-relational objects lying beneath their interactions with the environment. Against the traditional gesture of isolating the real from all its distorting associations, Latour holds that a thing becomes increasingly real *the more* associations it has. He is certainly not a full-blown antirealist, since he allows objects to do more work than phenomenologists or philosophers of language permit. In my view he is even more of a realist than the scientific naturalists are, since he does not begin by defining all realities out of existence other than clods of physical matter. He is clearly no social constructionist, since uranium and paraffin construct Joliot's existence every bit as much as French society molds and shapes them in turn. But Latour is definitely a *relationist*, and since relational philosophies often hold that human linguistic or social structures do all the work of relation, it is understandable why his position is confused with these others. Relationism, the view that a thing is defined solely by its effects and alliances rather than by a lonely inner kernel of essence, is the paradoxical heart of Latour's position, responsible for all his breakthroughs and possible excesses.

There is a worthwhile philosophical debate to be had over this point. It may be that relationism is unjustified. It may be (as I myself hold) that metaphysics *demands* a distinction between the inner reality of a thing and its relations with other entities. Yet it is not possible to side here with Latour's opponents, who commit the obvious blunder of assigning reality and relation to two specific *kinds* of entities: the natural object and the human subject, respectively. In other words, traditional realism thinks that nature is purely laced with objective reality, and the observing human being imposes false relational projections onto this reality, which the enlightened person must proceed to debunk and denounce. Nature does all the work of reality, and culture does all the work of distortion. But even if someone wishes to oppose Latour's relationism with a rift between the inner heart of a thing and its manifestations to other things (as I do), this chasm still cannot be a synonym for a cosmic gap lying between world and humans alone. It cannot be only humans who produce this dualism, or we have relapsed into the most dismal feature of modernity. By trying to apportion reality and relations along the human/world divide, traditional realists grant too much power to human beings by giving them the unique sorcerer's power of distorting the world. Latour abolishes this mistake once and for all, by giving all actors an equal kind of power: the power to relate and assemble. Let those who attack Latour attack him for relationism, and not on false charges of antirealism and social constructionism.

We have seen that the privileged rift between world and humans is, for Latour, the most regrettable feature of modernity. As he often declares, 'the philosophy of language makes it seem as if there exist two disjointed spheres separated by a unique and radical gap that must be reduced to the search for correspondence [...] between words and the world' (PH, p. 69). Much like Whitehead, Latour fragments this gap to infinity, placing it everywhere in the world. Everywhere, the universe is riddled with gaps. But they are by no means unbridgeable, since they are crossed constantly by the work of translation. In Chapter Two of *Pandora's Hope*, Latour gives us a typically wonderful case study: a trip to the Amazon to observe a dispute over whether a section of the jungle is receding from the savannah or advancing toward it (PH, pp. 24-79). Here we find a perfect case of 'science in action'. At no point in the story is the truth of the jungle visibly incarnate at a glance. Our knowledge of it emerges only through a long chain of mediating actors, whether intellectual or purely manual. First, there are the satellite maps that translate raw Amazon landscape into a series of accessible coloured shapes. The map tends to roll up if not pressed down firmly by paperweights or hands, which thereby become scientific instruments. The trees in the jungle must be labeled with numbers. The soil must be compared with colours on portable charts and even molded with the hands and subjectively judged: is it 'sandy clay' or 'clayey sand'? (PH, p. 63). Finally, the soil and plant samples must be physically removed from their natural context and taken to the university for further tests. If there are gaps in the argument of the scientists, their article may never appear in print. But the same will be true if the jeep crashes on the homeward drive and spills the samples, if a military coup lands the researchers in prison, or if a careless insult leads to broken friendships among the co-authors. The chain of mediators can be interrupted at any point: intellectual, physical, political, or moral. Wherever the break occurs, it will cut the unbroken electric circuit that the research requires.

Using the same term employed by Heidegger to speak of poets, Latour says that the truth of whether the jungle is advancing or receding is *instituted* (*gestiftet*, in Heidegger's German) by this lengthy chain of actors. There is never an immediate visibility of the fact, but only a series of mediations, each of them translating a more complicated reality into something whose forces can more easily be passed down the line. Though a skeptic might claim that these mediators are mere utensils that can be tossed aside at the end, there is no such thing as transport without transformation. Truth is *nothing but* a chain of translation without resemblance from one actor to the next. To focus only on the end-points is to distort the meaning of truth. Philosophers have taken subject and object, the two extremities of the chain, 'for the entire chain, as if they had tried to understand how a lamp and a switch could 'correspond' to each other after cutting the wire [...]' (PH, p. 73). This is the meaning of 'circulating reference'. As Latour puts it, 'when we say that Pasteur speaks truthfully about a real state of affairs, we no longer ask him to jump from words to world. [Instead,] we say something much like 'downtown expressway moving smoothly this morning' [...]' (PH, p.

149). We do not gain access to reality by subtracting the layers of distorting perception added to the world, but only by *increasing* the number of mediators: 'as if *the more filters there were the clearer the gaze was* [...]' (PH, p. 137). Truth is best described not by the optical or pictorial metaphor of copying a true state of affairs in our mind, but by an 'industrial' metaphor. For 'when [...] a student of industry insists that there have been a multitude of transformations and mediations between the oil trapped deep in the geological seams of Saudi Arabia and the gas I put into the tank of my car from the old pump in the little village of Jaligny in France, the claim to reality of the gas is in no way decreased' (PH, p. 137). For modern philosophy, all the problems of translation occur at the single critical point where human meets world. But for Latour, translation is ubiquitous: any relation is a mediation, never some pristine transmission of data across a noiseless vacuum. While Descartes fretted over the gap between mind and body, Latour is closer to Malebranche and his Arab ancestors, who needed God to enable even the collision of grains of dust—since here too there was a gap, though not one between minds and bodies. Instead of calling on divine intervention, Latour finds his mediators locally. For it was *Joliot* who connected neutrons with politics: 'it is only because of Joliot's work that this connection has been made' (PH, p. 92). Two actors are always mediated by a third; this is the ultimate lesson of the circulation of reference. This 'local occasionalism' in Latour marks an important breakthrough in metaphysics, and will be discussed in more detail in Part Two.

Latour's concept of the circulation of reference entails his democratic metaphysics of actors, each separated from the other by a gap as wide as that between human and world, each serving as a mediator or translator that leaves no message untransformed. His primary enemy is Kant's Copernican Revolution, with its *salto mortale* or deadly leap from inside to outside, criticized so forcefully by William James (PH, pp 73-4). Latour holds instead that the perilous leap occurs not once, but constantly, and that it is not always so perilous. This also changes our conception of the traditional matter/form distinction. Instead of assigning matter to one kind of entity (nature) and form to another kind (humans), Latour globalizes the distinction. Every actor now fills both roles at once:

> we load the precious cardboard boxes containing the earthworms preserved in formaldehyde, and the neatly tagged little bags of earth, into the jeep [...]. From the restaurant-laboratory we set out for another laboratory a thousand kilometers away, in Manaus, and from there to Jussieu University in Paris, another six thousand kilometers away [...]. As I have said, each stage is matter for what follows and form for what precedes it, each separated from the other by a gap as wide as the distance between that which counts as words and that which counts as things (PH, p. 74).

Among those philosophies that Latour accuses of reinforcing the bad unique gap between human and world is phenomenology, a school for which he has little sympathy. For 'phenomenology deals only with the world-for-a-human-consciousness'. And though it 'will [claim to] teach us a lot about how we never distance ourselves from what we see, how we never gaze at a distant spectacle, how we are always immersed in the world's rich and lived texture [...] we will never be able to escape from the narrow focus of human intentionality'. And this 'leaves us with the most dramatic split in this whole sad story: a world of science left entirely to itself, entirely cold, absolutely inhuman; and a rich lived world of intentional stances entirely limited to humans, absolutely divorced from what things are in and of themselves' (PH, p. 9). Latour's objection to phenomenology, namely, is its apparent deficit of *realism*. He makes a similar complaint, and with even more justice, about the scientific naturalism that opposes Descartes' mind/world dualism with a single real world of physical forces:

> Why not choose the opposite solution and forget the mind-in-a-vat altogether? Why not let the 'outside world' invade the scene, breaking the glassware, spill the bubbling liquid, and turn the mind into a brain, into a neuronal machine sitting inside a Darwinian animal struggling for its life? [...]. No, because the ingredients that make up this 'nature', this hegemonic and all-encompassing nature, which would now include the human species [as well], are the *very same ones* that have constituted the spectacle of a world viewed from inside the brain-in-a-vat. Inhuman, reductionist, causal, law-like, certain, objective, cold, unanimous, absolute—all these expressions do not pertain to nature *as such*, but [only] to nature as viewed through the deforming prism of the glass vessel (PH, pp. 9-10).

The reason phenomenology is not realist enough for Latour is that it brackets the world and focuses on a description of what appears to human consciousness, letting science deal with the nonhuman realm by means of a causal theory on which no further light is shed. Naturalism is also not realist enough, because it merely denies such bracketing and submits poignant human emotions to the same materialist treatment as neutrons and paraffin. Full-blown idealism is obviously not realist enough, since it merely flips naturalism upside-down and imprisons physical reality in the sphere of human perception. As different as these three positions might seem, all share the same basic mistake. Namely, all work within the framework of the modernist purification, in which there are exactly two possible kinds of being: free human consciousness and mechanical clockwork causation. They differ only by variously affirming this split and handing out one slice of reality to each type of being, or by attempting to reduce humans entirely to natural causes, or natural causes entirely to appearances in human consciousness. This is the same parceling out of Alexander's Empire, the same violation of a united Kurdistan, that we encountered in *We Have Never Been Modern*. None of these positions are realist enough, because none of them grant individual objects any reality. Latour justly takes pride in the alternative position of 'science studies', the name he uses in *Pandora's Hope* for his own metaphysics. In Latour's philosophy 'realism now returns in force', and the chapters of his book 'should look like milestones along the route to a more "realistic realism"' (PH, p. 15). Put differently, 'realism comes back like blood through the many vessels now reattached by the clever hands of the surgeons [...]. No one [should] even think of asking the bizarre question "Do you believe in reality?"—at least not of asking *us*!' (PH, p. 17). And finally, 'it should become clear how very unrealistic most of the philosophical discussions about realism have been' (PH, p. 24). The time has come to look a bit more closely at what Latour describes as his more realistic realism. For in a surprising step, Latour comes to identify reality with *relations*.

B. A REALISM OF RELATIONS

The translation model of truth renders the correspondence theory impossible. According to the correspondence version, knowledge in the human mind copies a reality outside it, with the usual proviso that this copying can only be 'asymptotic' and never arrive entirely at its goal. Progress in knowledge would mean making increasingly accurate copies of the world, just as improved cameras give ever more realistic images of what they depict. But if every relation is a translation rather than a copy, then the optical model fails. The description of a wine does not 'resemble' that wine, but amasses words and metaphors of various individual histories in order to evoke something like the *style* of the wine. Francis Parkman's history of Quebec does not 'resemble' the real events any more than less interesting histories of the same topic do. The gas in Jaligny does not 'resemble' the oil trapped deep in Arabian fissures; it has merely retained something of that oil, a kind of *nectar* of the oil expressed in terms comprehensible to the internal combustion engine. Now, it is often believed that abandoning the correspondence theory of truth entails the abandonment of realism as well. To jettison the model of truth as a copy, putting in its place a model of translations, apparently leaves no room to judge one translation as superior to another. If there is no correspondence between knowledge and world, it might seem that 'anything goes'. But this conclusion does not follow. There can still be better or worse translations, just as there can be limitless French versions of Shakespeare of varying ranges of quality. But here the metaphor seems to break down: after all, there really is an original text of Shakespeare (though philologists have a hard time establishing it) and by analogy we might hold that there is also an original world that is the subject of all translation by actors. But such a notion makes a poor fit with Latour's relationism. The analogy with Latour would apparently work only if Shakespeare's text existed only at the moment of being translated and were in fact defined by that very translation. Since this hardly seems like a realist theory of mind-independent reality, it is easy to understand why objections to Latour might still arise from mainstream realists. I leave this issue of an original, untranslated reality to the second half of the book.

Latour's relationism is clear enough. Unlike for traditional realism, things are not real by being less connected with others, but become more real the more they are linked with allies. While speaking of Pasteur's microbes, Latour remarks ironically that 'we imagine microbes must have a substance that is a little bit *more* than the series of its historical manifestations. We may be ready to grant that the set of [its] performances always remains inside the networks [...] but we cannot suppress the feeling that the substance travels with fewer constraints than the performances' (PH, p. 167). This feeling of substance as 'something a little bit more' is precisely what Latour opposes. Echoing Whitehead, Latour says that his position 'does not document the travel *through* time of an already existing *substance*' (PH, p. 162). A thing is not separate from its relations, and in fact 'each element is to be defined by its associations and is an event created at *the occasion* of each of those associations' (PH, p. 165, emphasis added). There follows a list of sometimes shocking examples: 'this is true for the lactic acid ferment, as well as for the city of Rouen, the Emperor, the laboratory on the rue d'Ulm, God, and Pasteur and Pouchet's own standing, psychology, and presuppositions' (PH, p. 165). God is not included on the list accidentally, or in a passing flippant moment. Latour's Catholicism does not compel him to think of God as an enduring substance any more than the other actors, nor does he respect 'the moderns' pathetic notion of a God-of-beyond' (PH, p. 267). Latour gives us not just a metaphysics of actors, but of actors that come to birth only *on the occasion* of their associations. Insofar as these associations shift constantly in both tiny and revolutionary ways, we have actors that perpetually perish rather than endure. The same notion led Whitehead to equate his 'actual entities' with 'actual *occasions*', a term meant to emphasize their utter transience, their utter exhaustion by a specific set of relations to the world that does not endure for longer than a flash. All of this clearly links both Whitehead and Latour with the great and underrated tradition of occasionalist philosophy stretching from medieval Iraq to Berkeley. But while occasionalism viewed God as a unique pillar of granite, an unyielding substance amidst the constant disintegration of other entities, the devout Latour does not exempt even God Himself from the river of alliances.

An actor is not a substance, but a kind of explorer testing what can and cannot be withstood. 'Any entity is such an exploration, such a series of events, such an experiment [...]. If Pouchet accepts the experiments of his adversary but loses the Academy and gains the popular anti-establishment press, his entity, spontaneous generation, will be a *different* entity. It is not a single substance spanning the nineteenth century unchanged' (, 162-3). Speaking equally of himself, Latour says that 'Pasteur is a good matist: for him essence is existence and existence is action' (PH, p. 123). As we read one page earlier: 'in his laboratory in Lille Pasteur is *designing* an *actor* [... He] designs trials for the actor to show its mettle. Why is an actor defined through trials? Because there is no other way to define an actor but through its action, and there is no other way to define an action but by asking what other actors are *modified, transformed, perturbed, or created* by the character that is the focus of attention' (PH, p. 122, emphasis added). And again, 'the accuracy of [a] statement is not related to a state of affairs out there, but to a traceability of a series of transformations' (PH, p. 123). And finally:

> The word 'substance' does not designate 'what remains beneath', impervious to history, but what gathers together a multiplicity of agents into a stable and coherent whole. A substance is more like the thread that holds the pearls of a necklace together than the rock bed that remains the same no matter what is built on it [...]. Substance is a name that designates the *stability* of an assemblage (PH, p. 151).

Alluding to a more traditional terminology, Latour dismisses those who 'want to have a substance *in addition* to attributes' (PH, p. 151). Here he implicitly sides with the tradition of British empiricism and its notion that 'substance' is nothing but a bundle of qualities, and against the phenomenological view that starts with unified objects and sees attributes as derivative. Independence is not the starting point for isolated individual things, but the end result of a long series of transformations: 'the more *Pasteur* works, the more *independent* is the substance on which he works [...]. We do not simply want to say that the ferment is [both] constructed and real as all artifacts are, but that it is *more real after* being transformed, as if, uncannily, there were more oil in Saudi Arabia because there is more gas in the tank of my car' (PH, p. 138).

Despite such remarks, it should be clear why Latour is not a social constructionist holding that the world is malleable clay subjected to the whims of a mighty human society. After all, neutrons and governments both resist Joliot, just as ferments and newspapers resist Pasteur. Humans both *shape* and are *shaped by* other actors, no more or less than they shape one another. If there is a point where Latour deviates from the usual realist spirit, it lies neither in his supposed preference for human society over the 'objective reality' of stones, nor in his actual rejection of the subject/object dualism, but only in his view that a thing is defined entirely by its relations. This relationist theory cuts against the grain of common sense, which affirms a world of unchanging physical solids occasionally shoved around by transient human whim. But metaphysics is not the handmaid of common sense. And furthermore, common sense itself is nothing but the sedimentation of a dubious and mediocre metaphysics. The foundation of this watery realism is the notion of objective 'states of affairs', in which real durable things sit around in the universe whether we like it or not, and sit around in the same way whether they are observed by Pasteur, Liebig, or no one at all. This is the same concept that Heidegger criticized under the name of *Vorhandenheit*, or presence-at-hand. Later in this book, I will suggest that this idea of objective physical states of affairs is saturated with an even more untenable form of relationism than the one Latour advocates. This makes Latour's relationism an 'obligatory passage point' for present-day metaphysics (PH, p. 191). For there are only two options here: we can either accept Latour's relational definitions of actors, or pursue a revived theory of substance apart from all its relations. But even if we choose the latter option, it will turn out that commonsense materialism is not of sufficient quality to do the job.

Borrowing an apt if colourless piece of terminology from Whitehead, Latour now speaks of 'propositions'. Normally propositions belong to the philosophy of language, as statements by a human subject about an outside world. But for Latour, 'propositions are not statements, or things, or any sort of intermediary between the two. They are, first of all, actants. Pasteur, the lactic acid ferment, the laboratory are all propositions' (PH, p. 141). While occasionalism made God the sole mediator between every least interaction in the universe, Latour distributes this divine power to Frédéric Joliot and every other actor in the cosmos. We have seen that Latour is probably the first thinker in history to invent a local option for occasional cause—one not passing through God (as in al-Ash'ari, Malebranche, and even Whitehead) or the human mind (as when Hume and Kant turn human habit or categories into the seat of all relations). In my view, this is Latour's single greatest breakthrough in metaphysics, one that will be associated with his name for centuries to come. As he puts it, '[propositions] are not positions, things, substances, or essences pertaining to a nature made up of mute objects facing a talkative mind, but *occasions* given to different entities to enter into contact' (PH, p. 141). In this new occasionalism it is Joliot rather than God who brings neutrons and politics into union, and other local mediators that bring any two entities into contact.

Occasions 'allow the entities to modify their definitions over the course of an event' (PH, p. 141) and this is what Latour means by a proposition. Every actor is a proposition: a surprising marriage of components that never expected to find themselves together, or which were at least surprised by the exact nature of their union. And 'the relation established between propositions is not that of a correspondence across a yawning gap, but what I will call *articulation*' (PH, p. 142). Since articulation does not occur across a gap, but is merely the improved articulation of a contact already in place, we have an interesting situation in which things must already be in relation before that relation is better articulated. Every articulation arises from a previous articulation, not *ex nihilo*. Pasteur and Pouchet articulate *something* in their theories: not an underlying substance, but an earlier proposition that was not as well articulated as the one they will soon create. Needless to say, it is not only humans who do this. It is difficult to find any social constructionism in the following passage by Latour: 'instead of being the privilege of a human mind surrounded by mute things, articulation becomes a very common property of propositions, in which many kinds of entities can participate' (PH, p. 142). Here we can safely replace 'many entities' with 'all entities', since Latour surely does not just wish to add intelligent whales and monkeys to the list while excluding clumps of metallic ore. The articulation of propositions is clearly meant as a general metaphysics of relations. 'Propositions do not have the fixed boundaries of objects. They are surprising events in the history of other entities. The more articulation there is, the better' (PH, p. 143). Actors for Latour are both human and nonhuman, lasting only as long as their alliance endures, more real the more alliances they have, and linked only through another actor capable of translating one into terms of the other.

We have seen that Latour's profound commitment to relations as the stuff of the world runs counter to common sense and mainstream science alike. It takes rare audacity to call oneself a realist while still uttering statements of the following kind: '"Did ferments exist before Pasteur discovered them?" There is no avoiding the answer: "No, they did not exist before he came along"—an answer that is obvious, natural, and even, as I will show commonsensical!' (PH, p. 145). Whatever the rhetorical value of this passage, even a fiery supporter of Latour's relationism would have to concede that there is nothing 'obvious', 'natural', or 'commonsensical' about the doctrine. Indeed, its entirely unobvious and unnatural character gives it much of its shocking appeal to those who uphold it. But Latour's motive here is obviously not a wish to allow the human mind to create reality from scratch. Instead, it is his commitment to relations that makes him say that the ferment is a proposition rather than a substance, and that a proposition requires multiple actors. The one baffling point is that Latour has already affirmed that propositions belong not just to Pasteur and his fellow humans, but to 'many' kinds of actors, by which he surely means 'all' actors. If Pasteur and the rest of humankind were exterminated, numerous actors would still remain on the scene; presumably, various materials would continue to ferment in our absence. But the real point for Latour is that these incidents would be different propositions, since Pasteur and our pasteurized modern society would no longer be involved in them. There might be 'propositions' linking chemicals with other chemicals and with wooden barrels, long after the great nuclear holocaust destroys all humans. Yet even such actors would not be objective states of affairs, since they would be fully determined by their associations with each other.

These views lead Latour to a retroactive theory of time that is anything but obvious and natural. He holds that the true reality of any moment in time is not something that slumbers beneath its surface articulations; rather, the moment is incarnated in those very articulations. To rethink the past for Latour means to produce an alternate version of the past *retroactively*, a time that never really existed at the moment in question:

> It is now possible for Pasteur to understand retrospectively what farm-
> ing and industry have been doing all along with knowing it [...]. Sowing
> germs in a culture medium is the rearticulation by Pasteur of what oth-
> ers before him, not understanding what it was, named disease, invasion,
> or mishap [...]. Pasteur *reinterpreted* the past practices of fermentation as
> fumbling around in the dark with entities against which one could now
> protect oneself (PH, p. 169).

This pushes Latour into a surprising series of remarks about historical time, remarks that will only confirm (understandably, though wrongly) the view that he is a social constructionist. 'What Pasteur did was to produce in 1864 a new version of the years 1863, 1862, 1861, which now included a new el-ement: "microbes fought unwittingly by faulty and haphazard practices"' (PH, p. 169). Just as Europeans rethought the history of German culture fol-lowing Auschwitz, Pasteur '*retrofitted* the past with his own microbiology: the year 1864 that was built *after* 1864 did not have the same components, tex-tures, and associations as the year 1864 produced *during 1864*' (PH, p. 170).

But to repeat, any objections to these views should be aimed at their root: Latour's metaphysics of relations. His point is not that 'history is what-ever we make of it by projecting our own selfish values onto it'. His point is that 1864, like any other year, is a fully articulated event without any cryp-tic reservoir of independent reality that had previously lain unexpressed. After all, Latour's relationist metaphysics rules out such an option from the start. Hence, if a new 1864 is unearthed by Pasteur's discoveries, this can-not be because it was always already present at the time and is now merely unveiled before the mind. Instead, the new 1864 can only be a new *proposi-tion*, in which Pasteur's microbes interact with a past year by rereading it in microbial terms. The problem here is that Latour focuses on a *human* actor, Pasteur. If we extend propositions to all actors, as Latour himself elsewhere intends, this means that there were other articulations of 1864 *during 1864 it-self* of which *humans* were simply not aware at the time. Microbes may have existed in the year 1800, interlocked in propositions with wine and broth, and even with human bodies, though not with the human medical knowl-edge of the time. For humans to become *aware* of the microbes does require a new proposition, one that links Pasteur with those past inanimate events. And Pasteur will invariably modify or transport those events in the course of the proposition, since that is what all actors must do.

Though Latour claims that his views on time are both obvious and com-monsensical, his shocking conclusions mass ever more heavily as the chapter proceeds. His metaphysics of relations forces him into a twofold theory of time, now split into 'linear' and 'sedimentary' kinds. In his own words, 'a year should be defined along two axes, not just one. The first axis registers the linear dimension of time [...] in that sense 1864 happens *before* 1865. But this is not all there is to say about the year 1864 [...]. There is also a portion of what happened in 1864 that is produced *after* 1864 and made retrospectively a part [...] of what happened in 1864' (PH, p. 172). And further, 'if we skip forward 130 years, there is still a year 1864 "of 1998" [...] maybe [including] a complete revision of the dispute in which, eventually, Pouchet is the winner because he anticipated some results of prebiotics' (PH, p. 172). If you feel yourself resisting this strange conclusion, Latour says that your resistance is the result of 'a very simple confusion' (PH, p. 172) between linear and sedimentary time. At the same time, he denies that his theory amounts to 'an absurd form of idealism, since most of the sedimentary segments of the year 1864 *do* include airborne germs. It is thus possible to say, without contradiction, both 'Airborne germs were made up in 1864', and 'They were there all along' [...]' (PH, pp. 172-3). Or to express it in a single sentence: '*After 1864* airborne germs were there all along' (PH, p. 173). Ending in the same exasperated spirit in which he began, Latour asserts that 'the answer to these apparent puzzles is so straightforward', and mockingly adds that 'the question is no longer whether to take such "mysteries" seriously, but why people take them as deep philosophical puzzles that would condemn science studies [i.e., Latour's philosophy] to absurdity' (PH, p. 173). But outright absurdity is not Latour's danger here, at least not from fair-minded readers. After all, his theory of time does follow with perfect rigor from his view that actors are fully articulated events with nothing held in reserve. I will contend below that there are compelling reasons to prefer this vision of actors to the mediocre realism wielded by Latour's detractors. But this does not require that we accept the entirety of his actor metaphysics. There are good reasons to revive a non-relational form of realism—but a much *weirder* realism than the kind endorsed by Alan Sokal and his science warriors.

C. ON BEHALF OF THE MOB

Before leaving the marvelous pages of *Pandora's Hope*, we should consider Latour's surprising criticism of Socrates, which occupies two full chapters of the book. Thanks to Nietzsche we have long been accustomed to diatribes against Socrates as a life-denying and decadent criminal type; at the same time, more recent authors have discovered new merit in the long-vilified Sophists. Even so, Latour's anti-Socratic views remain surprising. Geometers do not denounce Euclid, nor do Christian monks heap scorn on St. Paul. Hence it is worthy of note if Latour, a philosopher indeed, has nothing good to say about the founding hero of our discipline—a man who is usually presented to students in a spirit of pious awe. Latour is aware, half-apologetically, of the intensity of his attacks. Yet he can hardly avoid such attacks, since his negative views of Socrates follow from his relational meta-physics as directly as his astonishing theory of time.

Plato's dialogue *Gorgias* presents a discussion between Socrates and three Sophists of varying quality: Gorgias, Polus, and Callicles. Although Latour is well aware of the annoying sneers of Callicles, his assault on Socrates is much more relentless. Not since Nietzsche has a philosopher charged our ancestral role model with such a range of misdeeds. Socrates, 'having dis-couraged discussion' (PH, p. 219), conducts himself in a spirit of 'tranquil arrogance' (PH, p. 220). He is 'on very thin ice' (PH, p. 231), 'should have lost' (PH, p. 229) the argument with the Sophists, and was saved only by their inept concessions. Greeted sarcastically as 'Professor Socrates' (PH, p. 244), his failure in Athenian politics is met with the phrase 'tough luck' (PH, p. 238). Even his closing triumph in the underworld is mocked with an acid 'clap clap clap' (PH, p. 257). Guilty of a 'mind-boggling crime' (PH, p. 253), Socrates joins the Sophists in 'odious self-annihilation' (PH, p. 245). Nietzsche was right that Socrates is an anti-Midas who 'turns gold into mud' (PH, p. 240) and also right to put Socrates on his 'hit list of "men of *ressentiment*"' (PH, p. 253). Worse yet, the execution of Socrates by Athens was merely a 'political mistake' that 'made a martyr out of a mad scientist' (PH, p. 257). Plato receives equally rough treatment for his own 'perver-sity' (PH, p. 253) in 'holding all the puppet strings' and creating 'a straw Callicles' (PH, p. 221). Plato's staging of the dialogue is described by Latour as if by a nasty theater critic: 'A beautiful effect on the stage, to be sure, with naked shadows pacing a papier-mâché inferno and artificial fumes and fog lingering in the air' (PH, p. 227). Plato is also a hypocrite and a spoiled brat, since his *Gorgias* was written 'not by a barbaric invader, but by the most sophisticated, enlightened, literate of all writers, who all his life gorged himself on the beauty and wealth that he so foolishly destroys or deems irrelevant for producing political reason and reflection. *This* sort of "deconstruction," not the slow iconoclasm of present-day sophists, is worth our indignation [...]' (PH, p. 245).

But Latour's vitriolic attack deserves to be taken seriously, for two un-related reasons. First, those readers who have not visited the *Gorgias* re-cently may be surprised by Socrates' tone in the dialogue. This is not the lovable needling ironist found in our memories of Socrates, but a more ag-gressive and bitter interlocutor: he behaves, as we say in English, like a *jerk*. His treatment of Polus is especially appalling, with its useless twists of gram-mar and a dead-end sarcasm that rarely advances the debate as it does in other dialogues. Though I am more sympathetic to Platonism than Latour himself, on a purely emotional level I find myself cheering for Callicles in this dialogue, despite the shallowness of his sneers. But second, and more importantly, Latour's annoyance at Socrates comes in defense of an understandable cause. Socrates defends positions that are anathema to Latour's metaphysics. Moreover, it is not only the long-dead Socrates who does this, but also his emulators in the 1990's science wars. Latour cites Nobel Laureate Steven Weinberg from the *New York Times*: 'Our civilization has been profoundly affected by the discovery that nature is strictly governed by impersonal laws [...]. We will need to confirm and strengthen the vision of a rationally understandable world if we are to protect ourselves from the irrational tendencies that still beset humanity' (PH, p. 216).[1] It is hard to imagine a less Latourian passage than this. Weinberg endorses two opposed spheres: an impersonal nature governed by laws, and an arbitrary realm of irrational human belief. The latter must be condemned for its naïve prejudice so that humans can be made more rational. Yet one can easily imagine a postmodernist inversion of Weinberg on the same page of the *Times*: 'Our civilization has been profoundly affected by the discovery that "nature" has been viewed differently by different societies, each speaking with a different voice [...]. We will need to confirm and strengthen the vision of a world constructed by cultural presuppositions if we are to protect ourselves from the imperialist tendencies that still beset humanity'. Only the choice of option is different. The shallow opposition between two and *only* two spheres remains the same for Weinberg and postmodernists alike. And not only does Latour reject both options—his own position is regularly *confused* with both! It is little wonder if this situation provokes anger, and for this reason it is easy to forgive his vehement outburst against the Socrates/Weinberg axis.

Latour's basic insight into the dialogue is irrefutable. At first, the *Gorgias* seems to be a predictable morality play of might versus right. Power is all that counts for the Sophists, while Socrates sacrifices all power to the selfless search for truth. As he proudly puts it, 'last year I was on the Council [...] and [when] I had to put an issue to the vote, I made a fool of myself by not knowing the procedure for this [...]. I can't even begin to address people in large groups' (PH, p. 238).[2] The Sophists are concerned with getting their way through persuasive speech, but Socrates is concerned only with reaching the truth no matter what the cost in human terms. In a sense, this typical view is correct. But Latour is equally correct that Socrates and Callicles behave like Siamese twins, and that both have the same enemy: the Athenian mob. Although Socrates seems to represent 'right', and Callicles 'might', both wish at bottom to silence the crowd from a position of superiority. 'Socrates and Callicles have a common enemy: the people of Athens, the crowd assembled in the agora, talking endlessly, making the laws at their whim, behaving like children, like sick people, like animals, shifting

---

1. Weinberg cited by Latour from the August 8, 1996 edition of the *New York Times*, p. 15.
2. Latour's added italics to the passage from the *Gorgias* have been removed.

opinions whenever the wind changes direction' (PH, p. 219). The main problem with the people is that 'there are simply *too many* of them' (PH, p. 220). For Socrates, the people are dominated by flattery, *doxa*, custom, routine, which are inferior to the demonstrative truths discovered by geometry. For Callicles, the mob is merely a group of slaves and other fools, and their massed physical strength must be subordinated to the greater merit of superior individuals. In both cases, the plurality of actors ('the mob') is despised in accordance with a theory of what the real truth is. For Socrates, who here anticipates Heidegger's ontological/ontic distinction, there is truth in geometry but not in cooking. For Callicles, the only reality is power: the ability to do with impunity whatever one wishes. The truly superior man must outflank the muscular force of the mob with rhetoric. In other words, both Socrates and Callicles defend an ontology (and a politics) that is basically undemocratic. This puts both of them at the opposite pole from Latour, whose metaphysics, we have seen, holds that 'Golden Mountains, phlogiston, unicorns, bald kings of France, chimeras, spontaneous generation, black holes, cats on mats, and other black swans and white ravens [...] all occupy the same space-time as Hamlet, Popeye, and Ramses II' (PH, p. 161). Whether we say with Socrates that all these actors belong to a sphere of appearance and *doxa*, or say instead with Callicles that they exist only to be overpowered by the rhetorician, in either case we define such actors out of existence. We appeal to some expert *theory* of the true nature of things, and use this theory to annihilate whole armies of swans, ravens, unicorns, pharaohs, and Danish princes. This is precisely what Latour does not do.

In the *Gorgias*, might and right turn out not to be opposites at all. Both attempt to replace the democracy of actors with a monolithic ontology that reduces its opponents to dust: either we silence the irrational babble of the crowd with impersonal laws (Socrates, Weinberg) or we persuade the fickle mob of our own arbitrarily chosen perspective (Callicles, the postmodernists). For Latour, the truth lies not in some combination of these two flawed positions, but in a middle term that shares nothing in common with either: the 'Third Estate' or 'excluded middle' of the bustling mob of actors, all of them equally real. 'Instead of a dramatic opposition between force and reason, we will have to consider *three* different kinds of forces [...] the force of Socrates, the force of Callicles, and the force of the people' (PH, p. 235). In a useful image, Latour asks us to imagine a tug of war not between Socrates and Callicles, but between both of them on one side of the rope and the mob on the other.

Latour's commitment to democracy is not a form of pandering to the spirit of our age, but is an intimate part of his metaphysical position. The universe is nothing but countless actors, who gain in reality through complex negotiations and associations with one another: not as one against a crowd, but as one in the *shape* of a crowd of allies. We cannot appeal to some authority (geometry, power) lying outside the shifting alliances of networks. And for this reason, the turmoil of democracy cannot be silenced by the expertise that Socrates wants to use for this purpose. 'The assembled Body Politic, in order to make decisions, *cannot* rely on expert knowledge alone, given the constraints of number, totality, urgency, and priority that politics imposes' (PH, p. 228). A politics that does not rely on experts citing impersonal law 'requires a disseminated knowledge as multifarious as the multitude itself. The *knowledge of the whole needs the whole, not the few*. But that would be a scandal for Callicles and for Socrates, a scandal whose name has been the same at all periods: democracy' (PH, p. 229). By contrast with democracy, 'the disagreement of [Socrates and Callicles] is secondary to their agreement: the contest is about how to shut the mouths of the people faster and tighter' (PH, p. 229). When Socrates boasts that he would rather persuade one person than a crowd, Latour responds that 'canvassing for one vote is worse than a crime, it is a political mistake' (PH, p. 229).

By 'political mistake' Latour does not mean a tactical blunder in a regrettably corrupt world where the thinker must hustle the truth past self-interested fools. Recall that for Latour, political compromise is on exactly the same footing as Weinberg's 'impersonal' collisions between billiard balls. Talleyrand and Sarkozy are actors no less than paraffin and neutrons. A 'political' mistake is already an ontological mistake, because it means that an assemblage has been badly constructed. Latour is displeased that 'contempt for politicians is still today what creates the widest consensus in academic circles' (PH, p. 245). These academic circles are still made up of the warring disciples of Socrates and Callicles; all of them miss the excluded middle, and hence miss politics altogether. For Latour all reality is political, not because human power inexorably shapes the truth, but because truth and reality are assembled through chains of actors in the same way that bills go through Congress: slightly transformed and translated at each step, and failing as often as they succeed. All reality is political, but not all politics is human. Referring to the 'cosmopolitics' of his friend Isabelle Stengers, Latour speaks of a redefined political order that 'brings together stars, prions, cows, heavens, and people, the task being to turn this collective into a "cosmos" rather than an "unruly shambles"' (PH, p. 261). It is no accident that Latour's book *Politics of Nature* is translated into German as *Das Parlament der Dinge*: 'The Parliament of Things'. We must liberate politics from the narrowly human realm and allow prions and the ozone hole to speak as well. Whether babble is reduced by reason (Socrates) or by power (Callicles), in either case political *mediators* are eliminated. Latour's position is not just more politically attractive than this, but more metaphysically acute.

And yet, philosophers will wonder if there is nothing more to Socrates than this. Does his sole significance in the history of philosophy amount to silencing the crowd of actors in the arrogant name of reason? The answer, of course, is no. There is more to Socrates than this, and it amounts to the most pivotal discovery of Socratic-Platonic philosophy. Latour overlooks this additional element, not through ill will toward Socrates as a person, but because of his own metaphysics of relations. There are key passages of the *Gorgias* that play no role in Latour's account, and they resemble countless other passages in the *Meno*, the *Euthyphro*, the *Republic*, and almost every Platonic dialogue. These refer not to Socrates' contempt for the mob, but to his contempt for *power*. Since this element is more visible in his dispute with Polus than in the collision with Callicles, I will speak here of Polus.

Everything Latour says about Socrates and Callicles is true. They are certainly united in their contempt for the mob, and it is easy to imagine them teamed up in a tug of war against the unruly shambles of the people. Yet there is more to Socrates than meets the eye, and *not* more to the Sophists than meets the eye. Recall that Socrates is not merely the tranquil liquidator of the mob that we meet in the *Gorgias*, but also the legendary professor of ignorance. Socrates' famous statement that he 'only knows that he knows nothing' is not a mere pretense contradicted by his high-handed treatment of various interlocutors. For even if Socrates in the *Gorgias* imagines silencing the mob with demonstrations, there is no passage in any of the Platonic dialogues where he actually claims to have such demonstrations at his disposal. More important than his opposition between expert knowledge and the flattery and cooking of the people is his opposition between wisdom and power. This latter distinction is the 'inner truth and greatness' of Platonic philosophy.

Socrates' strategy is a familiar one for regular readers of Platonic dialogues. It begins harmlessly enough. In his dispute with Polus, Socrates denounces rhetoric as a mere knack or routine that produces gratification and pleasure. When Polus asks if such pleasure does not make rhetoric a fine thing, Socrates retorts: 'What, Polus? Have you already learned from me what I consider rhetoric to be, that you proceed to ask if I do not consider it a fine thing?'.[3] The tone is sardonic and impatient, but the point lies at the very heart of Western philosophy. The famous Socratic quest for definitions is equally famous for never providing any. The problem is not just that Polus needed to let Socrates finish, as if we could patiently wait another two or three pages for Socrates to define at last what rhetoric is. Socrates will never arrive at that destination: not through personal failings, but because no definition of anything will ever strike the target. Piety is never defined in the *Euthyphro*, nor justice in the *Republic*, nor the Sophist in the dialogue of the same name; even virtue receives only three or four vaguely approximate definitions in the *Meno*. Whereas Latour holds that a substance is constructed retroactively from its qualities, Socrates takes the opposite approach. For

3. Plato, 'Gorgias', trans. W.D. Woodhead, in *The Collected Dialogues of Plato*, Edith Hamilton and Huntington Cairns (eds.), Princeton, Princeton University Press, 1961, p. 245.

Socrates, we do have an approximate sense of what piety, justice, virtue, friendship, love, and Sophists really are—but all attempts to give exact definitions of these things become entangled in contradiction. Socrates is not striking a pose when he tells us in the *Meno* that he is unlike the stingray since he numbs himself as much as he numbs others. In fact, Socrates does not actually win any of the discussions in the dialogues—what wins are the never fully graspable forms of things, before which all definitions fall short.

In one sense, this even makes Socrates the ally of Latourian metaphysics. Latour's starting point is actors whose nature cannot be defined in advance. In similar fashion, what Socrates and Plato defend are realities that are vaguely known without being explicitly known. Their agreement with Latour is only partial, of course, since Latour grants full reality to everything that Plato would denounce as shadows on the cave wall: political speeches, Hamlet, subway trains. But nowhere do Socrates/Plato claim to grasp what lies outside the cave, since only a god could do this. For all his bullying ferocity in the *Gorgias*, Socrates does not oppose the mob with a knowledge that is actually possessed by any living human expert. After all, we remember that his entire career begins with a two-year period of systematically debunking all such experts, reaching the ultimate conclusion that there seem to be no experts in any field. Note that Socrates rarely seeks random members of the Athenian mob in Plato's dialogues, but makes a point of challenging the supposed experts in their very fields of expertise: he asks statesmen about politics, Meno about virtue, and Phaedrus about love. The expertise that Latour worries will be used to crush democracy is an expertise that Socrates finds in no living creature, including himself. In this sense, Latour and Socrates are oddly united in their *rejection* of privileged experts. Their main difference is that Plato's metaphysics seeks reality at a layer deeper than all articulation by qualities, while Latour thinks there is no reality outside such articulations. Hence, there could never be a Latourian myth of the cave.

In this respect it is easy to imagine Latour and Socrates joined on the same side of the rope in a different tug of war: pulling hard against Steven Weinberg, postmodernists, the Churchlands, and various pre-Socratics who think everything is made of water or air. For what Latour and Socrates have in common is an initial gesture of ignorance, even though they depart from this gesture in rather different ways. Platonic philosophy abandons ignorance through its double world of reality and appearance, which Latour opposes with his democracy of objects: an Adidas shoe is not just a shadow on a cave wall, but an actor every bit as real as justice itself. The Latourian metaphysics abandons ignorance through a pragmatist definition of actors, whose reality is defined by the impact they have on other actors. Socrates would oppose this definition for the same reason that he rejects all definitions: it turns things into a set of qualities, without grasping the things to which these qualities belong. Latour is the ultimate democrat in philosophy, allowing even widely despised consumer objects to enter the parliament of things. Yet they are allowed to enter only by virtue of their effect on other things, since Latour holds that there is never anything more to them than this.

We now turn to a related point that also recurs throughout the Platonic dialogues. In the *Gorgias*, Polus gives unsurprising praise of tyrants, which Socrates just as predictably condemns. In response, Polus wonders sarcastically if Socrates '[is not] jealous when [he sees] a man killing or imprisoning or depriving of property as seems good to him!'.[4] A bit later, Polus wishes that he were 'at liberty to do what I please in the state—to kill, to exile, and to follow my own pleasure in every act'.[5] As an example of his ideal success story, Polus offers the case of Archelaus of Macedonia, a worthy rival to any of Machiavelli's anti-heroes. Archelaus was born the son of a slave woman, and would always have remained a slave if he had acted justly. His rise to power required that he first intoxicate and murder his rivals, then drown his seven-year-old half-brother in a well while lying to the boy's mother that it was an accident. Polus has no doubt that Archelaus is happy.[6]

The Socratic response to this story had come a few pages in advance, when Socrates told an astonished Polus that rhetoricians are actually powerless. For 'how can rhetoricians or tyrants possess great power in our cities, unless Polus proves against [me] that they do what they will? [...] I deny that they do what they will'.[7] Cue the great old Platonic music, familiar from countless dialogues... For Socrates, humans do not will whatever it is that they happen to be doing at the moment, but only that *for the sake of which* they are doing it. This is clearer and more compelling than it sounds. We know from the *Republic* that the tyrant who tries to help his friends and hurt his enemies is rarely sure of who those friends and enemies are. Often the tyrant's corruption backfires, as he executes apparent enemies who are really loyal counselors, and pampers apparent friends who secretly conspire against him. Hence the only real virtue, for Socrates, is wisdom. All other virtues— intelligence, beauty, physical strength—can be misused to the detriment of others and oneself. Only wisdom governs these virtues in such a way that they always reach that for the sake of which they act; and in the end only a god is wise, not human experts. As Socrates says in the *Gorgias*: 'So too with those who sail the sea and engage in money-making in general—they do not will what they do on each occasion. For who desires to sail and suffer dangers and troubles? But they will, in my opinion, that for the sake of which they sail, namely wealth, for it is for wealth's sake that they sail'.[8] And further, 'if a man, whether tyrant or rhetorician, kills another or banishes

---

4. Plato, 'Gorgias', p. 251.

5. Plato, 'Gorgias', p. 253.

6. Plato, 'Gorgias', pp. 253-4.

7. Plato, 'Gorgias', p. 249.

8. Plato, 'Gorgias', pp. 249-50.

him or confiscates his property, because he thinks it is to his advantage, and it proves to be to his harm, the man surely does what seems good to him, does he not?'.[9] When Polus agrees, Socrates concludes: 'then I was right in saying that it is possible that a man who does what seems good to him in the state has no great power and does not do what he wills'.[10] Thus, the tyrant is not to be envied.

Just as Spinoza is the most fashionable great philosopher in our time, Plato must rank near the bottom of the list. Most contemporaries are united in establishing their credentials against Platonism; all compete to invert Platonism more radically than the next. And true enough, the Socratic defense of wisdom against power can often sound saccharine and insincere. But there is a sense in which this distinction is the founding gesture of Western philosophy. A thing is not a bundle of qualities, just as a tyrant is not a mere bundle of desires, because Socrates demonstrates that no qualities ever do justice to that which they seek to define. Virtue and love are real, if vaguely grasped; we define them in tentative fashion by way of attributes, but these traits never quite get at the thing itself. The power of a tyrant or rhetorician is insufficient, because these are merely superficial efforts at the mercy of a reality that only *wisdom* can probe, not power. The guiding insight of Socrates is the notion that reality is more than its current status, its current impact in the world here and now, its attributes, its relations, its alliances with other things. And here we find a more genuine point of opposition between Socrates and Latour. If confronted with Pasteur and his microbes, it is most unlikely that Socrates would encourage Pasteur to use his expertise to silence the babbling French mob. Instead, he would surely harass Pasteur for a *definition* of microbes, and we can already guess that Pasteur's efforts would never satisfy him. Latour would agree with Socrates that we cannot perfectly define microbes, since there will always be a 'slight surprise' in their action. What Latour denies is simply that this surprise comes from an additional hidden reality, a 'something more' lying beyond their basically pragmatist definition in terms of 'what other actors are modified, transformed, perturbed, or created by the character that is the focus of attention' (PH, p. 122). But Socrates is no pragmatist. If we had a Platonic dialogue called the *Latour*, it might contain an unfair scene along the following lines:

> *Socrates*: At the very beginning of our discussion, I praised you for being in my opinion well trained in these matters. So tell me, if you will, what is a microbe?

> *Latour*: Certainly, Socrates. What I say is that we do not know a microbe in itself, but only what other actors are modified, transformed, or perturbed by it.

---

9. Plato, 'Gorgias', p. 251.
10. Plato, 'Gorgias', p. 251.

Socrates: By the dog, my friend! Your definitions are as generous as your wineries! For is it not true that Bruno, son of Louis, is also knowledgeable of wines, the production of wines, and the numerous methods of shipping the casks in which wine is stored?

Latour: Yes, Socrates. What you say is true. My whole family has knowledge of these things, as you say.

Socrates: Now then, if I asked you to tell me what wine is, and you replied that wine comes in many sorts, is produced through many steps, and is shipped in boats, railcars, airplanes, and other vehicles, would this mean that wine is many things, or one thing produced and moved in many different ways?

Latour: It would seem to be only one thing, Socrates. For how could it be otherwise?

Socrates: Well then, great beloved of Dionysus the Liberator, be now the favourite of Asclepius the Healer as well!

Latour: How do you mean, Socrates?

Socrates: When I asked you what microbes are, you said that they modify, transform, and perturb other things.

Latour: I have said it, yes.

Socrates: And do microbes modify, transform, and perturb one man, or many? For surely you know of the plague during the time of Pericles, and other epidemics among the Persians and Scythians? And that there has been not just one outbreak of disease, but many epidemics in many different lands, and many men who have died from them?

Latour: Of course, Socrates. Everyone has heard of these things.

Socrates: And does the microbe remain one when it acts on many men in many lands, or is it a different sort of microbe in each case? Please, do not be angry, and answer my question.

Latour: I say that it is a different microbe in each case. For in each case it is allied with different people, and with other actors too.

Socrates: By Zeus! You are like the naiad in the myth who haunted the coves of Delos, or Lemnos if Pindar is to be believed. For have you not heard that the Greeks of old would place a single coin in her hand, and it would be returned as hundreds or even thousands of coins?

Latour: I have forgotten the details, Socrates, but I did hear of the myth.

Socrates: But instead of coins, you surprising man, I put one microbe in your hand, and it comes out as thousands! I'm afraid I am a poor rhetorician, but otherwise I should see fit to charge you in the law courts as a menace to the health of the city!

The tone is insufferable, but the dispute is revealing. In this fictional 'discussion', Socrates aims not to silence the crowd with a knowledge already in his possession, but only seeks to undermine Latour's claim to know that an actor is identical with its perturbations of other actors. Socrates/Plato deny that an actor can be defined in this way, or any other way for that matter. To make this denial, they pay the immense price of reducing actors as we know them to flickering shadows on a cave wall. Instead of holding that the true reality is water, atoms, or the boundless *apeiron*, Plato contends that it is the *eidei* or perfect forms. This is the genuine core of the *Gorgias*, as of nearly every other Platonic dialogue. But Latour is not interested in a unified reality lying beneath its various apparitions; in his own metaphysics, there is no place where he could possibly put an *eidos*.

Nonetheless, the similarities between Latour and Socrates are much greater than those between Latour and the Sophists. Latour's defense of democracy could be read as defending the same brand of learned ignorance that Socrates embodies, despite Plato's clear anti-democratic leanings. But to defend the Sophists would have precisely the opposite result. The slight surprise of action found in every actor means that Latour can never defend the notion that apparent power is the same as real power, or that an apparent actor is the actor itself. The question is only whether we grant sufficient reality to objects when we say that a thing is not just *known* by what it 'modifies, transforms, perturbs, or creates', but that it actually *is* nothing more than these effects. If the pragmatism of knowledge becomes a pragmatism of ontology, the very reality of things will be defined as their bundle of effects on other things. But in this way, the ignorance of Socrates is lost along with his arrogance.

objects and relations

5

Contributions

The first part of this book presented Bruno Latour as a metaphysician—a title denied him by librarians and publishing catalogs alike. Academic philosophy departments have little to do with Latour even as his ideas circulate widely in such fields as anthropology, geography, sociology, and the history of science. Indeed, his name is sometimes entirely unknown to professors of philosophy otherwise well versed in recent French thought. Bookstores shelve his titles in a variety of sections, but almost never assemble them under the 'Philosophy' heading, at least outside the Netherlands. Even Latour's admirers rarely come to his work primarily through an interest in metaphysics. Nonetheless, this second part of the book develops the claim that Latour gives us not only a metaphysics, but an obligatory passage point in the near future of the field. Chapter One reviews the contributions of Latour's metaphysical standpoint. Chapter Two identifies a range of shadowy issues never fully resolved by Latour himself. Finally, Chapter Three contends that Latour opens the gates on a new, object-oriented philosophy, but also claims that his rejection of non-relational entities is an unfortunate curb on the spirit of such a philosophy.

Let's begin with a brief consideration of how Latour differs from other recent figures of speculative philosophy. Since he has never had his moment on the stage of metaphysics, I have presented him largely as a self-contained figure, and made little attempt to trace the numerous influences and tacit rivalries detectable in his thinking. Such efforts are best left to a different sort of study. But it will be useful to give a brief geographical survey, distinguishing the most notable Latourian landmarks from those of other prominent contemporary schools. My purpose here is not to give a detailed history of recent philosophy, but only to sketch the landscape inhabited by vario

tribes of Iroquois, Hurons, Miamis, Cherokees, and Creeks. The possible
fuzzy borderlands between these groups are of less interest than the glaring differences between them. Speaking in Jerusalem in 1954, the ominous
Leo Strauss made passing reference to 'the four greatest philosophers of the
last forty years—Bergson, Whitehead, Husserl, and Heidegger'.[1] Though
Strauss himself lacks the imagination and intellectual warmth typical of
great philosophers, his evaluation of thinkers of that rank is always shrewd,
and often well worth noting. In the present case, it is easy (for me, at least)
to endorse his conclusion that Bergson, Whitehead, Husserl, and Heidegger
are the lasting names of philosophy from the period in question. So, we
might begin by asking what Latour adds to these 'four greatest philosophers'
of 1914-1954, and to other trends of the past century that have commanded
the most acclaim.

On this short list we find Husserl and Heidegger, teacher and student.
They can safely be combined under the label 'phenomenology', though the
differences between them have long been widely known. Though these two
figures rank among my dearest intellectual heroes, they are not Latour's,
and his lack of interest in this tradition is understandable. Husserl limits
himself to a description of phenomena present to human consciousness, and
hence remains an idealist despite his call for a return to the things themselves. Latour endorses this usual criticism of Husserl, which is largely accurate. As for Heidegger, though he never reduces entities to their presence in consciousness, he still belittles specific objects as merely 'ontic' and
draws the conclusion that ontology is commanded to deal with being itself and not specific entities. It should be obvious enough why Latour is no
Heideggerian. For Latour, philosophy plays out amidst microbes, tape re-
corders, windmills, apples, and any real or unreal actors that one might
imagine. Moreover, Latour has no interest in the pathos of depth: though
his actors can always surprise us, these surprises always emerge at the surface of the world, not from some veiled underworld ruled by the shades of
Eckhardt and Hölderlin. Now, my own view is that phenomenology harbors resources that lead it to converge with Latour's insights, however different their starting points may be. Read carefully, Husserl and Heidegger
veer from the previous sort of idealism thanks to their focus on *objects*, and
this trend is carried further in the works of later phenomenologists such as
Merleau-Ponty, Levinas, and Lingis.[2] Nonetheless, the usual sort of insider's
praise for phenomenology is directed more towards its vices than its virtues, and Latour is justified in condemning this ritual. Husserl's bracketing
of the world, Heidegger's contempt for all plastic and electrical things, and
Levinas's 'pathetic' notion of a God of the beyond are in no way compatible

---

1. Leo Strauss, *What is Political Philosophy?*, Chicago, University of Chicago Press, 1988, p. 17.

2. Harman, Graham, *Guerrilla Metaphysics: Phenomenology and the Carpentry of Things*,
Chicago, Open Court, 2005.

with the style of philosophy that we owe to Latour. Phenomenology *does* remain largely imprisoned in Kant's Copernican Revolution.

Outside the Husserl/Heidegger river valley, we find Jacques Lacan and his brilliant admirers Alain Badiou and Slavoj Žižek. However these figures may differ, it is safe to say that all three let the human subject bear the full load of philosophy and leave nothing to non-human entities. A Lacanian physics is unthinkable. Žižek openly proclaims that reality outside the subject is a naïve supposition, while Badiou holds that actors are units only when they are *counted* as units—and there is no evidence that he allows anyone but humans to do the counting. A Žižekian chemistry and a Badiouian zoology are equally unthinkable. By contrast, Latour lets non-human actors do as much ontological work as people do, even if the inanimate realm receives too little attention in his books compared with human scientific practice.

We turn to Bergson and his great successor Deleuze. The difference between Latour and these figures should be clear enough, and despite possible connections neither Bergson nor Deleuze is his ancestor in any crucial respect. What separates both figures from Latour is their disbelief that concrete actual entities are primary in the world. Bergson is widely and accurately described as a champion of pre-individual dynamism, an *élan* or *durée* that may harden into individual entities, but whose hardening is always derivative and generally lamentable. Indeed, Latour might even be described as the anti-Bergson, given his implicit opposition to any philosophy in which disembodied becoming trumps individual actors. Deleuze's notion of 'the virtual' is designed precisely to move philosophy away from actual freight trains and apricots; it is hard to imagine Deleuze taking Latour's 'actors' seriously. Recall that there is no such thing for Latour as a 'becoming' that would exceed individual actors. Nor is there any 'virtuality' that exceeds them, just as potentiality does not exceed them. The much-discussed difference between potential and virtual, so often wielded like a billy club in our time by Deleuzian hooligans, is irrelevant here—both terms fail Latour's standard for concreteness in exactly the same way.

We are now left with Whitehead, who is surely Latour's closest philosophical ancestor. The similarities between them are as obvious as they are pivotal. Whitehead's 'ontological principle' holds that the reasons for anything at all must always be sought in the constitution of some definite actual entity, a principle that neither Bergson nor Deleuze could possibly endorse. This suffices to demonstrate the sloppiness of trying to group all of these figures together under any single rubric, such as 'process philosophy'. Whitehead and Latour also share a great fondness for relations, which Whitehead calls 'prehensions'. The attempt to speak of a thing apart from its relations gives us only what Whitehead calls 'vacuous actuality', the same term he uses to dismiss materialism and other theories of substance. By now it should be clear that Latour offers the same basic criticism of such theories.

It is also true that Whitehead's philosophy displays a speculative cosmological spirit for which there is no equivalent in Latour. Though it would be misleading to call Latour a 'philosopher of science', it is revealing that no one ever calls him a 'philosopher of nature'—a term that might easily be applied to Whitehead. Nonetheless, I still prefer Latour's metaphysics to Whitehead's for one pivotal reason: the greater secularism of Latour's theory of relations. In Whitehead's model of prehensions between actual entities, we are led down the cul-de-sac of 'eternal objects', or universal qualities located in God himself. This is merely a variant of traditional occasionalism, and shares all the faults of that school. Latour takes the more daring step of ignoring eternal objects and keeping interactions on a local level: it is Joliot who links neutrons and politics, not God. In fact, for Latour *every actor is a Joliot*, a medium of translation able to link the most far-flung objects and equally capable of failing in this effort. The reason for preferring the secular model of relations is not because we must pander to the smug atheism of today's *avant garde*, but because when the problem of relations between actors is magically transferred to God it is solved merely by fiat. To put all relations in the hands of a deity is no better (though also no worse) than the Hume/Kant approach of locating all relations in the habits or categories of human beings. In both cases inanimate actors are stripped of autonomy, smothered in their infancy. By contrast, Latour gives us the first philosophy ever known in which the relations between objects are both a puzzling difficulty *and* are not monopolized by some privileged tyrant entity, whether human or divine. This last point provides the major theme for the remainder of the book.

A. THE CONCRETENESS OF ACTORS

As we have seen, the most typical feature of Latour's philosophy is the dignity it grants to all sizes and types of actors. Neutrons are actors and black holes are actors, but so are buildings, cities, humans, dogs, rocks, fictional characters, secret potions, and voodoo dolls. Some readers may tire (or pretend to tire) of these frequent lists, dismissing them as an 'incantation' or 'poetics' of objects. But most readers will not soon grow tired, since the rhetorical power of these rosters of beings stems from their direct opposition to the flaws of current mainstream philosophy. We cannot imagine Kant or Hegel invoking such a roll call of concrete entities, which shift the weight of philosophy toward specific actors themselves and away from all structures that might wish to subsume them. We find a tacit monism in philosophies of human access with their global apartheid where all breeds of objects are nothing more than equally non-human. The best stylistic antidote to this grim deadlock is a repeated sorcerer's chant of the multitude of things that resist any unified empire. Such lists are found not only in the present book, and not just in Latour himself, but in numerous authors who try to shift our focus from any onefold force to the muffled pluralities that arise from its ashes. Writing of the destruction of Hiroshima, Richard Rhodes launches a more extravagant poetry of objects than Latour or I have ever attempted:

> Destroyed, that is, were not only men, women and thousands of children but also restaurants and inns, laundries, theater groups, sports clubs, sewing clubs, boys' clubs, girls' clubs, love affairs, trees and gardens, grass, gates, gravestones, temples and shrines, family heirlooms, radios, classmates, books, courts of law, clothes, pets, groceries and markets, telephones, personal letters, automobiles, bicycles, horses—120 war-horses—musical instruments, medicines and medical equipment, life savings, eyeglasses, city records, sidewalks, family scrapbooks, monuments, engagements, marriages, employees, clocks and watches, public transportation, street signs, parents, works of art.[3]

Having been deeply disturbed by a personal visit to Hiroshima and Nagasaki, I mean no disrespect to the victims and ruined objects of Japan if I say that the same list of objects is destroyed in a different way by the various philosophies of human access. Human-centered philosophy is a Hiroshima of metaphysics, one that annihilates the objects invoked by Rhodes along with all others. But Latour does not share in this crime against humans and non-humans. Instead of dismissing grass, gates, gravestones, radios, classmates, and courts of law as mere ontic details, he allows them to be topics of philosophy again. Without being flippant, we should add that Latour also welcomes Hamlet, Popeye, phlogiston, subway trains, the Dutch East India Company, the Easter Bunny, and the Holy Spirit into a philosophical realm from which the materialists would cruelly banish them.

While Whitehead's ontological principle states that everything that happens is a consequence of the reality of specific entities, Latour's converse theorem is equally fruitful: all entities have consequences. To place all objects on equal footing erases the various two-world gaps found in the history of philosophy, as well as the numerous faux 'radical' efforts to glue the two worlds together from the start. The grass of Hiroshima is separated not just from some unknowable grass-in-itself, but also from the gravestones and musical instruments that inhabit the same plane of reality as the grass. Nor are the blades of grass mere present-at-hand entities outstripped by a unified rumbling being. Grass can do things in the world, just as atoms and Popeye can do things.

The necessary concreteness of actors also suspends any pre-individual reality that tries to claim a deeper status than specific entities. To take a bird seriously means to let the whole of reality pour into the actual bird, not to view it as the transient incarnation of some pre-avian 'diagram' or 'line of flight'. Mammals are real, and there is no good reason to hold that mammals

---

3. Richard Rhodes, *The Making of the Atomic Bomb*, New York, Touchstone, 1986, p. 733.

inhabit a topology that structures a space of possible vertebrates, as the wonderful Manuel DeLanda[4] wrongly argues. To shift the scene of philosophy
away from specific things is a superfluous gesture, one that makes sense only
if we lose faith in the concreteness of actors. Latour's gamble, of course, lies
in his notion that actors are defined entirely by their relations and alliances.
His model of ultra-concrete actors requires that they be fully relational in
character, with no distinction between object and accident, object and relation, or object and quality. This same model requires that actors not be
permitted to endure any shift in their alliances, since to change one's relations is to change one's reality. Entities for Latour *must* be a perpetual perishing, since they cannot survive even the tiniest change in their properties.
Whitehead partly escapes this consequence by contrasting 'societies' (which
can endure) with actual entities or occasions (which cannot). This distinction is less developed in Latour, but in my mind this counts to Latour's credit as a mark of bolder consistency. As we have seen, Latour does sometime
speaks of actors as 'trajectories' that cut across numerous moments, and implies that an actor acquires a 'history' when its allies shift rather than that it
perishes outright. For example, we might claim that Obama's White House
in 2009 is the same as Eisenhower's in 1959, since the changes on its periph-
ery do not really affect the trajectory of events that truly comprise the White
House. But recall that the very decision about what is important in a thing
requires a work of translation, since it cannot lie in the heart of an actor like
some traditional kernel of essence. Latour accepts no 'substantial form' of
the White House that could endure through the decades despite shifting inhabitants and changing coats of paint, because there is no automatic way in
his philosophy to separate the inner reality of the building from its transient
fluctuations through the work of birds and vandals. Some external Joliot will
always be needed to *establish* that the White House is the same thing at two
different moments fifty years apart.

   Individual actors are cut off in themselves, fully defined by their exact
relations with others at this very instant, unable to change those relations in
the least without perishing. It may sound paradoxical to stress this island-
like character of actors given Latour's obvious fondness for relations, but the
exact features of this paradox will be explored soon enough. Though an actor is defined by its relations with others, this does not mean for Latour that
it can barrel forward into a *different* set of relations thanks to some magical
élan, while still somehow remaining the same thing. If one actor were to contain its own future states in germ, or if it endured as an essential core over
time and withstood the rainstorm of shifting interactions, this would contradict the basic principle of Latourian metaphysics that nothing contains
anything else. Everything is external to everything else, and it takes difficult

---

4. See Manuel DeLanda, *A New Philosophy of Society: Assemblage Theory and Social Complexity*,
London, Continuum, 2006.

work to link any two things. Latour grants no initial principle of endurance over time, just as he accepts no force of temporal flux over and above specific actors themselves. Latour is no philosopher of becoming, no 'process philosopher' except in the trivial sense that he tries to account for changes in the world, as every thinker must. As we have seen, Latour goes so far as to claim that time is *produced* by the labour of actors, and that only such actors create an asymmetry of before and after. For exactly the same reason, the links between one instant and another must also be produced through the labour of actants, for they are not pre-given in some sort of internal drive or *conatus* in the heart of things that would free them from the prison of single instants. After all, the utter concreteness of actants actually requires that they be incarcerated in an instant. More occasionalist than Bergsonian, Latour's actors have no choice but to occupy punctiform cinematic frames. Otherwise they would endure, and endurance would imply an inner enduring kernel encrusted with shifting accidents—a most un-Latourian theme.

Latour's guiding principle is that an actor is defined by its alliances; if alliances shift, then *by definition* the actor has changed, and the two White Houses are linked as 'the same' White House only if some other actor is able to link them by showing an equivalence. It is sheer nonsense to claim that any Latourian actor 'points' toward another, or possesses some internal drive toward some future state of itself. That would be Leibniz, not Latour. For Latour an object 'points' only if some Joliot *makes* it point by forging a well-constructed link between that actor and another. If we want to claim that the White House 'points' to its own future states, we might as well claim that neutrons already 'point' to Belgian mining companies and commando operations, in direct contradiction of Latour's remarks on the pivotal role of Joliot. The issue is so clear for anyone who reads *Irreductions* carefully that I have often puzzled over the widespread resistance to reading Latour as a philosopher of isolated instants. What I suspect is that the resistance stems merely from the spirit of our age, which not only assumes (like Latour) that philosophy's enemy is rock-hard enduring substances, but also assumes (unlike Latour) that the only antidotes to such a poison would be process, flux, and flow. Since our *Zeitgeist* tends to assume that all intellectual freshness lies on the side of becoming as opposed to static being, it further assumes that anyone denying such ultra-flux in Latour must be accusing him of stupidity. The mistake here lies in the major premise: for the real novelty in philosophy no longer belongs to the tired old limerick of shifting fluxions and becomings, but to utterly concrete and utterly disconnected entities that cry aloud for mediators to bridge them. Latour's obsession with translation would make no sense if actors were always already linked or already pointed beyond themselves.

Thus, Latour's relational model of actors tilts him paradoxically toward an occasionalist theory of isolated instants. Yet it also shields him from the possible complaint that by admitting Popeye and unicorns to the same real-ist club as rocks and atoms he has multiplied entities to the point of absur-dity. This is because Latour's relationism gives him an obvious criterion for clearing the slum of superfluous actors: namely, a thing is real for Latour only if it affects or perturbs other things. Following a well-known pragma-tist axiom, he holds that an actor that makes no difference is not a real ac-tor. The possible entity assembled from Mars, the Mississippi River, and Charles Baudelaire is not a unified actor unless this perverse confederation somehow manages to perturb other actors. There is always the faint chance that someone might succeed in linking them ('*Tu es beau, mon fleuve, / comme la planète rouge…*') though this would presumably be more difficult than making the physical parts of a television achieve a genuine total effect.

Finally, we have seen that Latour's relationism allows him to replace the usual twofold rift of philosophy with a plurality of levels. Not only is the mournful human/world gap abolished, but the same happens with the sup-posed chasm between matter and form. There is no final stratum of brute material from which flimsier, more ostentatious entities would then be mold-ed. The Aristotle-Leibniz distinction between substance and aggregate is abolished, since 'nature' is a poor way to distinguish atoms on the one hand from machines and armies on the other. For Latour an actor is real not through nature-sans-artifice, but through its effects on other entities. There is no substance, only black boxes, and like Pandora's box they can be opened at will to examine the delicate internal negotiations that made them possi-ble. Traditional realism's hobgoblin of the 'mere aggregate' or 'mere thing of reason' is no longer a worry, since in the end everything is an aggregate, assembled carefully or carelessly from numerous components. Gaps multi-ply to infinity and are constantly crossed by the work of translation, not by the impossible perilous leap so deservedly ridiculed by James. In short, there is no final layer of reality from which all relations will have been cleansed. The stunning metaphysical implication here, which Latour never discusses openly, is an *infinite regress of actors*. If there are only black boxes and never a final substance, then we will never come to a final stage in any analysis. But notice that this infinite regress is not just a product of our own human analy-sis: Latour's black boxes belong to the world itself, not to our speeches about the world. The point is not just that we can keep opening black boxes *as far as we wish*, with some arbitrary cutoff point at the limits of human fatigue. More than this, his metaphysics entails that black boxes do in fact extend into infinite depths. Latour will shed no tears that this conclusion openly flouts Kant's Second Antinomy.

Thesis: Everything in the world is constituted out of the simple.

Antithesis: There is nothing simple, but everything is composite.[5]

---

5. Immanuel Kant, *Prolegomena to Any Future Metaphysics*, trans. Paul Carus and revised by

Though Kant forbids us to choose between the two, Latour's position implies the antithesis quite brazenly. Just as spring is announced by the songs of returning birds, the return of metaphysics will be known through the reappearance of birds driven south by the Antinomies. Latour's positions on the remaining three antinomies (finitude/infinity of space and time, freedom/mechanism, necessary being/no necessary being) are easy to guess as well. But they are less central to his thinking than the endless chain of composite black boxes stretching down to Hell and beyond.

B. AGAINST MATERIALISM

A more surprising historic parallel now emerges between Latour and Edmund Husserl: a figure for whom he has little sympathy. As we have seen, though Latour may be wrong to show such contempt for phenomenology, the reasons for his disdain are commendable. By bracketing the actual world and focusing on phenomena in consciousness, Husserl ratifies the most dismal aspect of Copernican philosophy. By contrast, Latour rejects idealism and maintains that there is no fixed gap between humans and other actors. All of this is true, and one must admit that Latour goes further than Husserl in abolishing the people-centered credo of continental philosophy.

Yet there is a striking similarity of method between the two thinkers: namely, both observe a rule of absolute pluralism that makes no sweeping distinction between real and unreal objects. Just as Latour initially places cartoon characters on the same level as rocks and atoms, Husserl asks that even the most ludicrous figments be described exactly as they appear to us and not quickly dismissed. This is the positive side of the idealist method of bracketing, since it allows Husserl to protect the unruly mob of phenomena from rapid decimation by critical debunkers. For this very reason Husserl and Latour often share the same angry opponents: hardcore reductionists who become enraged whenever centaurs and unicorns are allowed to graze freely in their field of neutrons. But there is an irony here. Since Latour forbids any schism between phenomena and the natural world, he is surely more of a realist than Husserl, who remains obstinately within the phenomenal realm. Yet this very fact makes Latour more obnoxious to materialists than Husserl could ever be. After all, since Husserl claims to do nothing more than describe the contents of consciousness, this leaves a full half of reality in which the naturalists can romp about and dominate. They will not feel threatened by whatever Husserl does in his homemade human castle, and can always seize it if they wish in the name of cognitive science. But Latour's claim to speak for the *whole* of reality, and his parallel claim that materialism is not a good description of that reality, suggests a rude invasion of scientific hunting grounds. As long as philosophers remain on the human

James W. Ellington, Indianapolis, Hackett, 1977, p. 74..

side of an artificial human/world divide they pose no danger to materialism, and are generally left in peaceful contempt. But as soon as they invade
the materialist kingdom itself, they are assaulted by angry scientific mili-
tias—as happened to Latour in the Sokal-driven 'Science Wars', but would
probably not have happened to Husserl if he had been alive in 1996.

Naturalism grants privilege to a world of real causes affecting all physical things equally, and thereby seeks to eliminate the Cartesian mind/world
dualism and its various heirs. Naturalism even grants physical causation the
right to invade the human realm, so that conscious phenomena no longer belong to a special zone immune from physical explanation. The mind becomes
a mere brain, not an enchanted spirit that punctures the fabric of causation
and rises above the world. In my view this attitude is both superior and inferior to the weary old dualism. In one sense it is superior, since it eliminates
the groundless dual monarchy of Human and World, which is ultimately no
better than the pre-Galilean double physics of heaven and earth. Cognition
does deserve to be treated by the physical sciences, and for those who are
tired of Copernican dogma the work of such figures as the Churchlands is
always strangely refreshing. But in another sense naturalism is inferior, since
it merely inverts the basic reductionist gesture of absolute idealism. Whereas
the idealists reduce inanimate collisions to their appearance in consciousness, the naturalists simply reduce in the opposite direction. Instead of turning fire into a mere phenomenon of fire, they turn this phenomenon into a
mere epiphenomenon of fire's true microphysical reality. In both cases the
two-world theory is taken as an article of faith, with one term elevated to the
throne and the other reduced to slavery. The situation resembles the trenches
of Flanders during the Great War, with neither side gaining more than a few
inches for every million bullets fired. To enlist with either side in a time of
trench warfare is foolish: movement is rare and lifespans are low. Whenever
we find that two sides of an intellectual dispute are merely the inverted forms
of one another, we have a stalemate. What is always needed to escape stalemate is some new strategy, some armored vehicle or shock troop tactic able
to pierce and outflank both trenches. In the present case, Latour's method of
placing all 'physical' and 'mental' actors on the same footing is the best way
to end the trench war between naturalism and idealism.

Materialism can safely be described as the default commonsense philosophy of our time, despite Weinberg's fear of 'lingering irrational tendencies'.
Today's educated castes silently assume, whether happily or sadly, that the
universe is basically made of hard physical matter. Naturalists openly celebrate this view, while dualists betray an equal faith in physical microparticles through their fearful retreat to the human castle—a special sanctuary
where they hope the blows of atoms will not apply. The 'intellectual Munich'
of the dualists lies in their refusal to conduct offensive operations in the realm
of inanimate matter, where they let the natural sciences dominate even while

consoling themselves with a feeble superiority in the fragile zone of human meaning. They boost their morale by repeating Heidegger's infamous and depressing claim that science does not think. Philosophy in our time is either materialist or it is intimidated by materialism—one of the two. The situation is intolerable. We can love and respect the sciences without accepting that philosophy is their handmaid. Science does think, but this does not mean it deserves the monopoly on thinking that the various intellectual Chamberlains have given it. What philosophy must do is address the inanimate world again, but in terms different from those of materialism, since the latter has surprisingly little to recommend it. The model of the world as a hard layer of impenetrable matter tells us only that matter can shove other matter out of the way or smack it forcefully, with the added sweetener that cognitive science will no longer allow the human mind to be exempt from this process. But this merely takes inanimate causation as an obvious given while doing nothing to explain how it occurs. It is a metaphysics fit for a two-year-old: 'da wed ball pusht da gween ball... an da gween ball fell on da fwoorr'.

Of Aristotle's famous four causes, only the efficient and material cause are retained, while the formal and final causes are dismissed as either illusory (final) or derivative (formal). More generally, relation is never treated as a *problem* by materialists, as it is by Latour. By showing that the relation between actors is always a form of translation, Latour begins to free philosophy from its fear of inanimate nature. He invites us to leave our drafty human castle, from which all non-human objects are banished under penalty of being reduced to images. Note that the idealist contempt for materialism amounts to nothing more than ignoring it, with the claim that philosophy has nothing to do with what happens beyond the river in the inanimate wilderness. In turn, materialism simply counters that it owns both banks of the river, since human reality is just as governed by physico-chemical laws as any soulless matter. Latour's contempt for materialism is more compelling than either option: there is not one river, but millions of them, and unbridged gaps between any two entities that exist. Science constantly crosses these gaps with great fruitfulness (as do gardening, juggling, and cookery) but it never tells us *how* they are crossed. This is the task of an object-oriented philosophy. Any metaphysics worthy of the name must be a metaphysics of objects and relations.

Latour is right to call materialism a form of idealism. He does this most lucidly in a 2007 article with the plaintive title 'Can We Get Our Materialism Back, Please?' The article declares that we need a 'new descriptive style that circumvents the limits of the materialist (in effect idealist) definition of material existence' (MB, p. 138). The problem is that 'materialism, in the short period in which it could be used as a discussion-closing trope, implied what now appears in retrospect as a rather idealist definition of matter and its agencies' (MB, p. 138). The origins of this idealist materialism lie in the distinction between primary and secondary qualities derived from Descartes and Locke. As Latour puts it: 'This is why the materialism of the recent past now looks so idealistic: it takes the idea of what things in themselves should be—that is, primary qualities—and then never stops gawking at the miracle that makes them "resemble" their geometrical reproduction in drawings' (MB, p. 139). To claim that reality is reducible to material factors is to make a dogmatic decision about what the primary qualities of actors really are, replacing the permanent mystery of actors with a dogmatic model of actors as extended solid things. In other words, a one-dimensional *idea* of actors replaces their reality, which is always partly surprising and opaque. Materialism turns out to be not a hardheaded realist doctrine, but one of the most blatant forms of idealism the world has ever known. It turns Socrates into a scientific expert, just as Latour feared. But since no one really knows what an actor is, to define it in terms of hard physical matter is a deeply unphilosophical step, one adopted mostly because it allows us to laugh at all the naïve tribal dupes who still believe in ghosts and omens. But as a rule, any theory that exists merely to unmask another as naïve is probably a bad one.

When Latour denies the materialist principle and puts all actors on the same footing, we may notice an inner feeling of resistance—as though some trick were being played and something were being lost. Namely, what seems to be lost is the critical weaponry that allows enlightenment to dismiss irrational phantoms and bring us to a true reality that exists 'whether we like it or not'. If Hamlet, Popeye, and bald kings of France are just as real as paraffin, then we seem to be in the land of 'anything goes'. By now it should be clear how this distorts Latour's position. Latour holds that all objects are equally real, not that all are equally *strong*. He would agree with materialists that a typical mountain has *more* reality than Popeye, or at least a more tenacious kind. Their point of disagreement concerns the criterion for reality. The iconoclastic method of critical debunking likes to measure reality according to the radical human/world split. It mistakenly identifies the 'world' side of the dualism with 'reality whether we like it or not', and gives to the 'human' side the sole responsibility for distorting this reality—perhaps undoing the distortion later in the name of correspondence and enlightenment. According to this standpoint things are real if they come from the 'world' side and unreal if added by the 'human' side. Enlightenment proceeds by *denouncing*, and exults as it punctures everyone's tissues of naiveté. In this way, iconoclasm solidifies both the unique human/world gap and the correspondence theory of truth. Latour's solution is entirely different. What makes an atom more real than a ghost is not that the former exists as a real state of affairs and the latter only in our minds. Instead, what makes the atom more real is that it has more allies, including allies stretching well beyond the human realm. Experiments testify to the atom's existence; instruments stabilize it and make it indirectly visible; the scientific profession is transformed by it; generations of children learn about atoms and pass the word along; Brownian motion shows that particles of water are moved by atoms, as argued by none other than Einstein himself. By contrast, the ghost has only a paltry number of allies bearing witness to its reality, such as hysterical children and a few old legends. But it might also happen that the atom's allies desert it one day too.

This Latourian approach to reality is both convincing and unconvincing, much like the subject/object dualism itself. Latour is right that human and world cannot serve as a dual tribunal of reality, with world getting all the reality and humans getting all of the unreality (at least until they grow up and learn to correspond with the world). When subject and object are identified with human and world, we have a disaster on our hands, since truth and falsity are now apportioned among two distinct *kinds* of beings. The same thing happens with the distinction between primary and secondary qualities, also rejected by Latour. According to this distinction the primary qualities of a thing (such as the physical structure of cloth or sugar) belong to it 'whether we like it or not', while the secondary qualities (such as the colour of a shirt or the taste of sugar) exist only for perception. Here, something that ought to be a global ontological distinction is carved up between two domains that Heidegger would call 'ontic': inanimate things have all the primary qualities, while humans and maybe a few smart animals add all the secondary ones.

But as already suggested, there is something else going on in these dualisms that is not as contemptible as Latour thinks. The repeated shouts against Latour that reality exists 'whether we like it or not' can immediately be dismissed when they are meant to endorse the human/world split that his democracy of actors destroys. But there is a more defensible side to 'reality whether we like it or not'—namely, the reality of a thing apart from its *relations* whether we like it or not. Since Latour is an absolute relationist in his theory of actors, he cannot look fondly upon this point. But the grain of truth in the physicist's scream is that an actor must already exist if other actors are to negotiate with it in the first place. For example, there is either something like a microbe at work in the pre-Pasteurian year 1700, or there is not. The retroactive production of the microbe, in the manner that Latour recommends, gives too much weight to the *human* awareness of it, and ignores the effect of the microbe on other non-human entities in 1700 'whether we like it or not'. Latour would surely be appalled by this objection, but here I think the old-time realists have a point. However, they quickly ruin their point by refusing Latour's justified abolition of the human/world divide and by denying all work of translation in the inanimate realm, which they regard as nothing but an objective and easily mirrorable state of objective affairs. What these science warriors overlook is that not only humans translate or distort the reality of the microbe. If they want to say that the microbe is there whether *we* like it or not, they should add that it is there whether dogs, milk, and wine like it or not. Entities such as horses and cheese confront this microbe no less than we do, and they too will give it 'secondary qualities' that do not entirely overlap with the microbe itself.

As we have seen, the usual approach of scientific realists is to assign primary qualities to things and secondary qualities to the human distortions of things. Latour's contrary strategy is to deny any difference at all between primary and secondary qualities, since he sees all qualities as constituted by relations, and thus all qualities are secondary—as Berkeley also holds, though with a more idealist twist. But there is still a third possibility. Namely, we can accept the distinction between primary and secondary (like the science warriors) while refusing to carve it up between the human and the inhuman respectively (as Latour himself refuses). For it is hard to see why only humans and animals would be able to generate secondary qualities in the things they encounter. If the smell and colour of cotton (for humans) are secondary qualities, then the flammability of cotton (for fire) is secondary as well. An object is grazed only lightly by another, not drained to the dregs. By placing secondary qualities solely in the human mind, humans are given the unique power to distort a true reality that is wrongly identified with inhuman nature. This falsely removes all problems of translation from the inanimate realm.

In short, Latour *does* lose something when he says that a microbe is nothing more than the chain of actors perturbed by the microbe's existence. For the relational theory of actors borders on a kind of 'verificationism' in which the reality of a thing is defined by the ways in which it is registered by other entities, with the important caveat that Latour allows inanimate actors to work on each other as well as on us. His view that an actor is real by virtue of perturbing other actors does veer away from one of the key principles of realism: namely, that a thing is real beyond the conditions of its accessibility. Latour's great achievement is to deny the modern oscillation between human and world as the wellspring of all enlightenment. But he pays the following price: while the gaps between entities are rightly multiplied to infinity, he leaves no gap at all between a thing's inherent reality and its effects on other things. But this is a far smaller price than that paid by traditional realism, with its strict segregation between humans and things, and its model of 'reality' as a dull independent state of affairs that the mind is forced to copy like a harassed student at some dreary provincial art school.

C. LOCAL OCCASIONALISM

We now return to what I have called the doctrine of local occasionalism. This is probably Latour's greatest achievement in philosophy, and provides (as far as I can see) an unprecedented theme in the long history of metaphysics. While mainstream realism is usually seen as the great champion of causality, it merely asserts the existence of causation against doubters while shedding no light on how it works. The causal power of nature is wielded as a sword against both extreme theists who deny it and skeptics who doubt it. Islamic occasionalism was opposed by Averroes, and Hume was opposed by any number of realist critics. But whenever natural causation is saved in this *ad hoc* way from its radical critics, an important insight is lost. For there is a true flash of genius shared by the occasionalists and the skeptics, and it comes from their willingness to cut things off in an inner life, refusing to let them bleed into each other without further explanation. In both the occasionalist and skeptical traditions, relations are external to the things that relate. The sole unlucky point is that occasionalists and skeptics do not push their insight to its maximum limit, since both systems are based on a crowning hypocrisy. As occasionalists see it, if fire cannot burn cotton then God can still do it. But since it is never clarified how God can burn cotton if fire cannot, only the shroud of official piety can bolster this brilliant but half-hearted doctrine. And while skeptics also claim to doubt the link between fire and cotton, they have always already linked these entities in the ramshackle form of custom or habit. After all, Hume never denies that I link fire, cotton, and burning in my mind; he merely disputes that they necessarily have autonomous power outside my experience of them.

The strength and weakness of these denials of causation should now be clear. Their strength lies in the deserved autonomy they grant to realities as purely external to one another—whether full-blown substances for the occasionalists or dismembodied qualities for the skeptics. Nothing 'points' toward anything else or bleeds into anything else. Everything withdraws into itself; all bridges are owned and operated either by God or the human mind. The weakness of both theories is the same: they allow a single pampered entity to break the ban on relations that is cruelly enforced on all others. Both theories flatter the feudal tyranny of a single actor allowed to dominate the rest. Nor is the dispute between these mirror-image philosophies just a dusty historical sideshow, since it continues to guide us today. For the duel between occasionalists and skeptics can be rewritten as that between the so-called rationalists and empiricists, who Kant claims to have unified in his own philosophy. Seventeenth century continental thought, from Descartes through Leibniz, proclaims the independence of substances mediated only by God (or identical with God, as in Spinoza's case). Meanwhile, the empiricists replace unified substances with qualities that are arbitrarily linked and bundled by the habits of human observers. The tyranny of God and substance plagues the first group, while the tyranny of mind and qualities enslaves the second. Both groups unite to suppress the private local actor, who is now reduced either to a puppet of the Deity or to a mere appearance in consciousness. On the other side of the fence, though the Aristotelian faith in direct causation is certainly admirable, it lacks the insight of these extremists through its failure to adopt the mutual externality of things, which the extremists affirm with a lucid extremism. Kantian merely blends the worst of both options: letting things link together in the mind as long as they claim no extra-phenomenal status, and allowing for real things-in-themselves while giving them no permission to interact. In this respect the Copernican standpoint gives us occasionalism and skepticism rolled into one, surrounded by enemies that choose only side or the other: German Idealism merely trumpets the human side of the dualism; naturalism takes the inhuman side, but never faces up to the occasionalist problem except to mock it once in awhile during introductory courses. None of these groups seem able to do two things at once; none of them know how to allow for local causation *and* pay respect to the absolute mutual exteriority of things.

To repeat, occasionalists and skeptics agree in denying individual things the autonomous power to enter relations. This seems to make them the opposite of Latour, since he is such an ardent champion of relations. Yet there is no contradiction at all in isolating things from one another *and* making them relational, as seen even before Latour in the cases of Leibniz and Whitehead. The Leibnizian monads are mirrors of other things, yet they are insular mirrors in direct contact only with God. For Whitehead, actual entities mutually prehend one another and are even made up entirely of relations, since otherwise they would be mere 'vacuous actualities'. Yet they do not prehend each other directly; this occurs by way of the 'eternal objects' that are found only in God. For Whitehead as for Latour, relations are a difficult *result*, not an easy starting point. Herein lies the close link of both authors with the occasionalist tradition. For Latour an actor is defined by its current alliances—but this does not mean that it has no problem entering new ones! The clearest proof of this fact can always be found in Latour's obsession with translation, along with his vehement denial that actors contain future states *in potentia*. Whitehead's appeal to God and eternal objects places him too firmly in the traditional occasionalist camp, with its central hypocrisy of a single entity mediating all relations. Latour avoids this pitfall, granting the former duties of God to Joliot and all other actors. In addition, Latour also escapes the deadlock of Kant and the empiricists by denying the claim of the human mind to have monopoly rights over relations. Human and non-human actors relate across countless gaps, and this bridging occurs constantly. The work of bridging always remains problematic, though it must be solved locally rather than by some god or human mind. For Latour, actors are linked only when some other actor *makes* them link. The term I have often used for this is 'vicarious causation', as opposed to the 'occasional causation' that too easily suggests a weatherbeaten theology.[6] Latour is one of the few to raise the problem of the very *nature* of causation,

6. See Graham Harman, 'On Vicarious Causation', *Collapse*, vol. II, Oxford, 2007.

which naturalists merely take for granted. Moreover, he plays the part of Galileo by denying that there are two kinds of causation, one for nature and another for the human realm. The impact of acid on seashells is no longer different *in kind* from Caesar's effect on Cato or Hawaiian steel guitars on Mississippi Delta blues. The point of a theory of causation is not to reduce humans to the atomic or molecular, but to give an account of causation that is broad enough to embrace everything from neutrons to armies of orcs from Mordor.

The occasionalist tradition first arose in early Islam, for theological reasons. Certain passages of the *Qur'an* suggest God's direct influence on even the minutest events, and some of the faithful drew broad conclusions. In their eyes, to grant any causal agency to created things would amount to making them miniature creators—a blasphemous result. Hence, God must be directly responsible for everything that happens, and must be capable even of the illogical and the malicious: such as making two plus two equal five, or sending a just man to Hell for no reason whatsoever. In the Ash'arite metaphysics of atoms and accidents, God intervenes to provide things with their accidents, and since endurance itself was viewed as just another sort of accident, entities would vanish with every passing moment if not sustained or recreated by Allah. With Descartes these themes make their belated appearance in the West and dominate the seventeenth century in various forms that are subtly distinguished while the wider point is missed. Descartes's problem, having split created substances into two distinct kinds, is how the thoughts of the mind could ever affect the motions of the body. God alone seems capable of bridging the gap. Once the Cartesian *res extensa* is fragmented into atoms by Cordemoy and others, Malebranche is forced to extend God's hand into the relations between bodies themselves. The limited mind-body problem turns into a body-body problem. Occasional cause becomes global once more, as it already was for the Ash'arite Muslims. For Bruno Latour the problem is global as well, since the link between one atom and another is no different in kind from that between the Red Army and the Pope. We have seen that Latour solves the problem without granting unique relational privileges to either God or the human mind. In this way, Bruno Latour is the first *secular occasionalist*: the founder of what I have called vicarious causation. Any entity is able to form the link between others that previously had no interactions at all. Latour also concedes that local causes might fail in their efforts: an interesting tragic side of causation that was always denied, for obvious reasons, to God. Joliot might succeed in linking politics with neutrons, or like Pouchet he might end his days as a discredited flop. Links are not easy to create, even though they happen everywhere all the time.

We return once more to the skeptical and empiricist traditions. It is well known that Hume was an admirer of Malebranche and greatly appreciated

his doubts about direct causal links. But for Hume there is still a link between things. Though not a real link made by God between substances,
it is an apparent one made by human habit between distinct impressions
or qualities. The human mind links bread with nourishment or fire with
pain despite no necessary connection between these realities. Human habit
is even responsible for shaping qualities into 'bundles', by habitually presum-
ing that the colour, texture, shape, and flavour of an apple all belong to one
and the same unified thing (a step that Husserl reverses, with his claim that
such qualities emanate from a prior unified apple). Despite all his skeptical
claims, Hume never denies that habit creates such links—*of course* it does. He
merely denies that we have proof of autonomous entities lying outside our
perceptions, with an inherent ability to form links in their own right when
human habit is not watching. Custom is to Hume what God is to the occasionalists: the only genuine link between separate realities, even though
these realities for him are qualities rather than substances. Latour's point of
agreement with Hume is clear enough, since both agree that things are not
different from their attributes. What saves Latour from skepticism is his denial that humans have the sole power to create links. Any actor is able to link
others. For Latour it is not *human habit* that links numerous machine-parts
into a single working machine, or many atoms into a single stone. Instead,
habit feels resisted by the machine and stone.

I have used 'Joliot' as a nickname for actors in general, since all actors
must do what Joliot did. Objects connect things that need not have been
connected, and sometimes they fail to do so. Latour's principle of irreduction taught us that nothing is inherently either reducible or irreducible to
anything else: work must be done to make a connection between them, and
this is always risky. In this way Latour grants the separation of actors and
tries to show how the gaps between them are bridged by the work of translation. This makes him the founder of a novel occasionalist theory in which
gaps are bridged locally. Like the occasionalists he sees actors as cut off from
one another, but *unlike* the occasionalists he thinks that local relations are
possible. Latour simply cannot be understood if this Janus-headed principle
is overlooked. Actors are defined by their relations, but *precisely for this reason*
they are cut off in their own relational microcosms, which endure for only
an instant before the actor is replaced by a similar actor. The work of mediation must be done at every moment to restore or maintain the links between
actors. While abundant paradoxes arise from this double outlook, they are
the very paradoxes that deserve to be the topic of philosophy today. Let the
Latourian school of metaphysics commence.

6

Questions

An old maxim states that there are two kinds of critics: those who want us to succeed, and those who want us to fail. Debate is always tedious when conducted with persons of the latter kind. Wherever we turn, they are popping balloons and spilling oil on the floor; we find ourselves confronted not only with arguments, but with unmistakable aggressions of voice and physical posture. Yet such gestures of supremacy yield no treasures even for the victors, and somehow always seem to solidify the *status quo*. It is analogous to 'critiquing' long-distance buses by puncturing their tyres, assuring that no one leaves town and nothing is risked. But fair play demands that we let the buses leave. If we make no concessions and play along with nothing, then our 'critical' claims merely endorse one of the prefabricated positions of the day, whichever one it may be. Today's critics stand not only for critique, but usually for a weary human/world dualism that is either affirmed or else falsely overcome by gluing two pieces together that should never have existed in the first place. If some random crank were to assert that everything in the world is made of either wood or metal, we would oppose him not by upholding a primal 'wood-metal' that prevents these two materials from ever existing in isolation, but simply by observing that wooden vs. metallic is not a fundamental rift. The same realization should occur with the dismal opposition and equally dismal reconciliation of human and world. Bruno Latour shows this more vividly than any author we have known. By starting with countless actors rather than a pre-given duality of two *types* of actors, he shifts philosophy from its stalemated trench war toward the richness of things themselves. Numerous breakthroughs follow from this decision, as the preceding pages have tried to show.

There are good reasons not to end this book with a 'critique' of Latour's philosophy, given that I wish him to succeed rather than fail. It is child's play to find mistakes and discrepancies in figures of the order of Plato, Augustine, or Hegel. Every great philosopher has been refuted countless times by critics long forgotten, yet we continue to read these thinkers while forgetting most of their critics. Aristotle notes that substance is only substance when it can support opposite qualities at different times. Likewise, a philosophy may be most substantial when it suggests the most possible contradictory readings. We cannot reduce a philosophy to a list of distinct arguments, because there is no philosopher (or at least no good one) who does not utter statements that are apparently at odds with one another. A philosophy is more like a substance or a person than a list of consistent statements, and for this reason it needs to be presented in the manner of biography, rather than as a chain of true and false utterances.

Latour often notes that critique makes things less real when the goal really ought to be to make them more real. The drama of human enlightenment is often portrayed as an elimination of gullible belief and an increase in critical distance toward the world. But never have humans believed in remoter and less accessible entities than today. In olden times there may have been more angels, omens, and saints than now, but in their place we have even weirder personae as our neighbors: quasars, black holes, neutrons, dinosaurs, continental drift, Neanderthals, the Oort Cloud, unconscious forces. Recent philosophy has not matched this feast of scientific entities, and oddly imagines that it becomes more like science the more it tears down every claim and explodes every entity in the name of 'parsimony'. Read a good popular work on science, then read an article by Bruno Latour and another by a mainstream analytic philosopher, and you will find that it is Latour who reminds you more of the scientists.

Instead of tripping and beating a philosophy for its supposed faults only to end up with the same range of mediocre biases with which we began, we ought to find a more vigorous means of engagement with philosophers. The method I propose is to replace the piously overvalued 'critical thinking' with a seldom-used *hyperbolic* thinking. For me at least, it is only books of the most stunning weakness that draw attention to *non sequiturs* and other logical fallacies. The books that stir us most are not those containing the fewest errors, but those that throw most light on unknown portions of the map. In the case of any author who interests us, we should not ask 'where are the mistakes here?', as if we hoped for nothing more than to avoid being fooled. We should ask instead: 'what if this book, this thinker, were the most important of the century? How would things need to change? And in what ways would we feel both liberated and imprisoned?' Such questions restore the proper scale of evaluation for intellectual work: demoting the pushy careerist sandbagger who remains within the bounds of the currently plausible and prudent, and promoting the gambler who uncovers new worlds. Nietzsche makes far more 'mistakes' than an average peer-reviewed journal article, but this does not stop intelligent adults from reading him all night long, while tossing the article aside for a day that never comes.

There is an obvious way to put the hyperbolic method into practice. Namely, we should begin by placing any given author in a position of maximum strength. This is best done by means of the imagination. Let's imagine that Latour's metaphysics someday achieves absolute victory. Though now positioned at the fringes of mainstream philosophy, he is eventually blessed with a stunning reversal of fortune. Through a variety of triumphs and lucky accidents Latour attains complete hegemony in the philosophical world. The analytic and continental schools fade from memory, as generations of young thinkers wholeheartedly adopt the metaphysics of Latour. In the year 2050, students worldwide are drilled in the maxims of *Irreductions*, while dissenters are marginalized and quickly fade from view. In Paris, Oxford, Boston, and Tokyo, compilers dispute the exact meaning of the Master, as most of the former puzzles of philosophy now seem to have been solved. We still find warring schools of Latourians and a few outlaw heresies, but there is no one who questions the basic principles of his work. To some extent we can imagine what this world would look like. A new empirical spirit pervades philosophy: everyone doing metaphysics is now doing 'experimental metaphysics', developing their categories through direct study of actual volcanoes, apricots, or trains. The old modern split between human and world is now a fossil ridiculed as severely as pre-Galilean physics, and decades of Kant-inspired analytic and continental publications seem like a tragic waste of paper. Elderly social constructionists and white-haired materialists are jeered from their podiums and harassed into retirement, cursing the name of Bruno Latour as they depart. Even the science wars have ended with a smashing victory for Latour—the new breed of physicist salutes him as a hero. Black boxes are now a staple of every philosophical dictionary, and substance is a faded memory of yesteryear. The entire history of modern philosophy is rewritten with Latour's emergence in mind. For me at least, it is a pleasant daydream—a far cry from the Derridean tyrannies of my student years. But there is no Eden in our world. If Latourian metaphysics were enforced with all the violence of dogma, it is likely that even his greatest admirers would feel misgivings. When thinking of a year 2050 in which Latour has become a figure of rigid orthodoxy, I try to imagine the various ways in which I would feel both happy and unhappy. What would be missing from this intellectual world? If I were to rebel against something in such a relative paradise, what would it be?

For me, there are perhaps five things that would be missing from such a world, points I would be willing to contest even at the cost of banishment from the Latourian citadel. First, there are problems arising from the relational model of entities. Second, the identity of a thing with its qualities might be suspected of additional problems. Third, although materialism is gravely wounded, it still has a final hiding place. Fourth, there are unresolved issues concerning the translation between actors. And fifth, many issues of cosmology have been left to the side, undeveloped. This chapter will briefly consider each of these questions, sketched forlornly as if in 2050, amidst the crushing dominance of the Latourian School.

A. RELATIONISM AND CORRELATIONISM

Early in 2006, Quentin Meillassoux published his outstanding book *Après la Finitude.*[1] Though the author uses 'metaphysics' as a negative term, his speculative philosophy is still a good example of metaphysics as defended in the present book. Instead of merely wringing his hands over obstructed pathways of human access to the world, Meillassoux reaches numerous distinct conclusions through reason alone: the independent reality of the world, the distinction between primary and secondary qualities, the necessary truth of the law of non-contradiction, and the necessary contingency of the laws of nature. After the long, cold winter of human-centered philosophy, the bluebird sings again! But the reason I cite Meillassoux's book here is for his central polemic, whose deserving target is a widespread doctrine he terms 'correlationism'. The correlationist holds that we cannot think of humans without world, nor world without humans, but only of a primal correlation or rapport between the two. For the correlationist, it is impossible to speak of a world that pre-existed humans *in itself,* but only of a world pre-existing humans *for humans.* The Big Bang is not an ancestral reality preceding human beings, but only happened in itself *for us,* a phrase openly endorsed by Merleau-Ponty and upheld by many others. A large portion of current philosophy evades realism with this correlationist dodge, which begins to dissolve before our eyes as soon as it has a name.

In many respects, Meillassoux's book is a highly un-Latourian product. His discussions of science make no appeal to mediators and pay no attention to actual scientific practice, which Latour takes as the hallmark of his method. The distinction between primary and secondary qualities is one that Latour could never accept, especially since Meillassoux holds that primary qualities are those that can be mathematized. But the interesting question is whether Latour could be described as a correlationist. In February 2007, Latour generously hosted a salon in Paris to discuss Meillassoux's book. Greatly curious about this event, I took the liberty of contacting the central figures, who gave uniformly warm accounts of the evening. Especially intriguing was Meillassoux's report of a self-deprecating

---

1. Quentin Meillassoux, *Après la finitude*, Paris, Editions du Seuil, 2006. The book has recently become available in English as *After Finitude*, but references in this chapter are to the original French version, and rendered into English by the present author.

joke played by his host. On the refreshments table, Latour had set a placard reading: 'Welcome to this correlationist house!'.[2] However unseriously the joke was meant, the question remains as to whether Latour really is a correlationist. In large part I have defended his claim to the mantle of realism. But Meillassoux's book denies that the correlationist can be a realist, since a permanent human-world correlate is not conducive to any reality that would escape such a rapport.

Let's begin by reviewing Latour's apparently most correlationist moment. In addressing the problem of whether microbes existed before Pasteur, Latour's conclusion was this: *'After 1864 airborne germs were there all along'* (PH, p. 173). In other words, microbes did not pre-exist Pasteur in the strict sense, but pre-existed Pasteur only *for Pasteur* and for those who inhabit his tradition. Past events are produced retroactively without having been there all along in their own right. Now, this is precisely the sort of statement that Meillassoux's first chapter assaults. He imagines the correlationist brotherhood saying that 'event x happens many years before humans—*for humans* [...]'.[3] They would find it absurd that there could be 'givenness of a being prior to its givenness',[4] and would conclude that '[a] being is not prior to givenness, but *is given* as prior to givenness'.[5] For correlationists, then, any past moment is a retroactive product rather than an independently pre-existing state of affairs. Meillassoux observes further that this attitude destroys the literal meaning of scientific statements. Indeed, he closes with a question that Latour might easily hear from Sokal or Weinberg instead: 'it is enough to pose the following question to the correlationist: *but what happened 4.56 million years ago?* Did the formation of the earth take place: yes or no?'[6] For Meillassoux the answer must be either yes or no, not Latour's qualified yes/no hybrid. The only answer that avoids correlationism would be 'yes, the earth was formed 4.56 million years ago... whether we like it or not'. At this point, Latour's flat on the rue Danton looks very much like a correlationist house.

Yet there is another side to the story that must not be forgotten. Correlationism is neither materialism nor absolute idealism, since it glues human and world together from the start, giving preference to neither. But we have often seen that glue is not Latour's preferred material for ending the human/world divide. Namely, he does not say that human and world cannot be separated because they are 'inextricably linked', but says instead that we should not speak of two such zones at all. Most actors are made of

---

2. Meillassoux. Personal Communication, electronic mail to Graham Harman of 21 February, 2007. trans. Graham Harman.

3. Meillassoux, *Après la finitude*, p. 30.

4. Meillassoux, *Après la finitude*, p. 32, emphasis removed.

5. Meillassoux, *Après la finitude*, p. 32.

6. Meillassoux, *Après la finitude*, p. 34.

so many human and nonhuman components that it would be ridiculous to assign them to one of these kingdoms or the other. In other words, Latour's *first step* in philosophy is to dismiss the very two terms that the correlationist wants to combine. Latour no more defends a human/world correlate than a solid/liquid correlate or a primal rapport of beasts and birds. While the correlationist holds that human and world are always linked, and *also* holds that nothing exists in itself apart from such a link, these are two separate accusations (Meillassoux does not separate the two claims, but in my view he should have done so). As for the first charge, Latour's denial that human and world are two privileged zones of the world saves him from the 'correlationist' label that he half-jokingly applied to himself. Soon I will suggest that his correlationist reading of the year 1864 is simply a bridge too far, not a core element of his thinking. As for the second charge, Latour *does* deny independent states of affairs that lie outside all links between actors. But remember that he never says that humans need to be witnesses to the link, and is sometimes explicit that they do not. Hence the charge should be downgraded from 'correlationism' to 'relationism', a lesser offense that some would prefer to decriminalize altogether (though I myself remain a hardline judge). To repeat, Latour's primal correlation between any actor and its allies is not the same thing as a correlation between human and world. A more accurate sign on Latour's dining table would read: 'Welcome to this *relationist* house!'

Let's consider the issue further. For the correlationist, not only are there no independent states of affairs apart from the primal rapport, but a human observer must also be one of the two ingredients of this rapport. But the case of Heidegger shows that one can believe that human and world are always linked without believing that the world is fully unveiled in this relationship. And the case of Whitehead shows how one can be a relationist without being a correlationist. For Whitehead, that proud rebel against Kant's Copernican turn, humans have no privilege at all; we can speak in the same way of the relation between humans and what they see and that between hailstones and tar. In *Irreductions*, Latour said that translations also occur between nonhuman things, and did not add the proviso that humans must be there to observe it. For this reason a Latourian physics is conceivable, unlike for most contemporary thinkers; his global focus on actors allows for a possible treatment of inanimate bodies by the same set of rules that are used to describe human translations. It is true that Latour's books focus overwhelmingly on scientific practice, and provide only the most flickering hints of networks devoid of human involvement. But this lack of emphasis on the inanimate realm is not enough to make someone a human/world correlationist, especially when that person began his career with the following words: 'For a long time it has been agreed that the relationship between one text and another is always a matter for interpretation. Why not accept that this is also true between so-called texts and so-called objects, *and*

even between so-called objects themselves?' (PF, p. 166, emphasis added). This mutual translation between all brands of objects is foreign to every form of correlationist philosophy.

Despite not living in a correlationist house, Latour does have correlationist moments. The example of microbes in 1864 seems to require that humans had to learn about microbes before they could retroactively begin to
exist in the past. This claim would enrage any realist, since it seems to deny
a world apart from human perception of that world. But as already suggested, this should be viewed merely as a bridge too far, not as a central feature
of Latour's position. The reason is that he not only *could* have avoided such a
theory of time, but even *should* have avoided it given his general views on actors. Latour's main point is that reality is made of *propositions*, in Whitehead's
sense of the term—defined not as verbal statements by conscious humans,
but mutual relations in which two things articulate each other ever more fully. Pasteur brings microbes into focus from the dubious grey matter and various symptoms through which they are announced; in turn, microbes bring
Pasteur into focus as a genius and national hero. Pasteur and the microbes
need one another. Though Latour limits himself to the statement 'after 1864
microbes were there all along', he would surely be willing to add the alternate version that 'after 1864 Pasteur was their discoverer all along'. This latter phenomenon is familiar to readers of the early chapters of biographies,
when we observe the childhoods of Pasteur, Hegel, Catherine the Great, or
Maxwell with their later achievements already in mind. There was nothing
clearly electromagnetic about the two-year-old Maxwell, and nothing evi-
dently philosophical about the newborn Hegel, yet their early lives and even
their ancestors tend to take on a retroactive halo of future breakthrough. For
the same reason, it seems to follow that there was nothing microbial about
microbes in the year 1492, since all the alliances through which they later
became known are missing.

The problem is that the two sides of the proposition are treated asymmetrically. First we have 'after 1864 microbes were there all along', and second 'after 1864 Pasteur was their discoverer all along'. Note that the second
statement is no threat to realism, since all it does is mildly condemn the well-
known human tendency to retroject later biographical events back into the
past. All that the statement denies is that Pasteur carried some latent genius
that pre-existed his dealings with microbes. Though I would personally disagree even here, the point is not hotly controversial, and Latour's lifelong
body of work does a great deal to bolster it. Actors co-produce one another;
Pasteur and the microbes need each other. Fair enough. The real controversy comes from the first statement, which seems to imply that Pasteur created
objects *ex nihilo* by discovering them. Latour never denies that *Pasteur* was already alive in 1850, but does seem to deny that microbes were present at that
date. He never says 'after 1864 *Pasteur* existed in 1850', but does say that 'after

1864 *microbes* existed in 1850'. The asymmetry is obvious.

And here is the bridge too far. It will widely be granted that Pasteur and microbes mutually articulate one another, although some have opposed this idea for flimsy reasons. Many will also grant (as I do not) that there is nothing more to these entities than their whole set of relations with other things. What *must not* be granted is that Pasteur has more right to exist before 1864 than microbes do. To avoid possible confusion, let's speak of 'Pasteur' and 'microbes' only as those actors that began to exist in 1864. We can then use the name 'pre-Pasteur' to point to the man before his discovery, and 'pre-microbe' to designate the entity he apparently discovered. We know that 'pre-Pasteur' was alive throughout the 1850's; it would be madness to claim otherwise. But what about 'pre-microbes'? Did they exist before 1864: yes or no? The answer must be yes. Something was performing multiple actions: spoiling wine, fermenting milk, killing sheep and children. Barring some drastic revision of current biology, the pre-microbe was that thing. Given that Latour's theory of actors does allow for the work of translation to occur even between non-human objects such as microbes, milk, and wine, it is unfortunate that he does not describe their relations apart from the presence of Pasteur.

But indeed, Latour's own Whiteheadian use of 'proposition' actually *requires* that the actors exist before they are linked; otherwise there would be nothing for either of them to articulate. He should have emphasized not only Pasteur's articulation of the microbe and its reciprocal articulation of him, but also the mutual rapport of microbes with milk and the human body, which long predates their rapport with medical knowledge. The failure to do this leads directly to correlationism, which requires humans to be one ingredient in everything that exists. But if this is a failure, then it is a tactical excess rather than a strategic flaw at the heart of Latour's work. After all, his philosophy demands that the two ingredients of alliance are not human and world, but any two actors whatever. My suspicion is that Latour crossed this dangerous bridge because of his view that an actor is no different from its sum total of qualities and effects. Since no one had formerly united the vague grey-coloured matter with the death of pigs and the curdling of milk, Pasteur becomes the Joliot who links them, and for this reason he might seem more the inventor than the discoverer of microbes. But this cannot be true. The microbes themselves were already mini-Joliots, linking their various 'allies' well before humans knew of them. Pasteur merely linked the microbe with a new set of allies: lab directors, hygienic practices, medical journals, France, and various honors and awards. Though infection and ferment had not yet been linked by human knowledge, they were already linked through the microbes themselves.

For this reason, it was unnecessary for Latour to say that the pre-microbe needed Pasteur to exist any more than Pasteur needed the microbe to continue life as normal, unheralded pre-Pasteur. But by contrast, it is a *central* Latourian theme that the microbe (or pre-microbe) cannot exist if it affects nothing at all. If the microbe caused no changes in wine or milk, the surrounding air, the bodies of animals, the mud of a creek, or anything else, then Latour would deny its existence altogether. This is what I have called Latour's *relationism*: Pasteur and the microbe are defined by their sum total of effects, not by an autonomous hidden essence. The rather different *correlationist* view, found for instance in Heidegger, is that the microbe did not exist until human Dasein unveiled it, since no reality makes any sense if human being is subtracted from the picture. If we imagine all human creatures wiped from the cosmos, we cannot imagine Heidegger's philosophy describing this situation. Yet one could surely develop a Latourian account of stellar clouds and black holes interacting with their neighbors both before and after the miserably brief lifespan of the human race. Latour is intrinsically a relationist but a correlationist only now and then. My purpose here is not to defend Latour from some future Meillassouxian critic, but only to ensure that he receives proper credit for exploding the human-world rapport of the correlationist. To escape the correlationist grip, it is not enough to deduce that something must pre-exist the correlate. We must also describe how the parts of this 'something' interact. Latour's democracy of actors is the best means I know of to deprive human beings of their illegal monopoly on relations, which is just as narrow as the earlier stranglehold granted to God or the human mind. There is a problem posed by the relation between *any* two actors, not just human and world.

Having dealt with the correlationist problem, the issue is now relationism itself. There is no question that Latour defines actors in terms of their relations. An object is no more than what it modifies, transforms, perturbs, or creates, as we read in *Pandora's Hope*. There is not a 'something more' for Latour, a latent substance hidden from public view beneath an actor's overt performance. An actor is completely actualized in any moment, inscribed without reserve in its current scheme of alliances. The term sometimes used for this doctrine is 'actualism', and some authors find it repellant. The specter of actualism drives Roy Bhaskar[7] from entities to the laws they must observe, and drives Manuel DeLanda[8] from entities to a topological space in which they unfold. By contrast, Latour shows a maximum commitment to actualism. Whitehead's ontological principle denies that we can pass beyond concrete entities when explaining anything, and this element of the Whiteheadian program is one from which Latour never veers.

We have seen that the actualist view of actors is reminiscent of the ancient Megarians, criticized by Aristotle with such fire and eloquence. The

7. See Roy Bhaskar, *A Realist Theory of Science*, London, Continuum, 2006.

8. See Manuel DeLanda, *Intensive Science and Virtual Philosophy*, London, Continuum, 2002.

Megarians hold that a thing only is what it is, with no secret inner chambers hidden in reserve. As Aristotle notes, this would entail that things have no potential, and would also entail that a thing is not hot or sweet unless it is touched or tasted. Latour would be happy to accept these implications; he gladly denies the potentiality of actors as well as their possession of primary qualities divorced from relations to other things. Latour would also dismiss Aristotle's complaint that according to the Megarian doctrine a sitting person will never be able to stand due to his lack of potency. For Latour a person does not stand up by drawing on an inner reservoir of potency, but through a series of mediations—nervous excitations acting on muscles, which then shift the body's weight onto a hard, unyielding floor. Numerous allies are brought into play even in the simplest movements of our bodies.

But here again there are two separate issues in play. Potentiality is one thing, and the distinction between primary and secondary qualities is another. Let's begin with potential. Latour's rejection of potency goes back to the principle of irreduction itself. To speak of something existing *in potentia* implies that it is already there but simply covered or suppressed. This is what Latour denies. For him a thing is only here once it is here, not sooner. To make something become actual is not to unfold a cryptic seed lying hidden in the ground, but to assemble a wide range of actors that begin in separation. For instance, it would make no sense to call Joliot 'the potential father of the atomic bomb', except in a purely literary way. What Joliot would have needed to do, and what Oppenheimer did do, is help piece together an assemblage of neutrons, heavy water, uranium, cannon assemblies, plutonium, implosion devices, distillation cascades, rural sites, metallurgists, security guards, loyalty oaths, government funds, physics articles, political allies, military allies, wounded egos, and target lists. The atomic bomb did not lie slumbering in any of these elements—not even in Oppenheimer himself, who became director of the Manhattan Project largely by accident, and to the great surprise of many who doubted his management skills. In this respect Latour's actualism should be applauded. By defending potentiality, Aristotle King of Realists veers strangely from autonomous reality toward an even more relation-dependent theory than Latour's own. For in what sense is an oak tree 'already in' the acorn? Only in the sense that the acorn contains *actual* features that get the first set of translations underway on the long and winding road to the oak. To say that something has potential is to define it in terms of the other things that it might someday affect. Latour does not mind defining an actor by what it affects, but he does not allow an actor to borrow its effects in advance. Payment in real time is demanded at every stage of the translation. In this sense, Latour never departs from the real by sneaking ahead to the end of the story, like a devious boy reading the finale of a Harry Potter tale before his brothers. For Aristotle, a thing is always more than what it is right now; for Latour, never. A thing changes by enrolling other actors, not by unveiling a pre-existent interior. The recourse to potentiality is a dodge that leaves actuality undetermined and finally uninteresting; it reduces what is currently actual to the transient costume of an emergent process across time, and makes the real work happen outside actuality itself. The same holds true if we replace 'the potential' with 'the virtual', notwithstanding their differences. In both cases, concrete actors themselves are deemed insufficient for the labour of the world and are indentured to hidden overlords: whether they be potential, virtual, veiled, topological, fluxional, or any adjective that tries to escape from what is actually here right now. On this point I can only salute Latour, the ancient Megarians, and other defenders of actualism.

Yet my agreement is suspended when they deny the difference between primary and secondary qualities. Here we have the crucial point: the very stronghold of relationism. I have already agreed with Latour that primary and secondary should not be identified with world and human—as if the world were made merely of objective states of affairs, and humans merely tainted them with distortion or copied them with correspondence. For two actors to enter into relation ('proposition'), those actors must exist in order to relate. And if the actors exist they must also have qualities, for otherwise they would be featureless lumps no different from one another. Latour might concede this point, but he would still have a powerful weapon in hand. Namely, while admitting that Pasteur the man must have certain qualities before discovering microbes, he would add that these qualities are themselves the result of alliances with a previous set of actors. And true enough, Pasteur during the 1850's was not floating in some otherworldly vacuum of essence, but was already in league with countless allies different from his later and more famous ones. At any moment of life, Pasteur seems to be defined by the allies he enrolls. This harks back to Merleau-Ponty's statement that 'the house itself is not the house seen from nowhere, but the house seen from *everywhere*'.[9] There is no Pasteur-in-himself, but only Pasteur in relation with everything that he modifies, transforms, perturbs, and creates. In this way, all of his qualities might be called secondary qualities just as Berkeley demands. Primary qualities have nowhere to exist, since Pasteur and everything else is stripped of any dark interior.

There are exactly two problems with this relationist model of the cosmos, and in my view they are severe enough that the model must be abandoned. First, relationism does injustice to the *future* of an actor, by not explaining how it can change. Second, relationism does injustice to the *present* of an actor, by not allowing it to be real outside the alliances that articulate it. Both problems were already sensed by Aristotle, however inadequate his solutions.

---

9. Maurice Merleau-Ponty, *Phenomenology of Perception*, trans. Christopher Smith, London: Routledge, 2002, p. 79, emphasis added.

1. As noted, Aristotle accused the Megarians of not allowing a sitting man to be able to stand up. For if the sitting man has no potency, there is no way to change any aspect of his current state. The man will be purely actual, purely defined by his current relations with the world, and hence cannot break free of his situation and enter a new one. Latour would even deny that the man is an enduring substance who undergoes adventures in many different postures, but that is a separate issue. The question for us here is what allows the sitting man to be replaced by a standing man. A good reason for siding with Latour in this dispute was that the actual cannot be pre-inscribed with potential, which merely borrows its potency from the other actors it might one day actually affect. The source of all change must be found *in the actual*, or it is a phantom. There is nothing on earth but the actual if we push Whitehead's principle a bit further than Whitehead did (by dumping the 'eternal objects'), and I gladly join Latour in doing so. There is nothing wrong with 'actualism'.

But if Aristotle is wrong in what he affirms, he is right in what he denies: Latour and the Megarians still cannot explain change. The problem is not that they defend the actual over the potential, but that *they identify the actual with the relational.* Only a non-relational version of actuality (and not potentiality, which is relational through and through) can explain change or movement. We do not empower the sitting man by sowing him with hidden seeds of movement, but only by somehow disengaging his actuality from his current situation. This cannot be done if we say that the man is the sum total of his alliances, because his current allies include the sitting posture and the soft cushions of the couch. If the sitting man is inherently 'sitting-man' through and through, then there is admittedly no way to turn him into 'standing-man'. What we are seeking instead is simply the 'man' who can either stand or sit.

What happens, in Latourian terms, if I cease to be a professor in Egypt and become a carpenter in my home state of Iowa? Let us grant that my years as a Cairo academic have changed my character in some way; that is beyond dispute. The question is this: what are the components of the *new* proposition when my life is changed? The new proposition includes Iowa, carpenter's tools, and *me myself*—not me-the-Egyptian-professor, since this proposition no longer exists, even if some historical traces of it may be left in the new me. Analogously, it is *Latour* who interacts with Sciences-Po to form a new proposition, not Latour-at-Ecole-des-Mines, an actor who no longer exists. While it may be true that Latour did not emerge unscathed and unaltered from his decades at the ENSMP,[10] he is still able to disengage from that ally and join with another. The years in his former office surely left many traces, but there is also plenty of 'information loss': many features of

---

10. ENSMP is the French abbreviation for Latour's long-time former employer: Ecole Nationale Supérieure des Mines de Paris.

the previous Latour-ENSMP alliance are gone forever. Those that continue in the new proposition Latour-Sciences-Po endure only if they are somehow etched into the actor Latour, not into a now-vanished former proposition that no longer walks the earth.

In short, things must be partially separated from their mutual articulations. If this were not the case, they would never be able to enter new propositions. This does not require that we accept the notion of 'potentiality'; it merely emphasizes that the actual is not the same as the relational. The proposition 'Pasteur-microbe' does not fully use up either Pasteur or the microbe, though it probably transforms them, and surely creates a new entity different from both. To say otherwise would amount to the claim that a proposition imports its components completely without loss or gain of energy—a very un-Latourian maxim. The relation 'Pasteur-microbe' does not fully sound the depths of either Pasteur or microbe, but merely deploys a tiny segment of both.

When Latour denies that a thing is different from its relations, he may be thinking of a related but separate issue. His philosophy suggests vividly that the 'I' who returns from Egypt to Iowa is not a simple monadic soul, but a black box containing all manner of swarming actors. This 'I' is surely a vast alliance composed of numerous elements: the friends and schools of my past, the books that have shaped me, the internal organs that keep me alive, the grain and beans I consume. But my reliance on internal components does not entail reliance on my outer relations. I cannot exist without my components, but can very well exist without my allies. These allies may shape me in turn: but what they are shaping is *me*, not my previous set of alliances, most of which are not preserved in my current self at all. If not for this basic asymmetry between an actor's components and its alliances, we would have a purely holistic cosmos. Everything would be defined to an equal degree by the actors above it as below it, and there would be no place in reality not defined utterly by its context. But this is by no means what happens. What happens instead is that components sometimes unite to form a new actor, an 'emergent' reality irreducible to its pieces. It can survive certain changes among its constituents, and even more easily survives the outer relations into which it is thrown. An actor is a firewall, preventing all tiny shifts in its components from affecting it, and also preventing its environment from entering the black box too easily. An object needs its components to some extent, but never needs its allies. Only the alliance as a whole requires the allies, but the alliance as a whole is a different entity from each of its components. Stated briefly: Pasteur is not the same thing as Pasteur-discoverer-of-microbes.

2. We have already touched on the second problem: even an actor's *present* is not adequately defined by its relations. When Merleau-Ponty speaks of 'the house seen from everywhere', what he means is the house seen from all

current points of view. But a simple thought experiment allows us to consider other points of view on the house. Imagine hundreds of new entities in contact with the house from previously untried angles, distances, or moods. This would certainly create new relations, but it would not create a new house. Now imagine (even though Cantor seems to forbid it) that the house is viewed by all *possible* actors from all *possible* angles under every conceivable condition. Even under this bizarre scenario, it is still not these viewpoints that are doing the work of the house. These infinitely many observers are not the ones who block the winds and keep the inhabitants dry: only the house itself does this. This implies that the house contains unknown realities never touched by any or all of its relations. Relations do not exhaust a thing—instead, they *rely* on the thing.

We have now approached the new model of objects that I propose to develop. Just as Latour teaches, there are countless actors of different sizes and types, constantly dueling and negotiating with each other. But objects are not defined by their relations: instead they are what enter into relations in the first place, and their allies can never fully mine their ores. In Heideggerian terms, objects enter relations but withdraw from them as well; objects are built of components, but exceed those components. Things exist not in relation, but in a strange sort of vacuum from which they only partly emerge into relation. Objects are purely actual, not potential. Yet this actuality is not defined by a set of relations with other things. This model of objects, a realism of autonomous things without matter, is admittedly rather weird. But this strangeness can be turned into a battle cry by using 'weird realism' as a synonym for object-oriented philosophy, in the manner of H.P. Lovecraft's 'weird fiction'.

Since relations are so important for Latour, he might seem unwilling to concede any reality outside articulations by way of alliances. Yet there are fleeting moments when he turns his gaze in this direction with his use of the term 'plasma', to which my attention was returned by Peter Erdélyi. There is a brief but intriguing discussion of this concept in at least two places: the 1998 work *Paris: Invisible City* (*Paris ville invisible*), authored jointly by Latour and Emilie Hermant,[11] and a somewhat more suggestive use of the term in *Reassembling the Social*,[12] Latour's lively 2005 introduction to actor-network theory. Early in the 2005 work, the new concept of plasma is heralded by surprising footnotes: 'we will encounter the strange figure of the "plasma," which takes the bottom out of any bottom line when accounting for action' (RS, p. 50 n. 48); 'we will deal [later] with the notion of "plasma." Emptiness

---

11. It was Edwin Sayes who drew my attention to the uses of the term 'plasma' in this work, where Latour links it explicitly with the now popular concept of 'the virtual'.

12. Erdélyi was the first to call my attention to the importance of the term 'plasma' in this work, in a post made on August 15, 2007 to the ANTHEM mailing list, which is so fruitfully devoted to the Latour/Heidegger connection.

is the key in following the *rare* conduits in which the social circulates' (RS, p. 132 n. 187). The latter statement is especially intriguing when coming from Latour. He always uses the title 'social' in such a way as to refer to non-human actors too, not just human ones. 'Society' for Latour is so ubiquitous that to hear him call it 'rare' is surprising indeed.

The main discussion of plasma comes at the end of the book. As Latour puts it, 'no understanding of the social can be provided if you don't turn your attention to another range of unformatted phenomena [...]. I call this background *plasma*, namely that which is not yet formatted, not yet measured, not yet socialized, not yet engaged in metrological chains, and not yet covered, surveyed, mobilized, or subjectified' (RS, pp. 243-4). He even estimates the size of this background plasma, just as astronomers indirectly size up the amount of dark matter: Latour says that if the social world of networks were the size of the London Underground, plasma would fill the remaining space of London. A truly vast space of unsocialized material! The plasma is '*in between* and not made of social stuff. It is not hidden, simply *unknown* [... like] a vast hinterland [..., like] the countryside for an urban dweller [..., like] the missing masses for a cosmologist trying to balance out the weight of the universe' (RS, p. 244).

In these startling pages, Latour amplifies the realism of *Irreductions* with a beautiful image: 'Hermeneutics is not a privilege of humans but, so to speak, a property of the world itself. The world is not a solid continent of facts sprinkled by a few lakes of uncertainties, but a vast ocean of uncertainties speckled by a few islands of calibrated and stabilized forms' (RS, p. 245). Latour's plasma is not a mere annoying remainder of academic bookkeeping, but is held responsible for all the change and movement we know. Above all, there is a stunning passage that one would never find in Heidegger:

> Why do fierce armies disappear in a week? Why do whole empires like the Soviet one vanish in a few months? Why do companies who cover the whole world go bankrupt after their next quarterly report? Why do the same companies, in less than two semesters, jump from being deep in the red to showing a massive profit? Why is it that quiet citizens turn into revolutionary crowds or that grim mass rallies break down into a joyous crowd of free citizens? Why is it that some dull individual is suddenly moved into action by an obscure piece of news? Why is it that such a stale academic musician is suddenly seized by the most daring rhythms? Generals, editorialists, managers, observers, moralists often say that those sudden changes have a soft, impalpable liquid quality about them. That's exactly the etymology of plasma (RS, p. 245).

These things happen because the articulated social world of relations leaves so much unarticulated: monsters and angels seep from the plasma, like rats and pigeons into the Underground. In his concluding summary of plasma, Latour even uses a term once banned from his personal lexicon: 'To every action I have described so far, you have to add an immense repertoire of missing masses [... And there] exists a *reserve*, a *reserve army*, an immense territory [...] for every formatted, localized, continuous, accountable action to be carried out in' (RS, p. 245, emphasis modified). Here Latour seems to understand that there is a problem with explaining how completely formatted actors could ever change their format. As his new thoughts indicate, the only possible solution is that actors are not fully formatted by alliances after all. Some reserve or reservoir must explain the sudden changes mentioned, and more gradual changes as well. To escape relationism means to establish a metaphysics of the plasma or missing mass to which Latour refers. Only one note of caution is needed: there is no good reason to agree with Latour that the plasma has no format, since this would imply that all format must come from relations. The plasma might still be formatted by other means than those of alliance, though he never considers the possibility. Formatting and networks are viewed as equivalent, and at best Latour verges on acknowledging a single plasma-in-itself, not a plurality of distinct entities withdrawn from all relation.

B. ACTORS ONEFOLD AND FOURFOLD

A rift has now opened within objects themselves. Latour has already multiplied gaps *between* entities like no one before him, and is patient enough not to link them through the instant *Ave Maria* of the occasionalist God. But for the most part, Latour envisions each actor as one: the tree is not split by a fissure from its own qualities, and is also not divided from some hidden tree-in-itself. The tree can move and perturb other actors, and like any black box it can always be opened to reveal its swarming components. But the tree remains a single actor utterly defined by its stance toward other things, not a cryptic nucleus hidden from view beneath shifting accidents. Yet the situation changes once we say that the object is not the same as its alliances. For reasons described in the previous section, Pasteur-for-the-microbe and the-microbe-for-Pasteur cannot be the same as Pasteur and the microbe themselves. Having distinguished an actor from its relations, we are now speaking of 'real' actors or objects as opposed to those encountered in an alliance, the latter of which are nothing but partly articulated stand-ins for the objects they articulate. Here we are no longer on strictly Latourian ground, though his basic vision remains intact: a democratic cosmos of actors engaged in networks, separated from each other by gaps that are bridged only by various Joliot-like mediators.

Relations do not exhaust the things that relate, and hence nothing can be defined as a sum total of alliances or even of possible alliances. Bring in new spectators to watch Merleau-Ponty's house from ever new angles, and what you will get are countless new propositions that include the house as a

component, not a new *house* each time. The house itself is subject to all manner
of relations without being generated by them. It is certainly composed of the
relations on its interior, but these have a different status from the relations on
the outside. (I am not speaking here of so-called 'internal relations', which are
merely external relations grafted into a thing's own heart.) The most extreme
instance of this would be Leibniz, who holds that any monad already harbors
relations to distant suns and planets and all future times. Here I agree with
those who accept nothing but external relations. Nothing is allowed to contain anything else; all objects are mutually external to other objects. But by
speaking of relations on the interior of a thing, I mean something quite different: the assembly of actors on the inside of any black box that enable it to exist. For lack of a better term, we might call these 'domestic' relations to avoid
confusion with the internal relations that deserve to be expelled from view. I
hold that there is an absolute distinction between the domestic relations that
a thing needs to some extent in order to exist, and the external alliances that
it does not need. But the actor itself cannot be identified with either. An object cannot be exhausted by a set of alliances. But neither is it exhausted by
a summary of its pieces, since any genuine object will be an emergent reality
over and above its components, oversimplifying those components and able
to withstand a certain degree of turbulent change in them.

It is not Latour's manner to speak of the hidden and the autonomous.
Nor is it Whitehead's. Somewhat surprisingly, the recent tradition most sympathetic to things apart from their relations is that of Martin Heidegger.
The next section will review his tool-analysis, which I have often discussed
elsewhere. Against the usual reading of Heidegger, his tools are in no way
relational, but withdraw entirely from relations while remaining real nonetheless. Heidegger is the unexpected champion of independent objects as opposed to those allied in networks; this runs counter to Latour's own views,
barring some unforeseen turn to a full-blown theory of plasma in his future
works. Yet Latour's points of superiority to Heidegger have already been described. His demand for translation is one that Heidegger never meets, since
for Heidegger the object is merely veiled, made gradually manifest through
the old 'asymptotic' model of truth. But Latour denies that we unveil something already cryptically present, and asks instead that we describe the instruments or mediators that allow that thing to emerge. It is actually a more
surprising and sophisticated model of truth than Heidegger's own, and derives from Latour's metaphysics of actors cut off in themselves and utterly
deployed in their current actuality. Furthermore, Heidegger's opposition between real and apparent objects, or *zuhanden and vorhanden*, does little to clarify the nature of withdrawn beings, and nothing at all to show what links the
two realms. If we ask Latour to subtract a thing from its allies, we must also
ask Heidegger to explain the relation between the real tree and the tree that
is present to our view.

But there is a second rift that must be considered. If Latour does not distinguish an actor from its relations, he also does not distinguish it from its qualities, a similar but not identical theme. For even if we refuse to descend into the Heideggerian underworld of veiled hammers, even if we remain in a world where things are all allied on a unified plane of mutual accessibility, it can still be questioned whether a thing is a package made of *all* its qualities. Experience shows that we can circle an object from different angles, thereby changing its specific visible profiles without changing the thing. But even if we were confined to a single instant without being able to circle the thing, it would still be the case that we look at *things*, not bundles of discrete qualities. In fact we pass right through these qualities to look directly at the unified object, ignoring the ever-present distortions produced by a tilted head or erratic lighting. No one ever really saw 'red'. We saw apple-red, ink-red or blood-red, infused with the style of the objects to which they belong. To speak of the same quality recurring in numerous objects requires a lengthy work of abstraction, as Latour would surely agree. For this reason it is somewhat surprising that he allows qualities to amass as individual things, given his much greater flair for concrete objects than the British Empiricists usually show. This difference between unified objects of perception and their numerous qualities is the great discovery of Husserl, whose pivotal concept is the 'intentional object'. Despite his idealism. Husserl is still a philosopher of objects—objects found only in consciousness, but still objects deeper than all their qualities and surface perturbations. If we focus only on Husserl's basic idealist gesture, we forget his startling rift between objects of experience and their qualities, which is found nowhere in previous idealisms. In what follows I will often refer to 'intentional objects' with the unconventional name 'sensual objects'. One motive for doing so is to replace the sterile, technical flavour of 'intentional' with something a bit more charming. Yet a second and more important motive is that Husserl uses 'intentional' to refer only to the unified objects of consciousness, while excluding the shifting surface qualities of things from the intentional domain. So-called 'sense data' are not intentional for Husserl, precisely because they are not object-oriented. For this reason, a new unified term is needed that covers both the enduring objects of consciousness and the overly specific facades through which they are always manifest.

In any case, the object is now divided from itself in a second sense. We saw that it is different from its relations, withdrawing into mysterious depths. But now it is also different from its qualities, and hence opens up a drama on the very surface of the world. Latour's magnificent circus of gaps between actors is now faced with the demand for further mediation *within objects themselves*. As we have seen, this mediation occurs in two directions. The tree itself must have qualities, under penalty of being a featureless lump no different from all others. Yet it must also be distinct from these qualities, since these can be altered to some extent without changing the tree. The tree as encountered by allies also has qualities, yet here as well it seems different from any particular set of those qualities, which can vary without changing it. Hence the two basic rifts in an object arise from its difference from its relations, and its difference from its qualities. The object becomes fourfold: a lucky clover whose leaves are linked by a plasma still unknown. In previous books I have described Heidegger's ridiculed *Geviert* (fourfold) as one of the great breakthroughs in the past century of philosophy. I have claimed further that the two axes of this fourfold arise from the two different concepts of objects found in Heidegger and Husserl, which are then joined by Heidegger himself. There is no need to recount the structure of Heidegger's fourfold here. Suffice it to say that earth and gods make up the concealed dimension that merely hints, while mortals and sky refer to the world in its presence to us. Each pair then has a further internal split, since earth and mortals refer to the unity of existence, and gods and sky to the plurality of qualities found either in withdrawal or in presence.

Heidegger never follows this path to the end. He badly needs Bruno Latour to help him develop his model of objects. Some Joliot needs to introduce these two thinkers, and the present book seeks to play this role. But in a sense, these authors can easily be linked thanks to Heidegger's own defects. For there are two especially glaring problems with Heidegger's fourfold: (1) he denies the fourfold to industrially produced goods while allowing it to peasant handicraft and ruined temples; (2) he gives no account of how the four poles interrelate, speaking vaguely instead of mirrors, dances, weddings, and songs. Latour is better equipped than anyone to solve both problems, because of (1) his democracy of objects and (2) his theory of translation between entities.

Though Latour's scattered remarks on Heidegger are rarely made in a spirit of praise, he seems to sense that they are neighbors on various themes. This is perhaps most clear in Latour's opening essay from *Making Things Public*, the catalog of an art exhibit held in Karlsruhe, Germany. Latour writes: 'as every reader of Heidegger knows [...] the old word "Thing" or "Ding" designated originally a certain type of archaic assembly' (MP, p. 22). in the sense of a parliament. He cites the Nordic parliamentary terms that remain so close to this etymology even now: *Storting* (Norway), *Althing* (Iceland), *Ting* (Isle of Man) (MP, p. 23). Humans assemble together with things, which are no longer expelled from a purified human political realm. Erdélyi, with his eagle eye for all things Heidegger/Latour, notes that an individual thing is already a parliament in its own right if crossed by rifts and fissures that make it a four.[13] Latour senses this too, invoking an altered

---

13. In Peter Erdélyi, 'ANT, the Fourfold, and the Thing in Common: A Multi-Case Study of Organising, Strategising and ICTs ine-Tailing SMEs in the UK', unpublished thesis proposal, Department of Management, London School of Economics, 2007.

version of Heidegger's fourfold to say that '*gatherings* is the translation that Heidegger used, to talk about those Things, those sites able to assemble mortals and gods, humans and non-humans' (MP, p. 23). He is right that 'there is more than a little irony in extending this meaning [of "thing"] to what Heidegger and his followers loved to hate, namely science, technology, commerce, industry and popular culture' (MP, p. 23). And reminding us of Heidegger's contrast between 'object' (bad) and 'thing' (good), Latour comments that 'the object, the *Gegenstand*, may remain outside of all assemblies but not the *Ding*. Hence the question we wish to raise: What are the various shapes of the *assemblies* that can make sense of all those *assemblages?*' (MP, p. 24). Here we find Latour's justified complaint about Heidegger's contempt for 'ontic' beings. Left unmentioned, however, is the fact that Heidegger's 'thing' cannot possibly be the same as Latour's famous 'matters of concern'. Something can only be of concern to stakeholders who are affected by it in some way. By contrast, Heidegger's jug is precisely what *does not* assemble with other things, and resides in itself, at least in part. Even so, Latour's philosophy of translation is our best hope of explaining how the four parts of an object belong together.

Whatever he might say about Heidegger, Latour's own proximity to the fourfold object is more visible elsewhere. I refer to his book *Politics of Nature*, first published in French in the same futuristic-sounding year that *Pandora's Hope* was born in English: 1999. In *Politics of Nature*, Latour is at war with the modern split between fact and value, so clearly linked with his old foe the world/human rift. 'Facts' are unshakeable states of affairs untainted by humans, while 'values' are the projection of human desires without any ties to criteria in the objective world. This gives us the same old miserable bicameral model that Latour's entire career has aimed to subvert. His usual means of attacking this split is to oppose the twofold world with a vast plurality of actors, a gesture that never disappears from his works. But the curious thing about *Politics of Nature* is that Latour opposes the bicameral world not with a vague plurality, but with a specifically quadricameral world (though he calls it a new bicameralism instead). That is to say, Latour salvages the fact/value split by *doubling* it. The old distinction between fact and value is crossed by a new one between 'taking into account' and 'putting in order' (PN, Chaps. 3-4). For all the different underlying assumptions of Latour and Heidegger, their fourfold mechanisms are surprisingly similar. 'Taking into account' confronts a world that is already there and must be addressed. In this sense it resembles the old 'fact' side of things, as do Heidegger's 'thrownness', 'past', or 'concealment'. By contrast, 'putting in order' must arrange what it finds, which clearly resembles the old 'value' pole, as do Heidegger's 'projection', 'future', or 'unveiling'.

There is also a second rift for Latour, just as for Heidegger. But this one is easier to grasp, since Latour openly declares which terms are the heirs

of fact and which of value. The power to take into account is split into perplexity (fact) and consultation (value). The power to arrange in rank order
is carved into institution (fact) and hierarchization (value). In short, there is
a fact/value split on the 'fact' side, and another fact/value split on the 'value' side. Heidegger's method is the same, giving us a being/beings split on
the being side (earth/gods) and another being/beings split on the beings
side (mortals/sky). The number of fourfold structures in the history of philosophy is so staggering that we should hardly be surprised when thinkers
generate new ones. Monisms are too pious and sugary in their holism, dualisms too static in their trench warfare, and triads too smug in their happy endings. But fourfold structures allow for tension no less than plurality,
and hence we find Empedocles, Plato, Aristotle, Scotus Eriugena, Francis
Bacon, Vico, Kant, Greimas, McLuhan, and others chopping the world in
four. It is important that the two principles of fission be chosen wisely, and
that some explanation be given for how the four zones interact. Assuming
these caveats, there is much to be said for viewing the cosmos as a reciprocal
pair of doubled mirrors. The main difference between our two thinkers here
is that Heidegger's four is found on the inside of specific jugs and bridges,
while Latour's four is a public creature, a matter of concern between multiple things. But these approaches may not be as different as they seem—
after all, if Latour opens any jug or bridge, he will always find another parliament of things.

C. THE BROTHERHOOD OF MATTER AND RELATIONS

It is said that in Puerto Rico, red and green traffic lights display a curious
reversal of roles. Drivers have flouted red lights to such a degree that the
practice is now contagious, so that cars approaching a green light must stop
from fear of those ignoring the red. Since my travels have never taken me to
Puerto Rico, I cannot verify these reports. But I will take the liberty of coin-
ing the phrase 'The Puerto Rico Effect' to describe a similar phenomenon
in readings of past philosophies. Since every great thinker is approached
through an initial aura of widespread clichés, the critical scholar is always
in a mood to reverse them. Good reasons should be given whenever this is
done, since we must always respect the rights of the obvious. But of course
there is nothing automatically false about such reversals.

As suggested earlier, it is typical of the greatest thinkers that they support opposite interpretations, just as Aristotelian substance can be both hot
and cold or happy and sad at different times or in different respects. Now, it
seems to me that conventional wisdom is falsely reversed when Nietzsche is
read as a democratic theorist, Spinoza as a thinker of plurality, Leibniz as
a thinker of monism, Aristotle as reducing substance to the human *logos*, or
Husserl as a realist, yet I have heard actual examples of all of these reversals.

But the cases are well worth hearing. What is interesting is that no one attempts such counterintuitive inversions with thinkers of *minor* stature—just as we reverse our understanding of Hamlet more easily than our reading of Batman. This suggests a good definition of a minor author, minor character, minor concept, minor invention, or minor argument: one that is reducible to *content*. The more a person, object, or idea can be summarized in a list of univocal assertions, the less substantial they are, since substance always wears different costumes when seen from various angles. This has important stylistic implications for philosophy. Against the program for philosophy written in 'good plain English', I hold that it should be written in good *vivid* English. Plain speech contains clear statements that are forgotten as soon as their spokesman closes his mouth, since they have already said all that they are capable of saying. But vivid speech forges new concepts that take on a life their own, like good fictional characters. It ensures that Leibniz's monad and Kant's *Ding an sich* will haunt the dreams of the future despite endless 'refutations' of both. Here we find the sole but towering advantage of continental philosophy over its analytic rival—the awareness that a philosophy is more than a list of true and false arguments. Yet the continentals waste this advantage by honoring great thinkers with shrines and prayer wheels rather than exploring the forest from which they came.

We now return to the Puerto Rico Effect. In my first book, *Tool-Being*,[14] I found it necessary to run a red light of my own. Heidegger makes a famous distinction between entities present-at-hand (*vorhanden*) and ready-to-hand (*zuhanden*). It might seem that presence-at-hand refers to objective physical substance while readiness-to-hand consists of tools used by humans. For Heidegger our primary way of encountering objects is in their readiness-to-hand; any sheer presence of things is derivative, and generally occurs through a malfunction or breakdown of tools. Since the ready-to-hand is described as a system of relations in which hammers draw their meaning from nails, nails from houses, and houses from humans who use them, Heidegger seems to defend a relational view of the world over a model of autonomous things. To some degree this was even his conscious intention. But a closer look soon requires us to invoke the Puerto Rico Effect: against all appearances, Heidegger's tool-analysis actually leads to the victory of autonomous objects over their relational fusion in a system.

Heidegger always uses the term 'presence-at-hand' negatively, as something that philosophy ought to overcome. It is seldom noted that he uses it for several different types of situations. Sometimes the present-at-hand is a broken tool, taken for granted in its moment of use but now lying obtrusively before us. Sometimes it is an object perceived in consciousness, like Husserl's phenomena, which Heidegger assails by pointing to a hidden

---

14. Graham Harman, *Tool-Being: Heidegger and the Metaphysics of Objects*, Chicago, Open Court, 2002.

depth in the things. Finally, the present-at-hand is sometimes the name for independent physical matter considered apart from the system of human praxis. This triple use of the term is no inconsistency on Heidegger's part, since all three moments share the same feature. For all are *relational*, reducible to their relation with human Dasein. This is immediately clear in the first two cases: phenomena and broken tools. Both are present-at-hand because both are seen only from the outside. A broken hammer, or a hammer as lucidly described by Edmund Husserl, do no justice to the hammer in its subterranean action. In such cases the hammer is viewed merely as a set of visible qualities, not in its underground *Vollzug* or 'execution'. For Heidegger, the hammer withdraws from any of its configurations in the mind. The broken or phenomenal hammer do not live up to this reality, but exist only in relation to us.

The case may seem harder to make when presence-at-hand refers to physical substance, since the physical realm seems to be uniquely independent of humans. Yet Latour's claim that materialism is a kind of idealism sheds new light on the problem with physical mass. To define a thing as material stuff that occupies space is to reduce it to a system of coordinates and measurable properties. Though it may seem that matter is autonomous, it is only autonomous insofar as humans define it according to certain properties, not in its own right. For Heidegger, the only way to escape presence-at-hand is to escape any form of representation at all—whether it be that of the surprised carpenter whose hammer falls apart, the phenomenologist who restricts the hammer to its manifestation to consciousness, or the physicist who defines it in terms of objective physical properties. In short, presence-at-hand is always relational to the core, and is in no way independent of Dasein.

For converse reasons, the ready-to-hand must be defined as autonomous and purely non-relational. The hammer withdraws from view. It surely cannot be described as an appearance in consciousness, since it does not appear to me at all until it fails. It is equally clear that a hammer is not the sum of what science tells us of its molecules, form, or dynamic properties, since for Heidegger it is a depth exceeding all such traits. It might still be claimed that the hammer used in unconscious praxis is the real one, and given that Heidegger tells us that equipment belongs to a system, the hammer itself might easily be taken for something relational. But this is the central falsehood of mainstream Heidegger studies. It is true that when I gaze at the hammer much of its reality escapes me. Yet it is equally true that the successful carpenter or mason do not exhaust the reality of the hammer when silently using it. Whether I am consciously aware of a thing or unconsciously exploit it, in either case the thing itself harbors secret reserves that my dealings with it never touch. If I shift roles from phenomenologist to manual labourer, I do not suddenly gain the magical power of exhausting a hammer to its depths. For this reason, *any* sort of human contact with a hammer changes it into a kind of presence-at-hand; the readiness-to-hand of equipment always lies deeper than the use we make of it, no less than the theories we make about it. Heidegger himself is not so clear about the issue in *Being and Time*, but it becomes quite vivid in his 1949 discussion of the thing,[15] where the jug is divorced from all human access and left to stand in itself whether humans use it or not.

But we must go a step further than Heidegger ever did, and say that not only *human* relations with a thing reduce it to presence-at-hand, but *any relations at all*. We have seen that Husserl does not exhaust the hammer by looking at it, the scientist by modeling it, the unlucky carpenter by surprise at its failure, or the lucky carpenter by reliably using it. But neither do ants and sparrows exhaust the hammer by touching it; nor do boards and nails do so by receiving its blows. There will always be more to the hammer than any possible contact with its being. Though Heidegger's tool analysis is usually glossed as 'unconscious practice vs. conscious seeing', this hollow interpretation must be replaced by a duel of 'thing vs. relations'. This is one red light that simply must be run, since the matter is urgent.

All of this serves as a background for the discussion of matter. Latour does a better job than Heidegger of showing why physical substance is not the product of hardheaded realism but is a purely idealist figment. We simply do not know what actors are, as both Heidegger and Latour would agree. We cannot assume that the hammer is made of molecules any more than of hammer-spirits. Any such theory is an attempt to format or formulate the hammer. This must not be confused with the hammer's own reality, to which no format ever does justice. And that is why Latour opposes materialism, though he rejects the withdrawn depths of the hammer in favour of its alliances with other things. Many readers, including a few materialists, are likely to see the force of this argument. But common sense will still rebel. Even if Latour convinces us that materialism is wrong, our inner faith will lag behind our intellectual agreement. It is difficult to abandon our customary belief that the world is made of hard, unyielding stuff, since the sole alternative seems to be that all things are fairies dancing before the mind.

Latour's equation of materialism with idealism is murderous in intent; he wants materialism to die. But it survives his attack, though just barely, because it still has a place to hide. The real, for Latour, is relational. Abstract physical matter is a failure for Latour because it allows primary qualities to exist apart from all relations. But for those with a nagging sense that reality *must* be independent of relations, it will be tempting to assume a layer of objective states of affairs lying beneath the social network of things. 'Let Latour have his networks of relations', they will say. 'Hard material bodies

---

15. See Martin Heidegger, 'Einblick in das was ist', in *Bremer und Freiburger Vorträge*, Frankfurt, Vittorio Klostermann, 1994.

still lie underneath them'. The only way to oppose such claims is to enter the lion's den of the supposed objective physical realities and show that they cannot be material either. Material bodies cannot possibly do justice to the reality of things themselves. Matter can only be relational, and hence it lacks the autonomy that real things demand.

Latour's critique of matter resembles Heidegger's assault on phenomenology. Both attack their rivals for reducing things to our conceptions of them, and claim that much is thereby lost. The first instinct of both Latour and Heidegger is to replace this model of solid objects with a system of things in reciprocal connection: the network, the tool-system. As already shown, Heidegger can and must be pushed in the opposite direction: the hammer is no more exhausted by its context than by human vision or handling, and thus the hammer in its being must be free of all relations. Presence-at-hand is generated not only by the abstracting human mind, or by the human praxis that brushes only a small portion of hammers, but by any relations at all. Fire does not exhaust the reality of cotton by burning it, nor does rain use up the glass that it moistens. An object might be measured or registered by its relations, but can never be fully defined by them. Pragmatism has value as a method, but fails as a metaphysical doctrine.

That is why materialism is still breathing, even after Heidegger's tool-analysis and Latour's important blow against matter. For both critiques set up an opposition in which the autonomous is always the merely ideal and the real is always the relational. This allows the materialist a way to sneak out of the trap. Namely, the materialist is free to concede that we over-abstract whenever we *think* of matter, while still holding that there is an unyielding physical stuff that is the true reality, deeper than any relational system. There is a hard physical reality occupying some position in space, a real state of affairs whether we like it or not. The problem is that everything said about matter, even if imagined in independence from our minds, is still modelled in purely relational terms. If physical things are described as firm and hard, this is clearly the case only for whatever tries to move them. The materialist might answer that prior to any experience of hardness or firmness there is physical matter occupying a position in space. Yet to occupy a point in space is nothing if not relational. To see this, we need not even take sides with Leibniz in his debate with Samuel Clarke.[16] In this famous exchange, Leibniz holds that time and space are not empty containers but are only the product of relations between monads. For Clarke (writing on behalf of Isaac Newton) time and space are containers indeed, and the things of the world must be positioned somewhere in absolute space. While Leibniz defines space as a relation between things, notice that Clarke also defines it as a relation: but a relation between a thing and *space*. To occupy a position

---

16. G. W. Leibniz and Samuel Clarke, *Correspondence*, Indianapolis, Hackett, 2000.

means to be a certain distance from other spaces, to fill up a vacant cavity, and other things of this sort. But these are all properties in relation with something else and cannot exhaust the inner reality of the thing. The thing may manifest itself in a spatial position, but this is no more identical with its reality than are its colour or smell. To use a somewhat ludicrous metaphor, the thing in itself and the thing as defined by relations are like the kernel of corn before and after being popped. The world is not filled with reciprocal networks of objects defined by their interchange and bundled together out of discrete qualities, but neither is it the refuge of solid physical puncta adrift in empty space. This leaves us with no option besides the strange model that will be developed in the final chapter of this book.

To summarize, the problem with phenomena, broken tools, and matter is not just that they are abstractions in our heads best countered by a reality outside our heads in which things dynamically interact. Instead, the problem is that the abstractions in our heads exist only in *relation* to us, thereby replacing their reality with simulacra. But not only the human head has the power to do this: mere unconscious use of a hammer already turns the hammer into a caricature. Physical collision between two balls reduces each ball to a shadow of its full plenitude, turning them into nothing but spatial obstacles while ignoring their colours and odours. And finally, the same holds true for matter stationed in space and touching nothing; even under this minimalist scenario of physics, the supposed properties of matter all turn out to be relational (inertia, solidity). In fact there is no such thing as matter, but only a descending chain of what used to be called substantial forms. These forms are not just real, but also purely non-relational. It is true that matter has no primary qualities but only secondary ones, since it is always in relation with other things. Yet primary qualities do exist outside matter: in the heart of substance itself.

D. TRANSLATORS

Latour gives us a world of actors that are not just relational, but also *self-contained*. Resistance to this reading of Latour is likely to continue, for understandable if misguided reasons. Since he defines actors in terms of their alliances, it may seem utterly impossible that they could be cut off in themselves. But the key point is that just because a thing is defined by its alliances does not mean that it can slide into new ones without explanation. Even if I am totally defined by my allies at this moment, this does not absolve me of the need to pass through a series of mediations in order to meet my new allies of a year, a week, or a second from now. Latour's notion of time is entirely occasionalist in spirit; if it were not, then translation would not loom as the major theme of his philosophy. For Latour there is no stream of 'becoming' compared to which momentary states are a mere abstraction: becoming is *produced* by actors, not presupposed by them. Nor do I contain my future states *in potentia* in the manner of Leibniz, since my present existence does not contain or 'point toward' anything outside itself. That would be cheating, since in Latour's philosophy nothing is allowed to contain anything else. This basic principle of *Irreductions* is never abandoned in his later career—an actor *is* an instant, since there is no time outside actors for Latour.

But there are several puzzles connected with translation, all of them pertaining to the medium in which it occurs. We have seen repeatedly that neutrons and politics do not 'point' to each other but need Joliot to link them. The cosmos is an army of human and non-human Joliots, all of them linking entities that would otherwise not be linked. The first problem that arises is simple: if Joliot is the bridge between politics and neutrons, then what is the bridge between Joliot and each of these things? If politics cannot touch neutrons directly, then how can Joliot touch them directly? The Latourian answer, of course, is that he cannot. Neutrons become visible only by a long chain of mediators, culminating in the scientific instruments through which their presence is announced. But how can Joliot even touch those final instruments directly? Perhaps through his eyes, his nervous system, his educational background, or other means that allow him to make sense of what he sees. Yet the same question can always be repeated, however far we retreat. It resembles the classic critique of intermediate points: the race staged by Zeno between Achilles and the tortoise. To reach one mediator we need another between them, but must first reach an additional mediator midway between those, and so forth. The same problem has often been raised concerning the theory of time as constructed out of instants, a doctrine I have ascribed to Latour as well. Such points are well taken. But they are merely problems to be solved, not outright refutations of the occasionalist stance. Note that the alternative theory of a primal whole of objects and primal flux of time is plagued with difficulties no less severe, since it cannot explain clearly how these wholes are segmented into distinct zones. The quantized world of occasionalism does have difficulty explaining leaps, but the continuum model of holistic flux or pulsations of intensity has problems explaining why the world is not a single molten whole, devoid of regions. It seems likely that the winning solution will be a model of the cosmos allowing for both aspects without watering down either of them.

This objection of infinite mediators between any two actors is not some smart-alecky trick designed merely to win an argument. Instead, it touches on the central problem of occasional causation. Namely, there cannot be *only* indirect links, since this would reduce to the absurdity of infinite mediators between any two points.[17] In the end, *something* must be capable of direct

---

17. The reader might wonder why this situation is held to be so harmful, given that I have already endorsed an infinite regress of ever-tinier black boxes. But that regress is merely strange; it does not contradict any known facts. Yet the imposition of infinite

action. It is true that we are always free to ignore the problem and proceed on a merely practical basis. Joliot's eyes and nervous system do not seem highly relevant to any link between science and politics in 1930's France, as long as blindness or insanity do not hamper his scientific abilities. Hence, we can ignore them in most cases. But while this method is sufficient for the sociology of science, it is impermissible for metaphysics. If we are trying to discover how objects interact, the phrase 'for all practical purposes' cannot be part of the solution. We cannot remain agnostic about the exact point where objects finally touch. There must be some medium in which Joliot finally touches *something*; at some point, mediation must give way to immediacy. As already seen, Latour avoids the cheap solutions of making God or the human mind the seat of all direct contact; his model requires causation to be secular, local, and plural. This requires that we identify the local site where things finally make contact. In the final chapter of this book, I will propose the solution that two actors can only touch on the inside of a third. Neutrons and politics meet only in Joliot's ether, where he touches both directly because they have already been translated into Joliot-language. This is what I have called the problem of 'vicarious causation', since the two actors are linked vicariously through a third.

The second problem results directly from the first. Since neutrons and politics must already be shaped by Joliot before they interact, we need a clearer notion of why their interaction was ever delayed in the first place. After all, politics and neutrons were both a part of Joliot's life for many years before he linked them, and both will remain part of his life whether he succeeds or fails in making the link. Work must be done to make them compatible, but since both are already accessible to him, they have already achieved a rough sort of compatibility in advance merely by both being a part of Joliot's life. What does it mean to do work on two actors so that they are no longer separate zones side by side in my life, but linked together in their own right? For example, one of the aims of the present book is to join Latour with Heidegger. This is not the easiest task: Latour does not like Heidegger, Heidegger would not have liked Latour, and their readership overlaps in a mere handful of people. Both were favourite thinkers of mine for many years before their point of interface became clear enough to be stated in writing. What happens if the present book is greatly successful, and Latour and Heidegger change from being merely two favoured authors side-by-side in a few random minds into figures whose link is established beyond all public doubt? A good mediator will tend to disappear, allowing the terms it links to flow more or less directly into each other. Hence, a successful link of Latour and Heidegger would render the agent of linkage increasingly irrelevant, just as engineers and contractors fade in importance when a bridge

---

mediators between any two points does contradict a known fact—after all, entities do influence one another rather than vaporizing into a mist of infinite intermediate points.

is finally completed. If Joliot succeeds in linking neutrons with politics, the effects may be largely outside his control; he may also fail, in which case the two actors will remain side by side in his mind, unable to join up. Since this implies that actors are already contiguous in a medium before making more direct contact, we can call this the problem of 'buffered causation'. Things are present together in the same medium before they are joined, preventing all causal relations from occurring in a flash, and ensuring that the world is riddled with missed opportunities. In fact, 'the site of missed opportunities' is the best definition of space that I can imagine.

The third and final problem stems from Latour's view that alliance is symmetrical: Pasteur articulates microbes and microbes articulate Pasteur in return. The motive for this symmetry was the commendable wish to efface the human/world divide by letting both actors cross the gap equally. But while this symmetry does sometimes occur, it does not *always* seem to occur. There may be cases where active and passive are irreversible—not just in the obvious sense that the sun affects us greatly and we affect it very little, but in the more absolute sense that one thing might affect another without being affected reciprocally in the least. Prime numbers may obsess a person who has no skill to affect them in the manner of Gauss or Riemann. Dead thinkers affect us all, and though we may be able to affect how their books are interpreted now, we cannot affect the dead. This kind of asymmetry is impossible for Latour: if one thing is allied to another, then the second is *ipso facto* allied to the first, and the alliance changes them both. Yet asymmetry may be the rule rather than the exception. If two things affect each other reciprocally, this may turn out to be a case of two different but simultaneous causal relations. This problem can be termed 'asymmetrical causation'.

The three problems meet when we reflect on the medium of relations, which I contend is the interior of some other object—some greater black box. Two actors link *vicariously* in the heart of a third. Since they must meet in that place for a short or long period before their interface is built, they are *buffered* from one another. And finally, it seems likely that they do not meet on equal footing in this medium, but that a real object meets only the shadow of another, thereby allowing effects to proceed *asymmetrically* in one direction alone. To summarize: mediating objects are always needed between any two objects, but a mediator would be needed to touch the mediator as well, and on to infinity. Hence, the world must also be filled with a non-objective gas or plasma in which direct contact is possible. That plasma is found on the interior of objects themselves.

E. COSMOLOGY

Recall that this chapter is written in the spirit of an imagined year 2050, with Latour's star at its zenith. It is a happy landscape worth exploring in the mind for hours, and even worth bringing into practice. Yet there is no such thing as paradise: even the beaches of Ipanema and the palm-lined cove of Palolem in Goa will darken one day with the feeling that something is missing. This chapter has covered several points where Latour's heirs in 2050 might wish to push things a bit further. First, there was the need to describe rifts in the actor itself. A thing is not just a duel with other actors, but also a strife between its own four dimensions; an object is split from its relations and from its qualities as well. Next, there was the sense that materialism was not yet buried by Latour's critique, since the real problem with materialism is not idealism, but its covert relationism. Finally, there was the question of the medium in which translation occurs—of how objects can meet without meeting, in the fiery inner core of a third.

But also missing are certain points of cosmology that Latour does not address, though he is far from alone in this silence. As we have seen, *We Have Never Been Modern* achieves a powerful dismantling of the Kantian gap between world and humans. Now, one of the famous results of this gap was Kant's elimination of all traditional questions of metaphysics. Is there life after death? Is everything purely determinate, or are there sparks of chance in the cosmic machine? Is there a necessary being, or are all beings contingent? By decree of Kant's Copernican Revolution such questions are now abandoned either to physics or to private prayer and confession. Philosophy shrinks back from these questions and holes up in the human castle while disputing whether it has the right to leave, with a few hotheads claiming that there is nothing beyond the castle in the first place. Pick up any random book of recent philosophy and you are likely to find dry, hesitant descriptions of the limits of human access to the world. But pick up a random book of recent physics, and you will find dazzling speculation on all manner of things: the creation and destruction of the universe, the existence of parallel worlds, chance and necessity, hidden spatial dimensions, time travel, and two-dimensional holograms that delude us into believing in three. Pick up a random book of history, and you will find countless actors exchanging surprises: generals, serfs, minerals, grain, animals, and germs. Even the New Age movement, despised by most intellectuals, speculates on themes of interest to any human: life after death, reincarnation, the meaning of dreams, the spirit uniting humans and animals, omens invading our lives to signal the future, and shared archetypes at work in multiple individuals. In Latour's own professional circle, where the questions are always too concrete for the Copernican gap to function smoothly, we find studies of every possible object. Yet so-called "first philosophy" remains paralyzed, and the source of its paralysis is clear: the obsession with the single human/world gap. We have even reached the point where I, a passionate reader of philosophy, prefer any section in bookstores *except* philosophy. Far better to read of the properties of salt, or the love story of a buccaneer and an Indian princess, than the latest measurements of the walls of our human prison. The elephant in the living room is this: philosophy has become *boring*. It is little wonder that Bruno Latour came to us from the outside; he could never have emerged from the wind-swept desert of our discipline. Science *does* think, and so do mathematics, history, anthropology, literature, politics, religion, and the occult. The question is whether philosophy wishes to join them.

Let's return briefly to Quentin Meillassoux. Another refreshing moment in his book lies near the end, when he defends questions such as 'Who are we?' and 'Where do we come from?'.[18] In our day these questions are tolerated from the novice as charming tokens of sincerity, but no trained philosopher would be caught dead posing them. They are deemed a sign of naiveté or proof of haphazard training. Many philosophers still wonder about such questions privately, in church or yoga groups, while reading books of popular physics, or in those lonely hours of the night when such questions press upon everyone. Yet only rarely do they appear in works of serious philosophy, a discipline long resigned to the 'intellectual Munich' of 1781. But Meillassoux's admirable view is that such questions are real. Though his own theory of radical contingency entails that they have no answer, this itself is an answer rather than the all-knowing smirk with which such questions are usually greeted.

Latour replaced the human-world gap with a democracy of actors, thereby toppling the central pillar of the Copernican turn. The next step would be to restore the speculative questions that seemed unanswerable for as long as the Kantian gap was in force. We have already seen Latour disobey the Antinomies by implying that there are no simples, only composites. Why not press further and try to take a stand on Kant's other illegal topics? Why not pursue a campaign to reclaim *all* the traditional questions of metaphysics? If we can take a stand on the infinite regress of objects, we might also welcome counterproofs suggesting that objects come to a halt after all. If the question proves undecidable, then this ought to be for reasons entirely different from those of Kant's human-world rift. The initial goal should be to reclaim all of the remaining Antinomies: freedom or necessity, infinity or finitude of time and space, and the existence or non-existence of a necessary being (on the latter question Meillassoux weighs in with a 'no'). Ever since 1781, an agnostic attitude to these questions has been seen as the prime philosophical virtue. But the spirit of a new era ought to treat agnosticism as a vice. Metaphysics can be rebuilt the way New Orleans could have been, with better engineering and more up-to-date materials.

---

18. Meillassoux, *Après la finitude*, p. 151.

7

Object-Oriented Philosophy

This book has described Latour as a pioneer of object-oriented philosophy. In this final chapter of the book I will try to clarify what this means, since 'object' signifies many things to many people. The most typical view of the term is that the object is whatever opposes the human subject—in this sense, the object would be a 'realist' concept pointing to a genuine reality independent of human access to it. But this is too restrictive to cover all senses of 'object', as can be seen from the case of Edmund Husserl. For Husserl is by no means a realist, since he brackets the real world out of consideration in his philosophy. Nonetheless, he remains an object-oriented philosopher, since even the most cursory reading of Husserl's major works shows objects to be among his most pivotal concepts. The object for Husserl is a unity over against its shifting series of outer *accidental* manifestations, since a house is the same house from no matter what direction or distance we view it. And in a second sense the house is an ideal unity over against its *essential* qualities, since we also cannot arrive at the house even by summing up all its non-accidental qualities. In Husserl, then, we find the strange case of an object-oriented idealism.

While it is true that objects cannot receive their full due from any non-realist philosophy, there remains the ironic fact that Husserl has made greater contributions to the philosophy of objects than most realists. It is not hard to see why. Realists are primarily concerned with asserting the existence of a world outside the human mind. And once they feel that this argument is won and their point is established, they are too often satisfied to let objects sit outside human knowledge as obvious and inarticulate physical lumps, with their philosophical mission already accomplished by their mere undercutting of idealism. But given that idealists confine themselves within the narrow compass of human access to the world, they are often forced to work harder *within* this human realm by identifying new features and new rifts.

A. RADICAL, CONSERVATIVE, AND POLARIZED APPROACHES TO OBJECTS

Whatever sense of the word 'object' we might consider, it always refers to something with a certain unity and autonomy. An object must be one, and it must also have a sort of independence from whatever it is not. An object stands apart—not just from its manifestation to humans, but possibly even from its own accidents, relations, qualities, moments, or pieces. Furthermore, insofar as an object is more than its relations it must stand apart from any supposed monism of the world-as-a-whole, since a homogeneous universe of this kind merely gives us the most radical form of relationism—with everything dissolving into everything else in a vast holistic stew. Now, any distinction between objects and the other terms mentioned above can also be rejected, provided good reasons are given. Indeed, most cutting-edge philosophies are distinguished precisely by their *denial* of one or more of the differences just mentioned. Let's use the phrase 'radical philosophy' to describe any claim that the object is nothing over and above one or more of the terms to which it might be opposed. This immediately evokes a landscape of possible radical philosophies:

1. Radical denial of the distinction between object and subject. Although Berkeley already reduced *esse* to *percipi*, a more prestigious denial of the subject/object distinction is found in Fichte and Hegel. For them Kant's thing-in-itself is superfluous, since it is posited as lying *outside* thought only *by* thought. A similar gesture can be found today in Žižek, for whom the Real is not something stationed beyond human access, but is instead posited by the human subject itself as its own constitutive lack.

2. Radical denial of the split between objects and relations. We find this extreme position in Whitehead (and later in Latour), for whom it makes no sense to speak of actual entities as enduring units that undergo adventures in space and time. An entity 'prehends' or relates to many other entities, and it is fully defined by these prehensions. If we claim that there is something more to the thing than all these relations, Whitehead calls this purported substratum a vacuous actuality, and he fully intends 'vacuous' to be an insult.

3. Radical denial of separate autonomous entities in the real world in favour of a primal whole. This is merely an extreme variant of the second radical position that reduces a thing to its relations. The more things are relationized, the less independence they have, and hence

the more we approach the limit case of a single homogeneous block, with the universe as an ominous rumbling unity. By implying that all things have some sort of unity at a level deeper than the actual, the genuine problem of communication between things is blithely eliminated. The earliest examples of such a position can be found in some of the pre-Socratic thinkers: whether in Parmenides (separate individuals are unreal figments of the senses as revealed by reason), Anaximander (the current differences between specific things are a transient injustice that will eventually pass away into a unified *apeiron*), Pythagoras (the original reality was an undifferentiated *apeiron* until it inhaled the Void and broke into fragments), or Anaxagoras (the original *apeiron* broke into pieces when rotated rapidly by *nous* or Mind). A more recent example can be found in the *Cause, Principle, and Unity* of Giordano Bruno, for whom everything swells up from a unified primal matter. Spinoza's *Ethics* invites the same accusation, since his attributes and modes belong to a single divine substance (although this relation is reversed by more chic present-day readers of Spinoza, the scene of his philosophy is still shifted away from individual things). We even find examples in twentieth century French thought. In *Existence and Existents*, Emmanuel Levinas harks back to Anaxagoras by imagining a rumbling primal *il y a* ('there is'), hypostatized into specific chunks only by human consciousness. Even more recently, Jean-Luc Nancy[1] has attempted a surprising theory of the world as a formless 'whatever' articulated only by the interactions among its parts.

4. Radical denial of any distinction between an object and its shifting accidents. At least four prominent thinkers besides Latour come to mind who take a radical position on this point. One is David Hume, who famously denies that an object exists as anything more than a bundle of qualities habitually linked together by the mind. Another is Alain Badiou, who sees the world as made up of 'consistent multiplicities' that are units only because they are *counted* as one, not through any inherent integrity of their own. Yet another example is found in the later 'reist' position of Husserl's teacher Franz Brentano, especially in the collection *The Theory of Categories*, where a thing is said to contain the sum total of *all* its features, not just a limited inner sanctum of essential ones. For Brentano's reism there is no enduring Socrates-nucleus deeper than the current Socrates who happens to be sitting, wearing a white robe, and drinking wine. Another famous example is Leibniz, who radically compresses every incident of the future into our monads from the dawn of time: Caesar crossing the Rubicon was

1. Jean-Luc Nancy, 'Corpus', trans. Claudette Sartiliot, in *The Birth to Presence*, trans Holmes & Others, Stanford, Stanford University Press, 1993.

not an accident, and neither is the fact that I am typing these words at 3:14 in the afternoon rather than 3:17, or that I have traveled to fifty-six countries rather than a mere fifty.

5. Radical denial that an object is different from its qualities. This is similar to Point 4 about accidents, but refers to the level of reality it-self rather than that of qualities experienced by the mind. Bertrand Russell[2] is one figure who sometimes takes a radical position here, denying that there is anything called 'substance' over and above the qualities that typify it.

6. Radical denial that an intentional object is different from its Husserlian *eidos*—from the *sum total* of essential qualities that it requires in order to be intended as what it is. A renegade fan of Husserl might uphold this radical point on the grounds that there is no purpose in positing an object over and above its essential traits.

7. Radical denial that an object is different from its pieces. This is clas-sic scientific reductionism. For radicals of this stripe, higher-level ob-jects are not emergent realities over and above the tiny material com-ponents of which they are formed. Many go so far as to say that even consciousness is reducible to the physical microparticles of which it is built. Even among those who deny that consciousness is reducible, there are many (such as David Chalmers and Galen Strawson) who still hold that all *physical* things can be reduced to microparticles—so that a table would be nothing over and above the quarks and electrons of which it is made, even if consciousness cannot thus be reduced.

These approaches can all be called 'radical' for reasons of etymology. While not all are radical in the sense of being new and unforeseen, all are trying to identify the single *radix*, the root of reality as a whole. By taking one side of any opposition as primary and the other as derivative, they resolve an ap-parent paradox by collapsing everything into one of two opposed terms.

The seven radical philosophies just cited all banish unified and autono-mous objects as a supposed figment of the reactionary mind, replacing ob-jects either with bundles of qualities, projections of human desire, function-al/environmental effects, subatomic particles, or a primal unified womb of becoming. By contrast with such radical gestures let's use the phrase 'conser-vative philosophy' to refer to those doctrines that leave initial oppositions in place rather than radically reducing them to one term, but with the major drawback of not giving adequate explanation of how the two terms interre-late. Examples of a conservative approach would be the Yin/Yang polarity, the mind/body dualism, the substance/aggregate distinction, the fact/value

---

2. Bertrand Russell, *The Analysis of Matter*, London, Kegan Paul, 1927.

opposition, the animate/inanimate rift, the phenomenal/noumenal split, or the Platonic gap between perfect forms and cave shadows. While all of these theories were 'radical' in their time in the sense of being innovative, none try to reduce the cosmos to a single *radix*. Instead, each offers some sort of unsurpassable duality, and hence can be called 'conservative' in the sense defined here. For all of these theories try to conserve two sides of the story, if at the cost of failing to link them effectively.

Most treatments of most philosophical problems adopt either a radical or a conservative strategy (and most thinkers are radical on some points and conservative on others). Hence, if we reject any radical approach that dissolves unitary objects into some other explanatory term, it might seem that we automatically lapse into some sort of conservative metaphysics that ratifies timeworn reactionary splits in the cosmos. After all, to defend objects means to refuse the radical assaults by Hegel on noumena, Hume on substance, Whitehead on vacuous actuality, Churchland on ghostly minds, Russell on substance, or Bruno on substantial forms. It might thereby seem that we are taking the side of boring common sense if we insist that all the polarizations surrounding objects must be taken seriously. But we are not, since we also aim to show clearly how the two terms of any polarization are able to interact. Whereas the radical gesture is always to say 'there is nothing more to S than P', our contrary gesture is to insist that 'there is *always* more to S than P'. Object-oriented philosophy is a proud defense of the 'something more'. And whereas the conservative gesture is to say that 'the world is made of opposed S-terms and P-terms', we should never forget the problem of how one term is inscribed in the other. Stated differently, radical philosophy holds that there is no problem of communication between opposites in the universe, because everything is ultimately of the same nature. (Example: Hume's skepticism, since everything that populates his philosophy stems from impressions.) Meanwhile, conservative philosophy holds that there are absolute gaps or dualities that must be respected, and which are generally only described or else solved by fiat. (Example: occasionalism, in which all entities and all instants of time are cut off from one another until God intervenes magically to link them.)

Although Kant is widely celebrated for carving up his predecessors into 'rationalists' and 'empiricists', these are merely terms for two ways of *knowing* the world (through reason or through experience) rather than two doctrines about the structure of the world itself. A deeper distinction is the one that lies between *occasionalism* ('conservative') and *skepticism* ('radical'), the most purified forms of the competing Continental and Anglo-Saxon schools of the seventeenth century. This revised terminology enables us to see that Kant's supposed synthesis of the two preceding camps of philosophy is no synthesis at all, but fully endorses the skeptical side over the occasionalist side. In Kant's philosophy everything knowable is radically reduced to the status of phenomena governed by categories. The only *conserved* duality for Kant is the one that lies between human and world. While the occasionalists boldly insist on preserving the gap between cotton and fire or raindrops and wood, Kant leaves such non-human relations outside of philosophy altogether. He maintains only a sickly, minimal occasionalist gap between humans on the one hand and *everything else* on the other. No wonder Fichte viewed this rump remnant of occasionalism in Kant as a withered vestigial organ, worthy of amputation. Thus, the things-in-themselves were booted from philosophy as naive. And in this way today's 'continental philosophy' actually *abandons* the vigorous Continental option of the seventeenth century and joins analytic thought in a little-noticed skeptical/radical consensus in which the difference between Hume and Kant is not so great. Everything is reduced to a question of human access to the world, and non-human relations are abandoned to the natural sciences.

By contrast, the method of object-oriented philosophy is neither radically skeptical nor conservatively occasionalist, but *polarized*. Objects exist as autonomous units, but they also exist in conjunction with their qualities, accidents, relations, and moments without being reducible to these. To show how these terms can convert into one another is the alchemical mission of the object-oriented thinker. The world is made up of a basic set of polarities—four of them, it turns out. They cannot be derived from a single radical root, but neither do they exist as incorruptible elements untransmutable into one another in the manner of the Empedoclean air, earth, fire, and water.

So far there has never been a perfect hero of object-oriented philosophy. Some of the polarizations of the object (versus the human subject, relations, the block-universe, accidents, qualities, *eidei*, and pieces) have been preserved by various thinkers, but only at the cost of denying the others. Bruno Latour is the closest figure I can think of to the ideal object-oriented hero. For in addition to the marvelous plurality of concrete objects found in his books, he is able to think two things at once in the manner that the polarized approach demands. For on the one hand, his actants are cut off from one another in their utterly concrete states and need mediators to bridge the gaps between them ('conservative'). But on the other hand, actants are defined entirely by their relations to other things ('radical'). My sole objection is that Latour's radical side is too radical, and his conservative side too conservative. By treating actants as entirely relational and not allowing an essential nuclear core in them to withdraw behind relations, he does not acknowledge the separation of things from their own traits. And by separating all things via mediators *ad infinitum* (Joliot and politics, Joliot and neutrons) he makes their communication impossible, since the mediators are left in the same boat as the two original actants that were not allowed to touch (politics and neutrons).

B. ESCAPING THE WHIRLPOOL OF RELATIONS

We now face several tasks. Since objects can be distinguished from at least seven contrary terms, we need to organize these opponents in cleaner fashion. Next, we need to pinpoint which side Latour takes in each of these controversies in order to know in what sense he is an object-oriented philosopher and in what sense not (no one has ever been object-oriented on every point). Finally, we should also explain why an object-oriented or polarized approach is superior to its radical and conservative alternatives on each count.

The first step is to notice that three of the differences mentioned (object vs. accident, moment, quality) refer to an internal split in the object itself, not in its relation to anything else. If we speak of a tree as different from the accidental profile that we experience of it, from the essential moments (*eidos*) of the tree as experienced, or of the qualities that the tree has even when nobody encounters it, these are all rifts *within* the real or intentional tree. None of these distinctions are of interest to Latour, and hence they can be safely ignored for the moment. After all, Latour's principle of the absolute concreteness of entities does not allow for any distinction to be drawn between the thing as a unit and the various features of which it is comprised. In this sense he is closer to the empiricist 'bundle of qualities' theory than to Husserl's model of a thing in tension with its own traits. Only in the next chapter will I return to these three rifts within objects themselves. Unlike these, the remaining four differences (object vs. world-block, the human subject, relations, and pieces) refer not to the articulation *within* a single object, but to the relation of that object with something else. And on these points Latour's views are mixed:

1. Latour clearly has no concept of a single block-world from which individuals are mere derivative chips (with the possible exception of his emerging theory of plasma, given that he seems to view it as an unformatted whole). In fact, his specific actors are completely cut off from one another. This is precisely why any two objects need a mediator if they are ever to make contact—a claim that one would never hear from Parmenides.

2. Clearly, Latour also means to distinguish between objects and their pieces. No one would mistake him for a scientific reductionist given that he allows Popeye and failed metro trains the same philosophical rights as quarks and electrons. An object for Latour is a black box concealing a vast internal drama, but it is never treated as a mere surface-effect of tiny unopenable microboxes lying at the bottom of all boxes. Indeed, I inferred earlier that Latour's theory of black boxes requires an infinite regress in which no box is ever final and unopenable, no matter how tiny. Nonetheless, if we ask what makes

complicated macro-entities genuine emergent realities for him, it turns out to be nothing inherent in their hearts, but has to do with their perturbations of other entities. In other words, the reason a subway train is not just a derivative cluster of tiny atoms is *because* it has larger subway-effects on other entities that cannot be explained in terms of the train's component atoms. In short, Latour veers toward a *functional* concept of emergence: a thing emerges as a real thing when it has new effects on the outside world, not because of any integral emergent reality in the thing itself. This leads to a certain tension in his theory of black boxes.

3. Latour's position is somewhat ambiguous when it comes to the subject/object dualism. Realist critics of Latour might take his claim that the microbe existed only when Pasteur discovered it, that it preexisted Pateur *only for Pasteur*, as grounds for inferring that he absorbs all reality into the human subject. These same critics might also be suspicious of the fact that the writings of Latour usually involve one or more humans in whatever network is under consideration. In Latour (unlike in Whitehead) we find little discussion of relations between inanimate entities when people are nowhere on the scene. For this reason the notion of a Latourian physics might seem impossible to some critics. Against these critics, two points could be raised to claim that Latour does allow for a reality independent of human access. First, there is the insistence in *Irreductions* (his key philosophical work) that interpretation occurs not just between humans and objects, but also between objects and objects. Second, there is the fact that actors for Latour are not reducible to our current human access to them: actors *resist,* after all. They do not always do what we ask of them, and this implies that they have some degree of autonomy from us.

4. But on the question of relations with other things Latour is a screaming radical, opposed to any attempt to distinguish between objects and relations. As we have seen, a thing for Latour is nothing more than its sum total of perturbations of other entities. There is no mysterious residue in the things hiding behind their relations with other things.

Point 4 is where Latour most clearly deviates from the object-oriented approach. Point 3 is more debatable, though I will repeat the pro-Latour case momentarily. But Points 1 and 2 are enough to establish Latour as one of the great object-oriented philosophers of all time. What makes Latour a great theorist of objects are the two following points:

A. He does not try to reduce various sizes of actors to some primal level of physical matter. He is not a materialist given that electrons, tables,

Popeye, and armies are equally objects. In terms of Point 2 above, he is not a radical who eliminates bulky macro-actors in favour of their tiny little micro-pieces.

B. At the same time, Latour sees these actors as cut off from one another. They can only be linked by some third term as their mediator, as when Joliot links politics and neutrons, neither of them inherently linkable or unlinkable prior to Joliot's act of translation. In terms of Point 1 above, Latour does not try to have his cake and eat it too by positing some unproblematic primal whole where communication is easy, but a whole that is *also* carved into 'pre-individual singularities' or some other equally vague phrase. There are nothing but actual objects. They come in all shapes and sizes, and all are equally sequestered by way of gaps that some third term must always bridge. Latour never cheats by invoking an unfalsifiable global deity to do this work. Instead he needs to call upon a local form of causation, and hence must count as what I call the first 'secular occasionalist'. And insofar as he finds these causal links to be problematic, and not just fodder for an arbitrarily invoked God of the gaps, he avoids the conservative approach to objects just as skillfully as most of the radical ones. The central problem of metaphysics is the interplay of objects and relations, and Latour sheds more light on both problems than perhaps any other contemporary thinker. It is odd that no one so far has seemed to realize this—bad luck for Latour, but once-in-a-lifetime good fortune for me, as the author of the first book on his metaphysics.

Although we have covered four separate points so far, all are concerned with a single question: are objects autonomous from their relations? My own view is that all four theses are different gradations of a single underlying thesis, so that all must be either affirmed or denied. Whereas Latour's position lies somewhere in the middle of the following continuum, I hold that all four of the following positions must be affirmed.

Objects are Not Derivative of a Primal Whole

The more we define a thing by its relations, the more we strip it of autonomous reality. This can be done to greater or lesser extremes. The most extreme version of a relational philosophy would be the pure monism of a single lump universe, a world devoid of any specific realities at all. Such a position claims not just that a stone or dolphin are both defined completely in terms of their relations to other objects, but even denies that stones and dolphins exist as two separate relational constellations. Instead, all ̶ ̶ ̶ Such philosophies are most abundant in the pre-Socratic era. We mi̶ that an undifferentiated world-lump, formless being, or boundless either existed in the past before it was shattered into pieces (Pythagoras, Anaxagoras), that it exists right now though our senses deceive us into thinking otherwise (Parmenides), or that it will exist in the distant future once justice destroys all opposite terms (Anaximander). As already mentioned, we find analogous theories in the more recent positions of Levinas and Nancy.

Assuming that one upholds such a theory, there is either some sort of relation between the undifferentiated world-lump and the specific beings we apparently encounter, or there is not. But in the former case it is hard to see how a homogeneous lump could be carved up later into distinct pieces, given the posited homogeneity of all portions of the lump. And in the latter case, that of no relation at all between the global lump and the specific beings, the unified world-mass is really just an irrelevant remainder playing no role for us, and we are left to confront the details of experience from a position indistinguishable from that of idealism. If Berkeley had claimed that behind all the perceptions there was a gigantic blob of objective indeterminate matter, this would have changed little about his philosophy.

Recently we have encountered a weaker but more sophisticated version of this position in the various philosophies of the virtual that have begun to proliferate in and around the works of Deleuze. These positions try to enjoy the best of both worlds, defining a unified realm beneath experience that is not *completely* unified. Instead of a total lump-world, it is one animated in advance by different 'pre-individual' zones that prevent the world from being purely homogeneous. This position has the following supposed benefits: it prevents things from being overdetermined by their current actuality (an admirable object-oriented gesture), while also slyly bridging the gap between things without doing the required work (a merely 'radical' move in the sense that must be rejected). For instance, DeLanda wishes to establish the possibility of a 'continuous, yet heterogeneous space'.[3] The same is true of Gilbert Simondon, that posthumous rising star. As Alberto Toscano describes Simondon's position, 'whilst [preindividual being] is yet to be individuated, [it] can already be regarded as affected by relationality. This preindividual relationality, which takes place between heterogeneous dimensions, forces or energetic tendencies, is nevertheless also a sort of nonrelation [...]. Being is thus said to be *more-than-one* to the extent that all of its potentials cannot be actualized at once'.[4] Simondon like DeLanda wants the world to be both heterogeneous and *not yet* parcelled out into individuals. In this way, specific realities lead a sort of halfhearted existence somewhere between one and many.

This is certainly not Latour's own position, since his actors are fully individual from the start; his philosophy contains no such concept as 'pre-

---

3. Manuel DeLanda, *Intensive Science and Virtual Philosophy*, London, Continuum, 2002, p. 27.

4. Alberto Toscano, *The Theatre of Production*, London, Palgrave, 2006, p. 138.

individual'. His actors are not blended together in a 'continuous yet heterogeneous' whole, but are basically cut off from one another. There is no continuum for Latour despite his relationism, and this thankfully entails that his relationism is *less* radical than it is for philosophies of the virtual (note that Latour's rare flirtations with monism seem to coincide with his equally rare flirtations with the term 'virtual'). Individual candles and apricots do exist for Latour. This means that they cannot *fully* dissolve into a global system of relations, not even of the 'continuous yet heterogeneous' kind advocated by DeLanda, who is otherwise a more hardcore realist than Latour himself. In Latour's metaphysics, even if a candle is nothing but its set of relations with other things it is still a specific *individual* set of relations different from those that assemble to give us an apricot. For Latour there are no pre-individual or virtual apricots—only actual apricots, defined entirely by their relations with other actants.

Objects are Irreducible to Their Components

If utter monism is the most extreme form of relationism, the halfway house of virtual philosophy is only barely less extreme. What would be the next incremental step away from the full-blown radicalism of the shapeless *apeiron*? It would be a position that Latour still rejects: materialism. This word can be defined in a number of different ways, so let's define it here as a philosophy claiming that all macro-sized entities can ultimately be reduced to a final layer of tiny pampered physical elements that are more real than everything else. If monism holds that there are no individual things at all, and virtualism holds that reality consists at best of *pre*-individuals, then materialism makes only a small additional concession: there are individuals indeed, but only at the level of ultimate microparticles. All larger entities can be explained away as relational composites. An apartment building is really just a big assembly of atoms, since the building exists *qua* building only in its relations with the people who use it. Only ultimate particles, whether they be quarks and electrons or unknown smaller pieces of the world, exist in and of themselves and need no relations with other things to earn their reality.

Here we still find Latour resisting relationism as too extreme. Rather than saying that all macro-sized actors are reducible to tiny material atoms, Latour allows for every possible size of object—new entities *emerge* at different scales of the world. One good list of criteria for emergent entities can be found in DeLanda's *A New Philosophy of Society* (a list drawn in part from Roy Bhaskar, an author DeLanda admires as much as I do). One obvious feature of emergent entities is that they must have 'emergent properties':[5] for instance, the Paris Metro has features not discernible in any of its cars,

---

5. Manuel DeLanda, *A New Philosophy of Society: Assemblage Theory and Social Complexity*, London, Continuum, 2006, p. 48.

tracks, turnstiles, or customers taken alone. Another feature is 'redundant causality':[6] the wheels of the Metro trains can be replaced with duplicates or even with completely different types of wheels without necessarily changing the Metro as a whole. Still another feature is that emergent wholes are able to act retroctively on their parts:[7] wheels in the Metro are perhaps subjected to more uniform frictional heat than they would in other possible contexts, and the global market for wheels, bearings, and tracks may become more standardized if the Paris Metro becomes their biggest customer. A final feature mentioned by DeLanda is that many parts of the emergent whole do not pre-exist that whole but are actually generated by it:[8] one can now have a special career as a Metro musician, flower vendor, or graffiti artist; one can become an academic scholar of the Paris Metro, or a Metro rat spending a lifetime in its tunnels. None of these were necessary initial parts for the Metro to be what it was, but all are now inseparable from its rich emergent life.

It should be clear enough that Latour's actors meet all of these criteria for emergence. This is true even for redundant causation, which might not sound very Latourian at first: if an entity contains *all* of its features and not just the supposedly 'essential' ones, wouldn't a different wheel mean a completely new Metro? Not at all. When Latour says that a thing is defined by its relations, he is talking about its outward relational effects on other things, not its real internal composition. If the Metro had one type of wheel rather than another, it would not necessarily be a different actor unless this change made it register different outward effects on *other* actors. At any moment we can choose to open up a black box and examine the components that gave rise to it. But the black box does not just screen its inner pieces from human view, for it also has a certain ability to endure internal changes (as in the case of the Metro wheel just mentioned). Most internal rearrangements of an actor's pieces are screened off from the external actors that the Metro affects, transforms, perturbs, or creates. Hence the black box is not just a temporary stopping point for humans who have not yet opened it, but also a genuine screen that blocks off unimportant changes from accessibility by all other objects.

However, I have already mentioned that there is a slight slippage toward relationism here. Why? Because Latour seems to view emergence as a *functional* matter. Namely, if a thing is real only because it transforms or perturbs some other entity, this means that it emerges only if it has an effect on something else. And this would imply that the Paris Metro does not exist if nothing is transformed by it. We cannot say that the Paris Metro exists 'potentially' before it is built, because there is no room for potential in Latour's philosophy; instead, the Metro will begin to exist only at the moment when

6. DeLanda, *A New Philosophy of Society*, p. 37.

7. DeLanda, *A New Philosophy of Society*, p. 34.

8. DeLanda, *A New Philosophy of Society*, p. 37.

it is affecting other things. But this cannot succeed as a concept of emergence, because it passes the hot potato of reality from the Metro itself to other entities—nothing in the Metro makes it something real over and above its constituent quarks and electrons. Real emergence cannot be merely functional/relational, but must amount to the generation of new autonomous things with new autonomous qualities *whether it relates to anything else or not*. Otherwise, we would have a final layer of atomic microparticles. All larger physical entities would be reduced to relational effects—as seen in the philosophy of David Chalmers, who thinks a table is real only in the functional sense of having table-effects, but is otherwise reducible to tiny pieces of micro-matter. But Latour's philosophy does not even allow for the existence of microparticles due to the infinite regress implied by his principle that black boxes can always be opened. Hence, it is all the more important for Latour that he allow genuine non-relational reality to emerge at each level of the world. And though he never passes the buck of reality *downward* to an artificial stopping point in the purported final kingdom of quarks, he does pass it *upward* to the outward effects an actant has on its neighbors. But the buck must never be passed in either direction. The reality of an object belongs to that object—not to its tiny internal constituents, and also not to the larger collectives in which it is immersed.

Objects Exceed Our Access to Them

Already, Latour has avoided the most extreme forms of relationism. He opposes the lump universe, the semi-lump universe of pre-individual 'heterogeneous continuua', and even the materialist poor house where tiny little particles are the world's only permitted entities. Against these extreme attempts to relationize the world, Latour maintains a fairly stalwart object-oriented stance—allowing for numerous entities of different sizes, and guaranteeing their autonomy by cutting them off from one another. But we now enter a cold, grey neutral zone where Latour begins to flirt with the relational model of entities, and soon enough will reach the weaker form of relationism that he openly defends. Following the three types of relationism that have already been described, the next more watered-down version would be this: 'the world is not just made of one kind of entity, such as atoms. Instead, there are *two* real entities: human and world. But they exist only in permanent rapport with one another. There cannot be real things-in-themselves lodged outside the human mind, because if we are thinking about them then we are *thinking* about them, and hence they are no longer independent of thought'. The reader will immediately recognize this position as the 'correlationism' brilliantly identified by name in the work of Meillassoux.

We have already seen that there are *flashes* of correlationism in the writings of Latour: microbes did not pre-exist Pateur's discovery of them, and

Ramses II could not have died of tuberculosis since it was not yet discovered in ancient Egypt.[9] But on the other hand there is also the Latour of
Irreductions, who makes it clear that objects interpret each other as much
as we interpret them. I have already suggested that the latter is closer to
Latour's true position, and that his intermittent correlationist moments
are a peripheral, dispensible element of his work. This view is seconded by
Meillassoux, who agreed in an e-mail that 'like you, I believe that Latour
is not a correlationist'.[10] Meillassoux actually holds Latour to be quite the
opposite: a relationist metaphysician who resembles Whitehead (and presumably Harman!) in hypostatizing the human relation with the world and
spreading it throughout the cosmos.[11] Although Meillassoux views this step
negatively and I view it positively, we both agree that Latour is not trapped
in a human/world correlate. It is ironic that we both agree on this point
even though Latour mocked *himself* as a correlationist.

Now, the most noteworthy feature of Meillassoux's own philosophical position was somewhat unclear to me on my first two readings of his
book, blinded as I was by my own strong distaste for correlationism.[12] For
Meillassoux is the only member of the 'Speculative Realist' circle who is actually *sympathetic* to the correlationist position. Rather than viewing it as a
sad degeneration from a robustly realist attitude, Meillassoux sees it as the
only path to a rigorous, rationalist philosophy. In other words, he holds that
correlationism must be radicalized from within, not dismissed from the outside. In this respect he has more in common with figures such as Lacan,
Badiou, and Žižek than with traditional realists. Now, in the Anglophone
world we usually hear Latour denounced as the latest French relativist who
subjectivizes the world and ruins science. For this reason it comes as a bit of
a shock to hear Meillassoux's opposite complaint (more common in France):
namely, that Latour is so addicted to hardheaded, old-fashioned realism
that he never develops the logic of the human-world correlate with sufficient

---

9. For the case of Ramses II and tuberculosis, see Latour, 'On the Partial Existence of
Existing and Nonexisting Objects' (PE).

10. Meillassoux, Personal Communication, 16 September, 2007. trans. Graham Harman.

11. Meillassoux, Personal Communication, 16 September, 2007.

12. See for instance my early review of Meillassoux's book, 'Quentin Meillassoux: A
New French Philosopher', *Philosophy Today*, vol. 51, no. 1, Spring 2007, pp. 104-117. There I
suggested that Meillassoux remained somewhat caught up in correlationism himself, not
fully realizing that this was precisely the point. In Meillassoux's view, correlationism can
only be overcome from within. Thus the early sections of his book on 'ancestrality' and
the 'arche-fossil' merely describe a paradox for the correlationist position, not a refutation
of it. This first became clear to me when hearing Meillassoux lecture in Maastricht on 4
October, 2007. The record shows that he had already made the point with equal clarity
in his 27 April, 2007 lecture at Goldsmiths College in London, but on that occasion severe
physical illness deprived me of full concentration despite having given my own lecture immediately before his.

rigor. In Meillassoux's presentation at the April 2007 Speculative Realist workshop in London, he refers to the anti-correlationist argument as

> a rhetoric of the fruitful concreteness of things, the revenge of descriptions and style on repetitive quibbles. Latour, sometimes, severs all links with correlationism in such a way, and does so with much talent and humour [....] But in the case of [his] 'Rich Elsewhere' rhetoric, it is clear that it is not an argument, but a disqualification of he who argues: the sickly and boring correlationist.[13]

Here the description of the correlationist as 'sickly and boring' is meant sarcastically. Although Meillassoux forcefully attacks the correlationist standpoint in his own writings, he still contends that it has a devastating point to make. It is clear from the remainder of Meillasoux's lecture that he has no sympathy for attempts to evade the correlationist deadlock from the start, as in Latour's case (and by implication my own).

Meillassoux defends the correlationist insight as follows. He speaks of the dominance of the human/world correlate in philosophy because he '[wants] to exhibit the essential argument of these "philosophies of access", as Harman calls them; and—I insist on this point—the essential *strength* of this [correlationist] argumentation, apparently and desperately implacable'.[14] On this point he stands bravely alone against his Speculative Realist colleagues, since Ray Brassier, Iain Hamilton Grant, and I concede no strength in the correlationist standpoint at all. Meillassoux accepts the Fichtean principle of 'no X without givenness of X, and no theory of X without a positing of X. If you speak about something, you speak about something that is given to you, and posited by you. Consequently, the sentence: "X is", means "X is the correlate of thinking" in a [broad] Cartesian sense [of thinking, namely...] X is the correlate of an affection, or a perception, a conception, or of any sort of subjective act'.[15] For Meillassoux as for Fichte, to *posit* X as *non-*posited is an obvious pragmatic contradiction,[16] and no realism is worthy of the name unless it somehow avoids this pitfall.[17]

Among those held guilty of falling into this trap is François Laruelle (whose escape from the correlationist circle toward a pre-philosophical Real is endorsed by Brassier). In Meillassoux's own words: 'if, like Laruelle, you posit something outside the circle of objectivity—in his case the Real outside "Philosophy"—this Real will still be, according to me, [inside] the circle of correlationism'.[18] Laruelle has abundant company, since Meillassoux holds

---

13. Brassier, Ray, Iain Grant, Harman Graham, and Quentin Meillassoux, 'Speculative Realism', *Collapse*, vol. III, Falmouth, Urbanomic, 2007, p. 423.

14. Brassier, et. al., 'Speculative Realism', p. 409.

15. Brassier, et. al., 'Speculative Realism', p. 409.

16. Brassier, et. al., 'Speculative Realism', p. 412.

17. Brassier, et. al., 'Speculative Realism', p. 413.

18. Brassier, et. al., 'Speculative Realism', p. 418.

that numerous contemporary thinkers are guilty of too much Real and not enough realism.[19] He also accuses standard realists of avoiding rational debate with the correlationist in favour of two illegitimate manoeuvres: (1) psychologizing the motives of the correlationist; (2) abandoning logical debate with the correlationist through appeal to a 'Rich Elsewhere'.

While Brassier praises Laruelle for upholding 'the radical autonomy of the Real towards thought [...] the essential asymmetry of the Real and thought',[20] Meillassoux views this gesture as a mere 'secession' from rational argument. It is insufficient when Laruelle tries to disarm the correlationist by *predicting* that the correlationist (Meillassoux's term, not Laruelle's) will resist the notion of a non-posited Real. For predicting that someone will resist a statement does not yet prove that they are wrong. Laruelle is still not off the hook: to think X is still *to think* X, and can never get us anything more than the X that is thought. Meillassoux finds that this correlationist argument is an *argument*, and deserves to be treated as such,[21] and also finds that many realists offer nothing but a disappointing *coup de force* exit from the correlational circle.

Nor is Laruelle alone in casting doubt on the psychology of correlationists and idealists rather than arguing with them. The same is even more obviously true of such figures as Marx, Freud, and Nietzsche: 'The realist fights every form of idealism by discovering the hidden reasons behind these discourses—reasons that do not concern the content of philosophies, but the shameful motivations of their supporters: class-interest, libido, *etc*'. The same holds true for 'the Nietzschean suspicion of the sickly Kantians of the university'.[22] However, 'you don't refuse a mathematical demonstration because the mathematicians are supposed to be sickly or full of frustrated libido, you just refuse what you refute!'.[23]

Along with the lazy psychologizing of one's opponents, Meillassoux is unimpressed by attempts to secede from the correlational circle in favour of a neglected 'Rich Elsewhere'. Here Latour is paired with Schopenhauer, perhaps the only time these two names have been linked. Meillassoux summarizes the attitude of this unexpected couple as follows: 'solipsism is a philosophy nobody can refute, but also one that nobody can believe. So let's leave the fortress as it is, and let's explore the world in all its vastness!' In this rhetoric of the Rich Elsewhere, 'the realist disqualifies the correlationist argument as uninteresting, producing arid idealities, boring academics, and pathological intellectuals'. Rather than judging correlationism by its motives in the manner of Laruelle, Nietzsche, Marx, and Freud, the Rich Elsewhere

---

19. Brassier, et. al., 'Speculative Realism', p. 435.
20. Brassier, et. al., 'Speculative Realism', p. 425.
21. Brassier, et. al., 'Speculative Realism', p. 426.
22. Brassier, et. al., 'Speculative Realism', p. 424.
23. Brassier, et. al., 'Speculative Realism', p. 426.

thinkers despise correlationism because of its boring results. Meillassoux admits that they have 'an attractive and powerful rhetoric [and] not in a pejorative sense'[24] [...]. They are forever annoyed by 'the same [correlationist] objection, tedious and irritating: if you posit X, then you *posit* X'.[25] But for Meillassoux, tedium is not a philosophical argument. For 'realism, in my view, must remain a rationalism',[26] not just an angry secession from whatever we dislike.

In response to Meillassoux's speech on behalf of the correlationist, I will try to do three things, though with greater brevity than all these points deserve. First, I want to suggest a more nuanced picture of human reasoning than Meillassoux presents with his split between rational argument on one side and psychologizing rhetoric on the other. Second, I will claim that the 'rhetoric of the Rich Elsewhere' is more *philosophically* powerful than Meillassoux allows, and not just a matter of impressive stylistic persuasion. Third, I will say that correlationism is actually not a powerful argument at all, despite its continuing fashionability in continental philosophy circles. But with Meillassoux as with Latour, I find myself in the strange position of not *wanting* to convince him that he is wrong. For in the first place, none of us can ever be sure that we have found the proper starting point for philosophy; even a successful annihilation of opposing positions merely strips diversity from the gene pool, which should only be done if we are absolutely sure that they are faulty genes. And in the second place, my disagreement with Meillassoux's pro-correlationist outlook does not lessen my admiration for all the exotic fruits and birds that spring from it. In what follows, I aim only to persuade readers of this book that correlationism is not an advisable foundation for philosophy. As for Meillassoux himself, it will be better if he continues to do what he is already doing, as will surely happen anyway.

One problem is that Meillassoux's lecture at Goldsmiths offers a picture in which rational, deductive argument on the correlationist side opposes sheer innuendo and florid rhetoric on the non-correlationist side. A similar model of thinking is proclaimed by analytic philosophy, with its assumption that tearing down the faulty logic of unsound arguments is the primary task of philosophy. For the analytics the great enemies of human thought are fuzziness, non sequiturs, lack of clarity, poetic self-indulgence, and insufficiently precise terminology. I disagree with this threat assessment. In my view these are all relatively minor problems in comparison with shallowness, false dichotomies, lack of imagination, robotic chains of reasoning, and the aggressive self-assurance that typifies analytic philosophers at their worst. When a desolate tax lawyer like Quine passes for a master of English prose simply because he always says exactly what he means, or when micro-

---

24. Brassier, et. al., 'Speculative Realism', p. 423.

25. Brassier, et. al., 'Speculative Realism', p. 421.

26. Brassier, et. al., 'Speculative Realism', p. 426.

debates over technical sub-issues eat up dozens of careers, then I think we need to question the assumptions of this entire school. When decades of analytic dominance build up a surplus of rigorous argument far exceeding global reserves of soybeans and hay, yet so few of the prominent analytic thinkers are obvious keepers for the centuries to come, then one has to wonder whether the constant focus on 'argument' is really getting us anywhere. To say that a philosophy is built of arguments is like saying that architecture is a matter of arranging steel girders. It is certainly true that no building can stand with faulty engineering, but there are always many ways to arrange steel beams and make them stand. Shifting to an analogy that hits closer to home: to say that a philosophy is built of explicit arguments is like saying that an apple is built of qualities, or that a person is built of all the things that can be known about them. We are not speaking here about aesthetic preferences for desert or jungle landscapes. Instead, we have a genuine *philosophical* dispute about whether or not an object or a truth is adequately rendered by specific statements or arguments about it.

Now, there is nothing even remotely sterile about the writings of Meillassoux, whose pages contain one magnificent surprise after another. His philosophical imagination is a source of constant fascination for me and others. His lucid pursuit of reasoned deduction, on a continental landscape that too often shuns such clarity, is a large part of what makes his approach so appealing. But though Meillassoux claims an irrefutable first principle as his starting point ('no escape from the correlational circle'), this strategy is opposed by no less a figure than Alfred North Whitehead. Early in *Process and Reality* we read these stirring words: 'It has been remarked that a system of philosophy *is never refuted; it is only abandoned*'.[27] This is not just inspiring historical rhetoric, but stems from purely philosophical considerations of deep importance to Whitehead. He continues: 'logical contradictions [...] are the most gratuitous of errors; and usually they are trivial. Thus, after criticism, systems do not exhibit mere illogicalities. They suffer from inadequacy and incoherence'.[28] Any cocky, well-trained analytic philosopher can make logical mincemeat of Plato's *Phaedo* or Spinoza's *Ethics* in ten minutes or less, yet everyone knows that the latter two authors are still the more impressive figures—and not merely due to their 'great historical importance'. Somehow, we all sense that getting the arguments right is not quite enough to build a philosophy.

Continuing further: 'the accurate expression of the final generalities is the *goal* of discussion and *not its origin*. Philosophy has been misled by the example of mathematics; and even in mathematics the statement of the ulti-

---

27. Alfred North Whitehead, *Process and Reality*, New York, Free Press, 1978, p. 6, emphasis added.

28. Whitehead, *Process and Reality*, p. 6.

mate logical principles is beset with difficulties, as yet insuperable'.[29] And 'the verification of a rationalistic scheme is to be sought in its general success, and not in the peculiar clarity, or initial clarity, of its first principles'.[30] And even more memorably: 'if we consider any scheme of philosophic categories as one complex assertion, and apply to it the logician's alternative, true or false, *the answer must be that the scheme is false*'.[31] And finally, 'the primary method of mathematics is deduction; the primary method of philosophy [by contrast] is descriptive generalization. Under the influence of mathematics, *deduction has been foisted upon philosophy as its standard method,* instead of taking its true place as an essential auxiliary mode of verification whereby to test the scope of generalities'.[32] I cite these words from Whitehead, a celebrated mathematician and one of the great philosophers of the last century, to raise initial concerns about Meillassoux's absolute split between lucid rationality on one side and rhetorical shadow on the other. This turns out to be more than a dispute over method, for it stems from a deeper metaphysical disagreement. For Whitehead, as for me, any statement of a philosophical argument is always an oversimplification not just of the world as a whole, but even of what the statement itself discusses. Rhetoric is not the devious art of non-rational persuasion, but the best tool we have for exposing the unstated assumptions that lie behind any surface proposition. The analytic contempt for rhetoric and metaphor must not be emulated—not just because this attitude leads to boring results, but because it is philosophically false.

Recall Meillassoux's complaint that the case against correlationism is often based on a frustrated appeal to a 'Rich Elsewhere' or an attack on the hidden motives of the correlationist rather than a genuine argument. Following Whitehead, my first objection is that this oversimplifies the workings of human reason. Consider the following possible statements that might be made against materialism:

A. 'Materialists, like all critical minds, are emotionally frustrated people. Their angry need to topple all traditional values in the name of a final substrate of physical atoms is a kind of needy protest at the world for letting them down. Indeed, a large number of materialists seem to come from broken homes, or to have other unresolved issues with their parents and siblings. Notice how aggressive they always are, just like the angriest children on the playground'.

B. 'The problem with materialism is that it reduces everything to purely *relational* properties such as hardness, resistance, and exact spatio-temporal coordinates. This means that materialism is not as realist

29. Whitehead, *Process and Reality*, p. 8, emphasis added.
30. Whitehead, *Process and Reality*, p. 8.
31. Whitehead, *Process and Reality*, p. 8, emphasis added.
32. Whitehead, *Process and Reality*, p. 10, emphasis added.

as it claims to be. It only gives us relations, while telling us nothing about *what* relates. Furthermore, materialism is purely arbitrary when it denies reality to intermediate macro-sized objects such as molecules, rocks, and animals and instead grants reality only to the mythical ultimate particles of sub-atomic physics—which even physics can never identify once and for all'.

Statement A is a good example of the sort of innuendo that Meillassoux would understandably reject. Statement B, by contrast, is what Meillassoux would call an 'argument'. Materialists would still call it a bad one, but it is clearly an argument formulated in the proper Meillassouxian spirit of rational disagreement. The difference between these two statements is obvious enough. Most people would agree that A is beyond the pale of acceptable philosophical discussion, but that B is a respectable argument even if it fails. But now consider an intermediate case of the following kind:

C. 'Too many materialists seem motivated by a predictable, pseudo-iconoclastic commitment to atheism and political leftism. Working from the false assumption that science makes progress through step-by-step critical debunking of gullible everyday belief, they try to annihilate all intermediate levels of meaning and accept only a final, physical substratum as a means of unmasking naive piety and bourgeois social structures. In other words, they are motivated more by off-the-shelf rationalist prejudice and their own inability to envisage more interesting alternatives than by any solid support from science itself'.

Here we have a more problematic case. Regardless of whether you find it convincing, is this a valid argument against materialism or mere psychologizing innuendo? The answer in my view is that Statement C is *neither* argument nor innuendo. Although Statement C surely fails to meet Meillassoux's threshold for counting as an argument, it still performs genuine cognitive labour. In the hours before someone hears Statement C for the first time, they may have a resigned sense that materialists hold the intellectual upper hand against their opponents, who are nothing but a gang of anti-scientific, dogmatic, pious reactionaries. 'Since I never want to be one of these horrible reactionary people', someone might silently assume, 'my only choice is to side with the materialists'. But Statement C hints at a different possibility. Statement C may not be an argument in the strict sense, but even Meillassoux might admit its effectiveness as 'powerful rhetoric' for a certain audience. And to repeat an earlier point, rhetoric does not mean 'irrational appeal to the emotions at the expense of reason, often by a deviously charismatic speaker or writer who favours style over substance'. As Whitehead observes, any explicit argument is always a vast oversimplification of whatever issue is at hand. One of the biases for which he criticizes analytic philosophy most severely is 'the trust in language as an adequate expression of

propositions'.[33] While argument merely plays with explicit dialectical figures, rhetoric pays attention to the unstated background assumptions of any
linguistic proposition. But such assumptions are part of our *cognitive* relation
to the world, not just our aesthetic or emotional one.

Let's return to Statement C, which apparently lies halfway between argument and ill-mannered insult. No one would claim that it gives a devastating refutation of materialism. Yet it still does important cognitive work—
not by destroying the materialist position, but by suggesting both the *need*
for new options and the *possibility* of new options. Previously the materialist
might have seemed like the only possible standard bearer for enlightened
reason against the hordes of obscurantist oppressors. But Statement C now
subtly warns us that the materialist may be guilty of: (a) overhasty zealotry,
(b) a destructive rush to eliminate all intermediate layers of the world in favour of some dogmatic substrate in a manner more reductive than the sciences themselves, and (c) a reflexive, nearly robotic distaste for religion and
current political forms. As Whitehead would surely agree, materialism (like
any philosophy) is never just an argument, but also comes fully equipped
with a rhetorical background and even an associated lifestyle. According to
its implicit grand narrative, materialists have scored repeated triumphs over
alchemists, astrologers, and spiritual obscurantists in the kingdom of nature,
while only irrational reactionary resistance has blocked the same progress
in political and intellectual matters. But Statement C offers a different picture, one in which materialism is zealous and hotheaded, motivated more
by what it wishes to destroy than what it is able to create. Even the open insult found in Statement A is not *entirely* lacking in cognitive value, since every
philosophical school tends to recruit and encourage certain human character types. Most of us avoid one or more intellectual groups simply because
we find them filled with generally repellent personalities (some of my friends
hate Heidegger for no better reason than this). But along with being rude
and uncivilized, Statement A also has the fatal flaw of being reversible: reduce materialism to the unresolved childhood anger of its adherents, and
ten materialists will respond with equally vicious speculations on your own
sordid motives for believing in Catholicism, liberal democracy, *élan vital*, reincarnation, Lamarckism, or whatever doctrine you might prefer to theirs.

Let's consider an analogous sort of rhetorical claim that I often make
myself. In past writings I have made statements running approximately
as follows:

D. 'Correlationists always confine philosophy to a human-centered ghetto,
    hoping in this way to build a privileged citadel immune to the blows of
    the natural sciences. Instead of this, we must take the fight to the sci-
    entists and build our own philosophical theory of inanimate relations'.

---

33. Whitehead, *Process and Reality*, p. xiii.

Is Statement D an 'argument' in Meillassoux's sense of the term? Not quite. But neither is it mere psychological innuendo. In other words, Statement D cannot be glossed as saying:

> D1. 'Correlationists are cowards who don't understand science, and that's why they lead philosophy into a narrowly human arena where they hope that scientists cannot enter. They are afraid to face reality. Many of them are probably not very skilled at mathematics, and this is why they fled into the humanities'.

Yes, some cognitive scientists might accept Statement D1 as the literal truth. But this is obviously never the meaning of Statement D when found in my own writings. Instead, the context always makes clear that I mean as follows:

> D2. 'Given the great prestige and success of the natural sciences, people are quick to assume that science already does philosophical justice to the *non*-human world. That is why philosophy since Kant clings too closely to the *human* world, under the false assumption that no philosophical work remains to be done on the inanimate side. But if correlationists realized how problematic inanimate causal relations truly are, they might be less satisfied with remaining trapped in the correlational circle. And this is precisely what I aim to show'.

In Meillassoux's sense D2 is not yet an 'argument', but would count at best as a 'powerful rhetoric'. Yet *qua* rhetoric it does ample cognitive work by exposing a key correlationist background assumption: namely, 'given that science is already wiping the table clean in the inanimate realm, the mission of philosophers is to work solely within the sphere of human access'. And I have found that merely *raising* the opposite possibility often has a profound philosophical effect on listeners, opening countless new doors and windows. The stale assumption that science monopolizes the inhuman sphere and hence philosophy must try to dominate the human-world correlate is far more universally crippling than any 'bad argument' of which I am aware.

In this respect, rhetoric is at least as potent a philosophical tool as explicit dialectic—the former unearths hidden presuppositions even as the latter tries to balance accounts on the level of explicit statement. Meillassoux himself often resorts to a similar 'good' rhetoric, as any effective thinker must. When the traditional realist opposes the correlationist by trying to posit a *non*-posited X, Meillassoux rhetorically compares him to Captain Haddock in the Tintin comics,[34] who angrily shifts a bandage from one finger to the other, frustrated that the bandage never leaves—just as the correlationist predicament supposedly never leaves us no matter how hard we try to escape it. After reading this point about Captain Haddock, someone might shout at Meillassoux: 'Haha! Hypocrisy! Now you're saying that the

---

34. Brassier, et. al., 'Speculative Realism', p. 421.

typical realist acts based on frustration and annoyance! You're psychologizing him! And that's just what you accused Laruelle, Nietzsche, Marx, and Freud of doing! Haha! You hypocrite!' But this response would miss the point. Meillassoux's reference to Captain Haddock's bandage was never meant as an 'argument'. Instead, it was meant as a powerful rhetorical appeal along the following lines:

E. 'The correlationist argument is that every X is a posited X—that if we try to think an object outside our thinking, we are still *thinking* it as outside our thinking. There is no escape from this circle… This is a powerful point that we must accept… What did you say, Mr. Latour? Please speak up… Yes, I realize that my point sounds so frustrating and tedious, especially since it often works to derail the most brilliant and fascinating philosophical arguments. Nonetheless, it is a rational argument, and we have no choice but to accept it. I understand and agree with your frustration, but please don't give in too quickly and fly away from reason. Bear with me here… We must work against correlationism by radicalizing it *from within*, into a form of absolute knowing. And if you follow me in trying this method, not only can we remain more rational than most realists are, but the results will be much more interesting and original than you expect. I have started to work this out in my book *After Finitude*. Have a look and see what you think. It's just a small sample of what I think is possible to do when we work patiently from within the correlationist assumption. And I think you'll find that it's an interesting book, not frustrating or tedious at all'.

While Meillassoux's 'argument' is clearly visible in this passage, it contains much more than an argument. It is really an interesting attempt to address the underlying assumptions and world-picture of his traditional realist opponents. Meillassoux reaches out in friendly acknowledgment, conceding that correlationism might sound like a tedious dead end. But he also insists with his usual mixture of personal warmth and steely resolve that there is no way around the correlationist argument. In closing he promises a form of compensation for our loss: we can eventually still arrive at a sort of realism *even though* we accept the rigorous and devastating objection of the correlationist. Just as Statement C accused the materialist of a failure of imagination, Meillassoux makes the same accusation against the Rich Elsewhere Realist.

And this is why I reject the suggestion of Meillassoux and many analytic thinkers that philosophy plays out primarily at the level of explicit, deductive argument from clear first principles. With Whitehead I hold that 'logical contradictions […] are the most gratuitous of errors; and usually they are trivial. [And that] after criticism, systems do not exhibit mere illogicalities. They suffer from inadequacy and incoherence'.[35] For the same reason Meillassoux is wrong to see so little of value in the 'Rich Elsewhere' objection. In fact, I think it is powerful evidence against a philosophy if it cannot do justice to the evident richness of the world. When Parmenides says 'being is, and non-being is not', this is refuted less by argument than by a glaring sense of its inadequacy to our experience of reality. In short, Parmenides is abandoned rather than refuted. And here again I quote Whitehead, who says that '[the] ideal of speculative philosophy has its rational side and its empirical side. The rational side is expressed by the terms "coherent" and "logical." The empirical side is expressed by the terms "applicable" and "adequate"'.[36]

Neither Meillassoux nor anyone else in philosophy simply follows a remorseless chain of deductions without stepping back from time to time and looking at whether these deductions describe the world accurately. Mathematics may proceed in this way, but I agree with Whitehead that philosophy cannot. And as for the natural sciences, not only do they not proceed through sheer logical deduction—they do not even acknowledge contradiction as their major principle of discovery. Although one falsifying instance is enough to decimate a mathematical proof, the same is not true (contra Popper) of the sciences. As Thomas Kuhn has observed, no scientific theory ever manages to overcome all falsifying evidence. Newton's theory of gravity was retained for a long time despite the anomalies in Mercury's orbit. Relativity and quantum theory are still mutually incompatible in the year 2009, yet no one is prepared to get rid of either—in this way they are already refuted but *not* already abandoned. In our time string theory remains institutionally dominant in particle physics despite its total lack of experimental evidence, solely because of its other virtues: mathematical elegance, the ability to unify gravity with quantum phenomena, and (so say its critics) the fact that people have invested so many years in strings that they are afraid to admit that the model is failing. Read the literature on contemporary physics, and along with numerous explicit arguments and pieces of empirical evidence, you will find numerous statements that are perfectly scientific despite amounting to nothing more than a hunch: 'something just doesn't feel quite right about the intellectual culture of the string community'; 'I have a vague feeling that we will eventually need to drop the Einstein-Minkowski model of four-dimensional space-time', and so forth. Consider the famous scientific 'paradigms' studied by Thomas Kuhn. Kuhn is often read as saying that these paradigms take power through mass social prejudice and replace one another at a level impermeable to reason. But this is incorrect. What paradigms really are is *objects*—scientific objects that guide

---

35. Whitehead, *Process and Reality*, p. 6.
36. Whitehead, *Process and Reality*, p. 3.

research for a time, not only *despite* the fact that we can never pin down their exact qualities, but precisely *because* of this. Rhetoric has as much power as argument in establishing new paradigms in both science and philosophy. This is not because 'people are not always rational and you sometimes have to appeal to their emotions to make them see the light'. Instead, it is due to Whitehead's point about the inability of arguments, propositions, explicit evidence, or tangible qualities to do full justice to the world. As Marshall McLuhan might say, to claim that a philosophy is built solely of arguments is like saying that a radio show is nothing more than the words that are said, with the background medium making no difference to the content.[37] To say that a philosophy is made of arguments is like saying that an apple is nothing but a bundle of qualities—that there is nothing more to the apple than the sum of its explicit traits.

Against this 'bundle of qualities' theory, I have said that we must uphold *objects*. And against the idea of philosophies as 'arguments', we must defend a model of philosophy as object-oriented. Analytic philosophy has given us more 'knockdown arguments' than the human race has ever known, yet it is not clear that we have achieved a Golden Age of philosophy in return. It is for this very reason that I uphold hyperbolic readings of philosophers against critical ones, since critique assumes that the major problem with any piece of writing are the logical errors it contains. By contrast, to hyperbolically imagine the complete victory of any philosophy is to simulate a social environment in which it is widely held to be *free* of logical blunders, and hence this method allows us to focus on what Whitehead calls the 'coherence and adequacy' of that philosophy. All of these points are closely linked. All rely on the fact that there is something more to the world over and above what can be explicitly stated about it. This does not require a 'non-*cognitive*' access to the world, as Meillassoux and Brassier[38] understandably fear,[39] but simply a non-*qualitative* access to the world. There is nothing especially mystical about such a view, since it can already be found in Saul Kripke's (1996) theory of names—which he views as 'rigid designators' that point to realities without being able to spell them out adequately in terms of definite descriptions.[40]

---

37. See any of McLuhan's books for important insights into the relative poverty of dialectical figures and arguments in comparison with their tacit ground or medium. The most theoretically persuasive may be Marshall McLuhan and Eric, *Laws of Media: The New Science*, Toronto, University of Toronto Press, 1988.

38. Ray Brassier, *Nihil Unbound: Enlightenment and Extinction*, London Palgrave, 2007, p. 28.

39. Brassier worries about the attempt by Heideggerians 'to deploy the figurative dimension of language in order to sound sub-experiential depths'. For Brassier the proper alternative to such poetry is to be found in 'investigating the sub-symbolic reality of phenomenal consciousness [by] using the formal and mathematical resources available to the third-person perspective' see Ray Brassier, *Nihil Unbound*, p. 29.

40. The famous dispute over whether Ruth Barkan Marcus developed the theory first

In short, the Rich Elsewhere is a fruitful rhetorical appeal, and I hold much more strongly than Meillassoux himself that a 'good rhetoric' is the key to philosophy. For rhetoric deals with veiled background assumptions rather than explicit dialectical figures—and if philosophy does not expose background assumptions and play counterpoint against them, then I do not know what philosophy is for. Plato, Spinoza, and Leibniz do not make fewer logical blunders than the average university professor, but are simply much vaster in adequacy, coherence, originality, relevance, and insight. This answers Jerry Fodor's puzzled question as to why lay readers have more interest in 'Kierkegaard [...] Heidegger [...] Kant, Hegel, and the pre-Socratics' than in mainstream analytic philosophy, even if we grant his point that 'anyhow, our arguments are better' (Fodor 2004). But I will not even playfully grant Fodor's bizarre additional claim that 'most of us write better than most of them', a ridiculous statement devoted to the fallacy that good writing means making as many explicit, univocal statements as possible while hinting at nothing more. In fact there are stunningly *few* good writers among the analytics, despite innumerable clear ones. Clarity is not yet vividness. An exact wax duplicate of Gandhi cannot free India of the Empire.

It is powerful evidence against correlationism that it arbitrarily treats the human/world relation as philosophically more important than any object/object relation. This may not be a 'knockdown argument', but it is certainly a strong warning sign. Meillassoux seems well aware that tedium is not a philosophical virtue, since he avoids it so skillfully in his own books. He does not endlessly repeat that 'X is always *posited* as X', but moves on to more abundant riches than I ever thought possible for anyone operating from his starting point. Speaking only for myself, I am drawn to Meillassoux's writings not so much through the deductive onslaught of his reasoning (which I find impressive but not decisive). Instead, his refreshingly strange *results* are what captivate me: his claims about the necessary contingency of the laws of nature, his shocking inferences about God, his magnificent speculations as to the nature of death or an ethics of regret. Meillassoux is not 'more logical' than Quine or Davidson, he is simply much more interesting. Indeed, the riches of Meillassoux's writings are so remarkable that one might suspect him of his own rhetorical commitment: a rejection of the Rich Elsewhere in favour of a converse doctrine of the Rich Homeland: 'Do not try to escape. Out there is merely grey matter subject to cold calculation. But just think of

---

is little more than a domestic controversy among analytic philosophers, since Husserl and even Aristotle already saw that names point to things deeper than their palpable attributes. What makes Kripke such a remarkable figure is that he was able to introduce this doctrine in an intellectual culture—analytic philosophy of language—that was so heavily devoted to the empiricist/positivist prejudice that things are reducible to bundles of attributes. And it was Kripke, not Marcus, who had this shocking cultural effect among the analytics.

all the luscious forms of logic and history that Hegel was able to spin out of the human-world correlate'. Meillassoux's own taste for richness is such that he might well abandon the circle of correlation if it had not been getting him anywhere. In any case, I hope he would agree that rhetorical appeal to richness does not belong in the same basket of 'irrational arguments' with wild claims about our opponent's frustrated libido.

This detour into rhetoric has been long, but it feeds directly into my own rejection of the correlationist standpoint. Yet we still need to answer the 'argument' part of Meillassoux's position, lest it seem that we have nothing to offer but poetic appeals to richness. Perhaps the biggest problem with Meillassoux's Goldsmiths lecture lies in its tacit assertion that no one has even *tried* to offer a rational refutation of the correlationist/idealist position—as if Fichte's 'X is posited as non-posited' had been met for the past two centuries only with mass innuendo and irrational appeals to the greater fertility of other theories. Meillassoux never makes this accusation openly, and surely he knows better. But nowhere does his article mention any of the realist counter-arguments to the human/world correlate. Nor are such arguments are hard to find. A simple Google search for 'refutation idealism' provides dozens of leads: Moore, Kant, Peirce, Candrakiirti, and Wittgenstein appear on the first search page alone. But Meillassoux proceeds in his Goldsmiths talk as though correlationism clearly occupied the high ground, so that the burden is on its opponents to charge up the hill and take volleys of arrows in return. Now, it is true that the human-world correlate is dominant in the Franco-German continental tradition where Meillassoux and I both do business. But this is much less the case among analytic philosophers. In fact, many analytic thinkers follow the late Australian David Stove (1991) in calling the correlationist argument 'the worst argument in the world' (Stove organized an actual *competition* before giving it first prize). This suggests that correlationists are in no position to play defense, like a basketball team icing a late forty-point lead. It still remains to show the fallacy at the heart of the correlationist argument. Rather than pursuing the objections made by analytic thinkers, I will oppose correlationism using the very thinker who unwittingly brought me to the realist party: Martin Heidegger.

The best way to show why I do not find the correlationist argument compelling is to speak of Husserl and Heidegger, and of Meillassoux's treatment of these two figures. Husserl and Heidegger might seem like a strange pair of thinkers to help us escape from the correlational circle—after all, Meillassoux is correct to say that both are correlationists. For Husserl this is obvious enough, since he 'brackets' any notion of an extraphenomenal world, insisting that we focus only on what appears to human consciousness. Although Husserl repeatedly denies that he is speaking of a merely immanent reality, this is only because he wants to distance himself from philosophical psychology in the style of Brentano. The ideal realm of meaning for Husserl is not something contained inside a human mind as opposed to a world outside that mind, but is equal to the *whole* of reality. Husserl repeatedly calls for a return to the things themselves, but these are in no way Kant's noumenal things-in-themselves lying beyond all possible human access—a nonsensical notion for Husserl. The city of Berlin present in consciousness is the same as the city of Berlin itself. In principle we *can* have an intuition of the essence of any object; they do not lie in some transcendent realm beyond consciousness, but are embedded within it.

Our first question is whether the same is true of Heidegger. Meillassoux's case that Heidegger is a correlationist runs as follows:

> for Heidegger, it is certainly a case of pinpointing the occlusion of being or presence inherent in every metaphysical conception of representation and the privileging of the present-at-hand entity considered as object. *Yet on the other hand*, to think such an occlusion at the heart of the unconcealment of the entity requires, for Heidegger, that one take into account the co-propriation of man and being, which he calls Ereignis [... which] means that neither being nor man can be posited as subsisting 'in-themselves' [... since] both terms of the appropriation are originarily constituted through their reciprocal relation.[41]

In this way, Heidegger apparently remains faithful to the correlationist injunction that runs from Kant to Husserl. But in the passage above I have emphasized the phrase 'yet on the other hand' because it signals a point where Meillassoux shifts gears. In the first part of the passage he concedes that Heidegger is a philosopher of occlusion, veiling, hiddenness, and withdrawal from all presence to humans (which would be a difficult thing to say about Husserl). But in the second part of the passage Meillassoux implies that this veiling is then swallowed up by Heidegger's Sein/Dasein correlate anyway. But this is untrue. The problem is that Meillassoux's wonderful term 'correlationism' (which deserves to be a permanent part of our philosophical lexicon) makes a subtle *twofold* claim. In its major sense correlationism means that neither human nor world can exist without the other. This is definitely true of Heidegger, for whom *Sein* (being) and *Dasein* (human being) always come as a pair. Indeed, it is true to such an extent that Heidegger famously claims that Newton's laws would be neither true nor untrue if humans did not exist.

Nonetheless, it is quite a different claim if we say that the two terms being and Dasein are *mutually exhausted* by their interrelation. Consider the case of two lovers so attached to each other that they are never found apart and would literally die if separated. This obviously does not entail that the lovers are fully constituted by their mutual interactions. *Au contraire.* For these lovers can never fully grasp each other to the ultimate depths, even if they

---

41. Quentin Meillassoux, *After Finitude*, trans. Ray Brassier, London, Continuum, 2008, p. 8, emphasis modified.

are never apart for one second during the rest of their lives. In Heidegger's hands, being and human being are a love story of this kind. Attempts are often made to say that for Heidegger being is nothing more than its series of manifestations to Dasein with nothing hiding behind the series. Being would then become an 'emergent process' circumscribed within the human/world correlate instead of something altogether deeper than the correlate. Yet Heidegger's own writings offer little support for such an interpretation, which merely stems from the pervasive correlationist fashion in the continental philosophy of our time. It is simply *assumed* that any belief in non-phenomenal reality is so glaringly naïve that a thinker as ingenious as Heidegger could not have held such a stupid view.

In short, if we call Heidegger a correlationist in the same sense that Husserl is a correlationist, the important difference between them is lost. There is a good reason that Heidegger talks so much about occlusion, veiling, and withdrawing though these terms play no role whatsoever in such figures as Fichte, Hegel, and Husserl. There is also a good reason why Heidegger thinks that both Hegel and Husserl are equally guilty of reducing being to its presence-at-hand configurations, and why he turns our attention to the veiling of being instead. Meillassoux tries to account for this passion by briefly adding 'the cloistered outside'[42] to a list of views supposedly shared by all correlationists. But it is difficult to find any uniform notion of a cloistered outside that can be applied simultaneously to Heidegger, Husserl, Hegel, Fichte, and Kant. In fact the cloistered outside plays vastly different roles in all these figures: denied altogether by Fichte, Hegel, and Husserl, probably accepted by Kant (noumena) and absolutely accepted by Heidegger (withdrawn being, sheltering earth, and gods that hint without appearing). To jump from Heidegger's obvious acceptance of a permanent human/world correlate to his supposed but nonexistent view that there is nothing mysterious to being outside its manifestation to humans is to present a Hegelized version of Heidegger, or to melt Heidegger and Husserl together into one.[43]

We should not forget that Heidegger repeatedly claims to be doing something more innovative than Husserl. For Meillassoux to say that both are correlationists in the same way carries the implication that Heidegger is wrong to think himself radical, and that he remains instead within the same human-world correlate as Husserl despite his attempt to do otherwise. This is a problematic consequence of Meillassoux's reading of Heidegger. In fact, Heidegger belongs to a species of thinker that he seems to regard as impossible: a *correlationist realist*. With this phrase I do not mean Meillassoux's own

---

42. Meillassoux, *After Finitude*, p. 8.

43. A similar problem can be found in the idealist reading of Heidegger by Lee Braver in his outstanding encyclopedic work *A Thing of This World: A History of Continental Anti-Realism*, Evanston, Northwestern University Press, 2007.

project of establishing realism *by way of* correlationism, but an actual simultaneous belief in correlationism and realism. That is to say, Heidegger holds
that human and world must always come as a package, but he also holds
that being is not fully manifest to humans. And though I cannot endorse this
monstrous hybrid doctrine, there is no doubt that Heidegger upholds it.

In order to see the genuine difference between Husserl and Heidegger,
we turn to the famous example of a hammer. For Husserl the hammer is a
so-called 'intentional object'. It does not exist in some independent world
forever hidden from human view; there is no noumenal hammer-in-itself.
Instead, the hammer exists only as a correlate of consciousness—which for
Husserl can mean the consciousness of humans, animals, or extraterrestri-
al creatures. We never see all faces of the hammer at once, but always see it
from a certain angle and distance, in a certain colour and intensity of light,
and always in a specific mood. In this sense the hammer only appears in
the form of specific profiles or adumbrations (*Abschattungen* in German). For
Husserl the object 'hammer' is not made up of the full series of appearances
of the hammer, but is an ideal *unity* over and above these appearances and
even above all *possible* appearances. In principle this unity or essence of the
hammer can be grasped through eidetic intuition in a fully evident way, even
though we only approach this ideal by degrees and never quite reach it.

Now, Husserl is often said to believe that humans can only perceive adumbrations, so that the hammer itself never appears. Although this view
is quite understandable (I thought so myself until the fall of 2004), it is er-
roneous. For it does not matter that we can never see the whole series of
hammer-adumbrations—*this series is not the hammer.* For Husserl, the hammer is the ideal unity that makes each profile a profile of the *same* hammer;
the hammer is not a series of appearances of any sort. Hence, our inability to run through the infinite series of possible hammer-appearances de-
prives us of nothing as concerns the object. Nothing is 'hidden' behind the
adumbrations for Husserl; the hammer itself lies *within* each adumbration,
as an eidos encrusted with accidents. In other words, for Husserl the eidos
of an intentional object is already with us from the very moment we intend
it, and is not hidden or veiled in the manner of Heidegger's tools. To think,
wish, or imagine that we have a chair before us means that the eidos of the
chair is already present to us. We do not get this eidos by running quickly
through a permanently absent infinite set of chair-profiles, but by clearing
away the inessential debris that always accompanies our intention of the
chair. It is a kind of *subtractive* process, since the essential chair is encrusted
at every moment with inessential surface fluctuations that eidetic analysis
must try to strip away.

Clearly, Heidegger views the situation differently. The whole of
Heidegger's philosophy is designed as a critique of 'presence-at-hand'. Among
other things, this means that the being of any object is always deeper than

how that object appears to us. In the eyes of Heidegger, Husserl's phenomena are merely present-at-hand in consciousness, exhausted by their appearance to us. Yet Heidegger holds that the hammer cannot be reduced to a set of visible features—not even essential ones—because these features are not what do the work of hammering in the world. The hammer as a Husserlian intentional object is always already present as soon as we acknowledge it, and is merely encrusted with non-essential features. By contrast, the hammer for Heidegger is a real entity that invisibly does its work in the cosmos. It is withdrawn or veiled from view and tends to be noticed only when it breaks. To use Meillassouxian terminology, Husserl would agree that the hammer is always a 'posited' hammer or hammer thought by us, since it has being only as a correlate of thinking. But for Heidegger this is not the case, since the 'posited' hammer that I think about is only the hammer suspended and chloroformed, reduced to presence-at-hand, which is not the same as the hammer at work in its subterranean tool-being.

In Meillassoux's eyes it must look as though Heidegger is merely enacting the Laruellian brand of *coup de force* by impossibly trying to posit the hammer as non-posited. Conversely, Heidegger would accuse Meillassoux of forgetting the question of being. After all, by insisting that whatever we talk or think about is automatically a thing talked about or thought about, Meillassoux holds that we cannot escape from what Heidegger calls *Vorhandeheit*, or presence-at-hand. This situation is essentially the same as in Heidegger's intermittent dispute with Hegel. And these are very much the two traditions in play here, since Hegel is ultimately Meillassoux's philosophical hero just as Heidegger is my own. Those who are convinced by Hegel's approach will tend to be sympathetic to Meillassoux; those who believe that Heidegger struck a death-blow against Hegel's version of being are likely to give a sympathetic hearing to the object-oriented position of this book.

Now, Meillassoux's Fichtean point at Goldsmiths can also be restated in Heideggerian terms. Heidegger wants to speak of the tool's readiness-to-hand completely apart from its presence to human Dasein. But precisely because we speak of it, the tool is really nothing but present-at-hand: to *say* that the tool withdraws from all access means that the tool is *said* to withdraw from all access. Therefore any attempt to establish a hidden *Zuhandenheit* must always revert into a present *Vorhandenheit*. Veiling is impossible, because when we speak of something veiled our speaking already unveils it. This amounts to a tacit rejection of Heidegger's entire philosophical enterprise, and is also a variant of what David Stove calls the 'worst argument in the world' (widely known in analytic circles as 'Stove's Gem').

Let's accept Meillassoux's broad use of the term 'thinking' in the Descartes/Husserl sense to refer to all forms of mental act, to include seeing, wishing, hating, expecting, and so forth. This having been done, the correlationist critique of Heidegger will then run roughly as follows:[44]

1. I cannot think of the hammer's being without thinking it. In other words, thinking of the hammer is a necessary condition for thinking it.

This is sheer tautology, of course, and no one will deny it. The problem comes with the next step.

2. Therefore, the hammer is no more than the being-thought of the hammer.

But this second step is much more than a tautology, and requires an additional unspoken premise: namely, that there is no hammer without its being thought. As Brassier summarizes the Gem: 'from the fact that [the hammer's being thought] is a necessary condition for my relation to [it,] I spuriously infer that it is a necessary condition for [the hammer] *tout court*'.[45]

In fact this argument was already refuted in Part One when rejecting Latour's fleeting correlationist claim about Pasteur and the microbes in *Pandora's Hope*. As the reader will recall, Latour concludes that 'after 1864' microbes had existed all along; they were given a retroactive reality only by Pasteur's discovery of them. The main problem with this argument, I suggested, comes from its asymmetry. Latour's initial point is that Pasteur and the microbes co-articulate each other: Pasteur would not have been famous without the microbes, while the microbes might be seen differently if another discoverer or a non-French medical tradition had chosen to emphasize different aspects of them. This is both interesting and somewhat debatable (though I fully accept it), but it is largely harmless in its metaphysical suppositions. Yet from this symmetrical starting point, Latour draws a strange asymmetrical conclusion. For on Pasteur's side of the relation, Latour holds that Pasteur was merely modified, perturbed, and transformed by his encounter with microbes. But on the microbe's side of the relation, he holds that the microbes were first *created* in 1864, as if *ex nihilo*. There is a slight additional complication to the picture, of course, since Latour's strict relationism does not really allow that Pasteur in 1845 and Pasteur in 1864 are quite the same person. But he at least allows that there was someone in 1845 who was fairly similar to the 1864 Pasteur, while he makes no allowance at all for a microbe-like object in 1845 that fermented and infected various entities without humans knowing about it. We begin with a two-way correlate and end with a one-way tyranny. We were promised that Pasteur and the microbe co-define each other, and end up ascribing godlike powers to Pasteur and mere nullity to the microbes.

---

44. I am indebted to Ray Brassier for stating the problem in this particular fashion, and for calling my attention to the efforts by Stove and other analytic philosophers to address it.

45. Ray Brassier, Personal Communiction, electronic mail to Graham Harman of 12 August, 2008.

But there is an even more vivid way to shed light on the problems with this argument. Namely, we can *reverse* the final asymmetry and see what happens. Imagine that Bruno Latour has a proverbial 'evil twin'. The obscure Professor Benno Latour—for so we shall call him—remained in Dijon as his brother achieved fame and fortune in Paris, and in his seething resentment Benno devoted himself to an especially perverse upheaval of his brother Bruno's work. In response to Bruno's chapter on Pasteur and the microbe, Benno Latour maintains precisely the opposite doctrine. For Benno it is the inanimate physical universe that must always have priority, since everything else arises from it. Namely, for Benno there can be no question that microbes have always existed, or at least have existed since their emergence on our hot planet billions of years ago. By contrast, humans are fragile, ephemeral, and not of especial importance. Microbes have existed all along—but only when Pasteur discovered them did *he* begin to exist. Only after 1864 did *Pasteur* exist all along! But not the microbes, whose existence all along is beyond all dispute.

A similar reversal can be used to plague the Fichtean argument about 'positing X as non-posited'. For we can imagine another evil twin named 'Anton Meillassoux', Benno Latour's star student in Dijon. In the same manner as just described, Anton holds that his more famous brother Quentin has it backwards. He accepts the human-world correlate but reverses the basic asymmetry. Instead of saying that a hammer exists only when it is *posited* as a hammer, he holds that hammers always exist, while the human who views it is *posited* as a human for the first time only by his thinking of the hammer. Almost everyone will denounce the views of Benno and Anton as absurd, yet the deductive force of their arguments is every bit as strong as those of their brothers. We call these inverted arguments perverse only because it seems so impossibly counterintuitive that Pasteur and a hammering carpenter could be summoned *ex nihilo* by the inanimate entities they confront. By contrast, four centuries of Western idealism have trained us to see the reverse doctrine as not so very strange—namely, that microbes and hammers exist only as correlates *of us*.

The problem is the same in both cases. We begin with a basic symmetry between human and world. From this symmetry, in which the hammer and the human exist only as part of a human-world correlate, we strangely deduce an *asymmetry* in which one half of the correlate is allowed to dominate the other. This becomes clear only when we see how bizarre the reverse domination would be. And notice that the reason we find these inversions absurd is *not* because their logical argumentation is worse than the originals, but only because we have an everyday intuitive sense of ourselves as individuals enduring through time, while we lack such immediate access to the careers of microbes and hammers.

But I have found that even those who accept this argument against correlationism often retreat to a weaker version of the doctrine. Though they will no longer claim that it makes *no sense* to speak of things-in-themselves apart from human access, they will still say that *we have nothing to say* about things insofar as they exceed our access them. Here is another example of the 'Rich Homeland' rhetoric that so many use against realism: 'Go ahead and speak abstractly about noumenal things-in-themselves. But you bore me, because it is impossible to say anything about them'. Even if things-in-themselves exist, they are completely uninteresting. This is a far less interesting and rigorous attitude than Meillassoux's radical stance, and unfortunately it is far more common. Worst of all, it is hopelessly false. An example of why it is false comes from physics, which offers numerous theories about the wildly popular object known as a black hole. No entity in the physical universe makes a better analogy with Heidegger's inaccessible tool-beings than the black hole. Its gravity is so strong that no information can escape; hence, we never see the black hole or have direct access to anything about it. Does this make the black hole 'boring' to physicists, or 'not worth talking about'? Hardly! The fact that we cannot encounter the black hole directly does not mean that we cannot speak about it.

Numerous properties of black holes can be inferred, despite our inability to receive direct information from them. If you ask an astrophysicist about these objects, you will not receive a bored shrug and a response of: 'Who cares? We can't know anything about them, so there's no point raising the subject. Astronomy should confine itself to those objects to which we have direct access'. Instead, you will be informed that a black hole has various effects on surrounding matter, that quantum theory has certain problems accounting for black holes, and that they apparently leak a certain amount of energy over time in the so-called 'Hawking radiation'. Numerous other deductions and speculations have been made about these 'uninteresting' black holes, which may actually be the most interesting objects in the entire universe. Their surface area seems to be more relevant than their volume, leading some theorists to suggest that they are holograms rather than solid objects. Certain deductions can even be made about what will happen to any object that falls into a black hole. Lee Smolin has theorized, and not without reasons, that each black hole might contain a universe of its own.

Granted, someone might object that the black hole is known only through its effects on surrounding entities, and that it can only be interesting because these effects are visible to us. To this I have two responses: (1) Withdrawn objects in metaphysics, such as Heidegger's tool-beings, also have effects on other objects. Hence, if this is enough to make veiled objects interesting to you, then you have already conceded my point that a philosophy of objects is not boring. (2) Even if the effects of the black hole or the object may be what alerts us to their existence, these objects are not *identical* with their sum total of effects. For we can discover new features of the black hole at any time, and this does not mean that the black hole is no longer a black hole. Our picture of astrophysics would be hopelessly incomplete if there were a pious Wittgensteinian ban requiring us to 'pass over in silence' the inaccessible interior of black holes. In similar fashion, metaphysics reaches a ruinous state if it forbids all discussion of reality subtracted from all relations.

But to return in closing to the main point, it is Heidegger's tool-analysis that convinces me that the correlationist standpoint is wrong. If I say that the hammer in its tool-being is that which exists in concealed subterranean form without being reducible to its presence to us, the correlationist will respond that I am now *talking about* this subterranean tool-being and thereby converting it into a form of presence. But this is to confuse words or thoughts about tool-beings with those beings themselves. The fact that we can allude to concealed hammers by way of language or thought does not entail that the hammers are exhausted by such allusion. Thus the correlationist standpoint fails for the same reasons as the relationist standpoint, but even more quickly, since it is a basically weaker position than relationism.

Another way of describing the correlationist standpoint is to call it a 'radical' philosophy that claims an entity is nothing more than its determinate manner of givenness to thought. But this is false for both Husserlian and Heidegger reasons. For on the one hand Husserl's hammer is always *less* than what it seems—a minimalistic core of eidetic features that can support all possible varieties of surface variation. And on the other hand Heidegger's hammer is always *more* than what it seems—a rumbling underground reality that can never become present without distortion. If we hint at the concealed hammer, the hinting is certainly something present to thought, but the concealed hammer at which we hint is not. Everyone knows the old Chinese proverb about the finger pointing at the moon and the fool looking at the finger. But correlationism is even worse, since it claims that the moon is made of fingers. This is not just folly, but a form of madness.

Objects are Irreducible to their Effects on Other Objects

We have seen that Latour rejects the lump universe, the virtual universe of pre-individuals, and the reduced universe made solely of material particles. The next weaker version of relationism is *correlationism*, in which human and world are the sole realities and are mutually determined by their permanent rapport. Meillassoux agrees with me that Latour is not a correlationist, though we disagree as to whether this avoidance of the correlate counts as a vice or a virtue. But there is still a final stage of relational philosophy that Latour continues to uphold, and it can be given the generic name 'relationism'. For Latour an actor is never anything more than what it 'modifies, transforms, perturbs, or creates'. And it is clear that we must oppose even this weakest form of relationism.

The non-correlationist Latour is refreshing in many of the same ways as Whitehead, since both explode the basic dogma of Kant's Copernican Revolution. Kant held that behind the phenomenal appearances are the unknowable things-in-themselves. Too much attention has been paid to this side of Kant, with endless arguments over whether it makes sense to posit such noumena, and whether Kant himself actually believed in them. But these are merely side issues. The greater defect of the Copernican philosophy is that even if we accept the existence of things-in-themselves, still does not give us much of a realism. For the only function of things-in-themselves in Kant's philosophy is to haunt human knowledge as a sort of ghoulish residue. The major defect is that no discussion is possible about how things-in-themselves relate *to each other.* The tree-in-itself, if it were even granted to exist, would be left with no other function than to differ from the phenomenal tree, just as shadows have no reality apart from their more tangible doubles. Nothing is said about the relation between tree-in-itself and fire-in-itself, since for Kant this is something we can never talk about. If a fire burns a tree, chemists and foresters can talk about how this happens, not philosophers. But notice that the sciences can only do this for natural physical objects. It took Whitehead and Latour to put the relations between *all* types and sizes of objects on the same footing, so that the relation of fictional characters such as Bilbo and Smaug must be treated in the same way as those of fire and cotton or human and world. Whereas the correlationist is obsessed with the single human-world correlate, relationism gives us trillions of different correlates between all the things that exist: trees, flames, dogs, chewing gum, violins, unicorns, diamonds, numbers, incense, and moons. This already makes a refreshing break with Kant's Copernican Revolution and its various correlationist heirs.

Nonetheless, relationism still suffers from the same basic problem as correlationism. It vastly broadens the scope of correlationist philosophy by allowing any two entities to relate without a human witness. Yet it never frees actors from *every* witness; indeed, it allows objects to exist only insofar as they have an effect on other objects. Earlier I suggested that there are two basic problems with the relationist thesis that a thing is nothing more than its effects: namely, it does an injustice to the present and future of the object in question. Take the example of a great philosophical work—say, Heidegger's *Being and Time.* The relationist would say that this book is no more than what it 'modifies, transforms, perturbs, or creates'. At this very moment, *Being and Time* is modifying, transforming, perturbing, and creating a certain number of objects, mostly human ones. But is this really the whole of its reality? We can easily perform the thought-experiment of imagining other interpreters coming onto the scene. What they would be interpreting in this case is *Being and Time* itself, not the sum total of other interpretations. In other words, an actor *is not* identical with whatever it modifies, transforms, perturbs, or creates, but always remains *underdetermined* by those effects. The effects cannot occur without the object, but the object might well exist without those effects, and perhaps even without *any* effects.

Second, we have reviewed and accepted Aristotle's critique of the Megarians: if a thing is entirely relational, then there would be no reason for it to change. The thing would be fully deployed or exhausted in its reality here and now, and the same would be true of all of the things with which it relates. Why, then, would the universe ever change? But while Aristotle uses this argument to establish the need for potentiality along with actuality, I read it instead as establishing a reality beyond all relationality. A thing can be actual without being registered by other things, or at least without being registered fully by them. Latour and Aristotle strangely agree in placing actual and relational together on one side, and potential and non-relational on the other, with the sole disagreement that Latour grants no existence at all to the second pair. But the pairing is false from the outset. The potential can only mean a potential *for future relations*, and the actual can only mean what is in and of itself actual *apart from any relations*. Unless the thing holds something in reserve behind its current relations, nothing would ever change. This secret reservoir cannot be the 'potential', because the potential needs to be inscribed somewhere actual right now, and if the actual is entirely determined by its relations then this gets us nowhere. And the reserve also cannot be called the 'virtual', since this term merely plays the double game of saying that true reality in the universe is both connected and separate, both continuous and heterogeneous. The only thing that will fit the bill is a *non-relational actuality*: objects that exist quite apart from their relation to other objects, and even apart from their relation to their own pieces.

Conclusion

In this section I have tried to save objects from four of the 'radical' attempts to deny their existence. First, objects are different from any supposed primordial world-lump, and hence they are not derivative of a primal whole. Second, objects are irreducible to their pieces and have a genuine emergent reality, which entails that materialist reduction will not work for metaphysics, and that it is of limited use even in the sciences. Third, objects are irreducible to their appearance in human consciousness, just as Heidegger's tool-analysis shows. Latour would surely agree on the first two counts, and would probably agree on the third. The only case where he would not agree is number four: objects are irreducible to their relations with other things, and always hold something in reserve from these relations.

All four theses are really just different degrees of the same thesis: an attempt to claim that a thing's reality is dependent on its relations with other things. This is sometimes called a 'theory of internal relations'. Against such theories, we should insist on the old maxim that relations are external to their terms, that things are cut off in themselves and the relations between them are something quite other than those things. The thesis (however it might be worded) is associated at various times with Deleuze, Russell, or British Empiricism. But an even older reference would be to the Arab and French occasionalist traditions, for which a thing does not relate to other things at all unless it passes through the mediation of God. (Empiricism, we have seen, merely replaces God with the human mind.)

But we must stay attentive to two separate points here. On the one hand an object is separated by firewalls from whatever it modifies, transforms, perturbs, or creates. It is completely independent of these, since it can shift into any new environment and still remain the same thing. On the other hand, an object is also separated by firewalls from its own pieces, since the thing emerges as something over and above those pieces, and since 'redundant causation' means that these pieces can be shifted or replaced to some extent without changing the thing. But there is a slight asymmetry in the two considerations, because whereas a thing is completely independent of its relations, it is not completely independent of its own pieces. To remove Whitehead from Harvard and put him at Stanford would only destroy Whitehead for those (such as Whitehead himself) who accept the strange doctrine that a thing is entirely defined by its relations. Far more drastic than forcing Whitehead to leave Harvard would be to remove all of his body parts, or to shatter his soul in the bowels of the underworld. In these latter cases the effect would be truly destructive. Nonetheless, all the cells in Whitehead's body can be replaced by similar ones without destroying Whitehead, and in this sense an object is partly independent of its own pieces just as it is fully independent of its relations with other things.

In this sense, an object is a sort of invisible railway junction between its own pieces and its outer effects. An object is *weird*—it is never replaceable by any sum total of qualities or effects. It is a real thing apart from all foreign relations with the world, and apart from all domestic relations with its own pieces. Stated in more traditional terms, both the foreign and domestic relations of an object are external relations rather than internal ones. Neither of them makes direct contact with the object, though both are capable of destroying it in different ways.

C. IMMANENT OBJECTIVITY

We know that one of Latour's signature moves is his elimination of the modernist human/world gap, as seen most clearly in *We Have Never Been Modern*. Instead of an objective nature filled with genuine realities and a subjective cultural sphere filled with fabricated fictions, there is a single plane of actors that encompasses neutrinos, stars, palm trees, rivers, cats, armies, nations, superheroes, unicorns, and square circles. All objects are treated in the same way. Latour justifies this with his broad conception of an actor as anything that has an effect on other things. In this sense, he is right to let Popeye inhabit the same region of the cosmos as copper and neon. When scientific realists respond with outrage to this mixture of fact and fiction, Latour adds that if all entities are equally real, all are not equally *strong*. Fictional characters and myths have weaker legions of allies testifying to their existence than do lumps of coal. Hence, we can democratize the world of actors and still avoid the free-for-all of social construction.

But there is still a problem. Brassier, who is more sympathetic than I am to scientific materialism, sometimes asks in conversation why the tooth fairy should be just as real as quarks. Allow me to respond to Brassier's very reasonable question with a different example. While writing this section I am hosting Falaki and Tara, two cats who belong to a traveling colleague. These animals obviously qualify as actors in the Latourian sense, since they transform, modify, perturb, and create any number of things in my apartment each day. But I now turn away from the cats and repose in imagination. After a few moments of relaxation I fabricate a new fictional entity—a 'Monster X' possessing a truly abhorrent array of qualities. In order to preserve the absolute isolation of this creature in my own mind, I refuse to describe any of its qualities here, but can assure the reader that their combination is unprecedented in the annals of fiction. Now, Monster X is also an actor in the Latourian sense: it partially disturbs my mood, enters into the current book as an example vaguely affecting the mood of future readers even after I am dead, and leads me to reflect on the parallels between Monster X and the creatures of H.P. Lovecraft. Since the cats and the monster are equally capable of entering into networks and transforming other entities, Latour would reject any assignment of the cats to 'nature' and the monster to 'culture'. These two domains do not exist for him. We cannot apportion the world in such a way that nature is praised for all the reality and humans are blamed for all the distortion.

The truth of this can be seen most easily if we take a third example: the Speculative Realism movement, which I myself helped to 'socially construct' in the year 2006. Despite the humanly fabricated character of Speculative Realism, it is obviously real in a way that Monster X is not. In fact, it is real in the same way that the cats are real. Note for instance that this philosophical movement has a certain independence from those who created it. Within certain limits, one or more members can sleep, resign, or die without exterminating this intellectual trend. Indeed, it might one day be hijacked and transformed by hostile newcomers, which is precisely what happened to phenomenology in Husserl's eyes. In short, the fact that humans create something does not make it less real than entities springing from the bosom of inanimate nature. If societies are real (and they are), then the objects of sociology are every bit as real as the objects of physics. And here Latour is correct.

But this deplorable human/world divide is subtly different from a similar gap that Latour mixes with it, though in my view they are two separate things. I refer to the difference between real and intentional objects, which takes various forms in the Brentano School of Austrian philosophy from which Husserl emerged. Consider the example of the cats and the monster. Unlike the celebrated creatures of Lovecraft, Monster X was created in my mind less than ten minutes ago, and I solemnly swear that none of its traits will ever be divulged even to my dearest friends. This means that if I fall tonight into a dreamless sleep, the monster will cease to exist. Monster X is entirely dependent on my thinking of it. The same is by no means true of the cats, since I will surely awaken tomorrow to find various personal items missing or displaced due to their nocturnal actions. Now, notice that the cats are not *only* real. They also lead a certain existence in my own mind, their properties objectified and caricatured by some in some specific manner. *Qua* objects in my mind, the cats will vanish along with Monster X as soon as I fall asleep. But unlike the monster, the cats will remain autonomous forces unleashed in my apartment despite my lack of awareness of their activities.

This example suggests that we cannot fully accept Latour's democracy of actors, which entails that all objects are of the exact same breed. While agreeing with Latour that the split between nature and culture is untenable, we need to reintroduce a split between real objects and sensual ones. That this new difference is not the same as the old one can be seen from the preceding examples. The modernist system deplored by Latour would assign the cats to 'nature' and Speculative Realism to 'culture'. But although cats breed without human permission while philosophical movements must be created by humans, this is irrelevant for the purposes of ontology. The cats are obviously *real* objects, but they also exist for me as *sensual* objects that vanish when I pay them no heed; sleep temporarily kills off the sensual cats while leaving the real ones untouched. Speculative Realism may seem to be only a *sensual* object insofar as it was created, developed, and preserved by humans. Yet it is also a *real* object independent of its creators and consumers—for none of us can control it, guarantee its success, or envision how and why it will end. Indeed, at this point no human being can even give a satisfactory definition of Speculative Realism. This means that the real/sensual distinction is not a mere reworking of the dismal old nature/culture gap. Yet it does provide an obvious way to assuage the fears of scientific realists about allowing a democracy of objects. We can still distinguish between merely sensual objects and autonomous real ones even after abandoning the nature/culture divide. The only small concession Brassier needs to make is that the tooth fairy has a 'real' dimension qua actor in stories and myths, even if not as a genuine winged fairy flying through genuine air. But even more importantly, to allow both real and sensual objects opens additional fissures in the heart of objects that none of the various 'radical' philosophies are able to recognize. We are speaking here of a new *polarization* of objects, not a new radix to which all else must be reduced.

The *locus classicus* for intentionality in philosophy is Franz Brentano's still underrated *Psychology from an Empirical Standpoint*, first published in 1874. Throughout the book, Brentano shows an unnerving gift for pushing classical themes in fresh directions:

> Every mental phenomenon is characterized by what the Scholastics of the Middle Ages called the intentional (or mental) inexistence of an object [...] or immanent objectivity. Every mental phenomenon includes something as object within itself, although they do not all do so in the same way. In presentation something is presented, in judgment something is affirmed or denied, in love loved, in hate hated, in desire desired and so on.

> This intentional in-existence is characteristic exclusively of mental phenomena. No physical phenomenon exhibits anything like it. We can, therefore, define mental phenomena by saying that they are those phenomena which contain an object intentionally within themselves.[46]

Brentano was not only one of the seminal thinkers in the philosophy of recent centuries, but probably one of the most charismatic teachers of all time. His concept of 'immanent objectivity' sparked a long-running debate, sometimes acrimonious, between Brentano and his most gifted disciples: especially Anton Marty, Kazimierz Twardowski, Alexius Meinong, and Husserl.

Twardowski (1866-1938) is little known to the average Anglophone reader. But he is a giant in Polish philosophy, and deservedly so. His Vienna habilitation thesis of 1894 is entitled *On the Content and Object of Presentations,*[47] and perhaps played as great a role as Brentano himself in stimulating Husserlian phenomenology. In one sense Twardowski views Brentano as a hero, and trumpets his basic insight as if it were a commonplace: 'It is one of the best known positions of psychology, hardly contested by anyone, that every mental phenomenon intends an immanent object'.[48] But when Brentano speaks of immanent objectivity in the mind, Twardowski notes several difficulties. Among them is one already noted by Brentano's student Alois Höfler, quoted by Twardowski as follows:

> The words 'thing' and 'object' are used [by Brentano] in two senses: on the one hand for that *independently* existing entity [...] at which our

46. Franz Brentano, *Psychology from an Empirical Standpoint*, trans. A. Rancurello, D. Terrell, and L. McAlister, New York, Routledge, 1995, pp. 88-9.

47. Kasimir Twardowski, *On the Content and Object of Presentations*, trans. by Reinhard Grossmann, The Hague, Martinus Nijhoff, 1977.

48. Twardowski, *On the Content and Object of Presentations*, p. 1.

presentation and judgment aim, as it were; on the other hand, for the mental, more or less approximate 'picture' of that real entity which *exists 'in' us* [...].

In distinction to the thing or object, which is assumed to be independent of thinking, one also calls the content of a presentation and judgment (similarly: of a feeling and willing) the *'immanent or intentional* object' of these mental phenomena.[49]

By accepting this distinction, Twardowski sets up a simple opposition between two terms. On the one hand we have the object in the real world, which he calls simply 'object'. On the other hand we have the intentional object, the picture that exists in the mind, which he himself calls 'content'. The title of Twardowski's book could thus be rewritten as *On Intentional and Real Objects*. Like his better-known fellow student Meinong, Twardowski envisions a global theory of objects that would outflank the sciences, which focus too narrowly on one specific *kind* of object. In Twardowski's stirring words:

metaphysics must be definable as the science of objects in general, taking this word in the sense here proposed [....] The natural sciences, in the widest sense of the word, for example, are concerned with the peculiarities of those objects which one calls inorganic and organic bodies; psychology investigates the properties and laws characteristic of mental phenomena, of mental objects. [By contrast,] metaphysics is a science which considers all objects, physical—organic and inorganic—as well as mental, real as well as nonreal, existing objects as well as nonexisting objects; investigates those laws which objects in general obey, not just a certain group of objects [...]. Everything which is in the widest sense 'something' is called 'object', first of all in regard to a subject, but then also regardless of this relationship.[50]

Barry Smith's fine book on the Austrian philosophical tradition relates a statement of the later Polish phenomenologist Roman Ingarden that Twardowski's book represents 'so far as I know, the first consistently constructed theory of objects manifesting a certain theoretical unity since the times of scholasticism and of the 'ontology' of [the celebrated Leibnizian] Christian Wolff'.[51]

---

49. Twardowski, *On the Content and Object of Presentations*, p. 1, cited from Alois Höfler and Alexius Meinong, *Logic*, Vienna, 1890.

50. Twardowski, *On the Content and Object of Presentations*, p. 36-7.

51. Barry Smith, *Austrian Philosophy: The Legacy of Franz Brentano*, Chicago, Open Court, 1994, p. 159. Smith translates the citation from page 99 of T. Schnelle, *Ludwik Fleck—Leben und Denken*, Freiburg i.B., Hochschulverlag, 1982. In turn, Schnelle refers to page 258 of Roman Ingarden's Polish article, 'Dzialalnosc naukowa Twardowskiego', found in the collection *Kazimierz Twardowski: Nauczyciel—Uczony—Obywatel* (Lvov, 1938), making this the most convoluted reference of my career, all as a result of my (and presumably Smith's) inability to read Polish.

The reaction of Husserl to Twardowski shows the sort of ambivalence typical only of our most important human relationships. Husserl's letters to his Polish colleague are friendly and respectful, and his repeated references to Twardowski's book throughout his career are far too numerous to suggest anything but profound respect. Yet we sometimes also find harsh or dismissive remarks about Twardowski, whose object/content distinction is sometimes dismissed as untenable or even confused. Throughout the 1890's Husserl struggled to write his essay 'Intentional Objects', in which many of his later themes appear in germinal form.[52] It is Twardowski even more than Brentano who serves as his rival and catalyst in these early years. Husserl's general attitude toward intentional objects is easy to understand. As he sees it, 'the masses' (including Twardowski) falsely think that our mind is filled with mental images of objects that point toward real ones, although the masses concede that in cases of error these images fail to point to anything real.[53] But for Husserl, the object is not doubled up between real and merely intentional versions; instead, the real and intentional object are one and the same. As he wittily puts it, 'the same Berlin which I represent also exists, and the same would no longer exist if judgment fell upon it as upon Sodom and Gomorrah'.[54]

However, for Husserl is less a matter of rejecting Twardowski's distinction than of *displacing* it. Husserl and Twardowski both agree that there is a distinction between object and content. But Husserl's great innovation is to transplant this tension into the phenomenal realm itself, with Twardowski's real world disappearing from the picture. For Husserl we do not point at some object out there somewhere on the basis of internal mental content. Instead, *experience itself* is split in half between unified objects and the diverse contents through which they become manifest. Imagine for instance that we perceive a tree. For Twardowski the 'object' is the real tree lying outside of us, while the 'content' or ('immanent object') is whatever we have in consciousness as an image of the tree. For Husserl it is different. The tree as object does not lie in some remote objective world, but inhabits every perception of the tree—every tree-content that we ever experience. At the same time, Husserl denies that the tree-object and tree-content are imprisoned in the immanence of the human mind. We are not trapped in the mind, since by intending the tree we are reaching out toward an object. This tree-object is not a psychological phantasm, but a truly valid ideal unity. Whether he admits it or not, this step does confine Husserl within an idealist philosophy, since he refuses to let us speak of anything in itself beyond the bounds of possible experience.

---

52. Edmund Husserl, 'Intentional Objects', in *Early Writings in the Philosophy of Logic and Mathematics*, trans. Dallas Willard, Dordrecht, Kluwer, 1993.

53. Husserl, 'Intentional Objects', p. 345.

54. Husserl, 'Intentional Objects', pp. 347-8.

Yet this very idealist gesture is what allows him to describe an unprecedented split *within* the ideal realm, precisely by importing Twardowski's object/content distinction into the phenomenal sphere. In fact, this new rift within phenomena should be seen as Husserl's most fertile contribution to philosophy. For if we perceive a tree or chair, what we perceive is not merely content, since no content is ever quite adequate. Whether I look at a building or a friend, the explicit 'content' seems to be only the front side that I now observe. But no one thinks they are looking at a mere surface, even though the surface is all that we directly see. As Husserl puts it later in the *Logical Investigations*:

> The object is not actually given, it is not given wholly and entirely as that which it itself is. It is only given 'from the front', only 'perspectively foreshortened and projected' etc [...]. The elements of the invisible rear side, the interior etc., are no doubt subsidiarily intended in more or less definite fashion [...]. *On this hinges the possibility of indefinitely many percepts of the same object, all differing in content.*[55]

Imagine circling a tree from different angles and distances at different times of day in ever-shifting moods. For Twardowski every tiniest change in the *content* of perception means a new immanent object; what remains identical through all these changes is the *real* tree lying outside experience. For Husserl it is different: no 'real' tree exists outside our possible experience of it, which is why Husserl is an idealist and Twardowski is not. But in another sense this difference is minor. Both agree that the content shifts constantly even as the object remains the same. The major difference between them is that Twardowski, like Brentano, assumes that our *experience* is always of definite content, so that the enduring object must lie somewhere outside. But Husserl, for probably the first time in the history of philosophy, holds that the realm of appearance is doubled in its own right between enduring unitary objects and shifting accidental profiles. This breakthrough has generally been lost amidst all the polemics and counter-polemics surrounding Husserl's idealism. But here both his friends and his foes miss the point: Husserl's original insights are not to be found in the realism/idealism dispute (where he is really just another correlationist) but in his fracturing of the phenomenal realm itself. And this has decisive consequences for us today.

In the previous section I claimed that objects cannot be defined in terms of their relations with anything else in the world. Real objects withdraw from our access to them, in fully Heideggerian fashion. The metaphors of concealment, veiling, sheltering, harboring, and protecting are all relevant here. The real cats continue to do their work even as I sleep. These cats are not equivalent to my conception of them, and not even equivalent to their own *self*-conceptions; nor are they exhausted by their various modifications

---

55. Edmund Husserl, *Logical Investigations*, 2 Vols., trans. J.N. Findlay, London, Routledge and Kegan Paul, 1970, pp. 712-3, emphasis added.

and perturbations of the objects they handle or damage during the night. The cats themselves exist at a level deeper than their effects on anything. Real objects are non-relational. This was the lesson of the earlier section.

But now we have intentional or sensual objects as well. Monster X or the cats-for-me (as opposed to the cats themselves) clearly cannot be subtracted from all relation, since they exist only insofar as I pay attention to them. When I close my eyes and fall asleep, the intentional cats vanish from existence no less than Monster X does. This distinction between real and intentional objects might sound like the old-fashioned difference between primary and secondary qualities, but it is not. For one thing, primary qualities are usually described in terms of underlying *physical* properties (such as mass, shape, position) unaffected by human perception. But I have claimed that such qualities are purely relational, and hence not deep enough to qualify for the status of 'primary'. Meanwhile, secondary qualities are always supposed to be made up of mere *qualities*, such as 'sweet', 'red', and so forth. But for Husserl experience is not made up of free-floating qualities, but of objects: the door slamming, the sailboat cruising down the lake. The empiricist model, according to which we experience discrete color-patches and arbitrarily weave them together into larger units through habit, is rejected by Husserl and all later phenomenologists as sheer ideology. For Husserl the phenomenal realm is not just excluded from the real one, but is also divided in itself.

Real Objects are Not Bundles of Relations

Our working model now runs as follows. We have real objects, which withdraw from all human view and even from all relations with each other. This was the conclusion of the previous section, which rejected all 'radical' attempts to collapse objects into a monistic world-lump, a virtual realm of pre-individuals, a reductionist cosmos of rock-hard atoms entering larger 'functional' units, a correlational circle of human and world, or a global relational network à la Whitehead and Latour. Real objects belong to a pre-relational dimension in which they cannot make direct contact of any sort. But the phenomenal level of the cosmos now seems to be split in two, with a strife between intentional objects and their accidental content at any given moment: the mailbox remains the same mailbox no matter what transient façade it happens to present in any instant. If real objects are hidden and never present enough, intentional objects are always already present. They are merely encrusted with inessential accidents that need to be stripped away by the phenomenologist in the method Husserl describes as 'eidetic reduction'. Real objects exist 'whether we like it or not', but intentional objects can be vaporized by a simple act of shifting our mind elsewhere. (Husserl would not agree with this point, since he holds that the mailbox is an 'ideal' unity that remains the same even if no one is looking, but we need not follow him here.) Finally, since real objects withdraw from all relations, they cannot make any contact with each other. By contrast, intentional objects are always intended or touched by me, since they are a genuine part of my life at this instant. And since there are always multiple intentional objects in my mind at any moment, they are contiguous with one another in my experience, not totally cut off from each other like real objects are. In the previous section I considered the difference between real objects and their mere relational profiles, and criticized several 'radical' attempts to collapse this difference, which in my estimation must be preserved or even deepened at all costs. Here I will consider several other rifts within objects that need to be maintained. Unlike the 'objects vs. relations' difference, these additional rifts are ones that Latour does not even bother denying. For only the phenomenological tradition gives us the needed strife *within* objects that establishes these additional polarities, and the phenomenological tradition has had little influence on Latour.

Sensual Objects are Not Bundles of Accidental Qualities

It is generally the case that Latour, like Whitehead, is satisfied with the empiricist doctrine that a thing is not different from its qualities. In any case there would be no way for Latour to make such a distinction, since it would require him to locate an enduring kernel in objects different from its palpable qualities, and this would be a rather un-Latourian task. What I have called a 'radical' philosophical position (not the same thing as an 'original' one) amounts to saying something along these lines: 'philosophers formerly distinguished between X and Y. But Y is merely a figment of traditional prejudice, and we can now see that it reduces completely to X'. Radical philosophies are reductive in spirit, and hence Latour's *Irreductions* makes him an anti-radical in spirit, as does his oft-repeated maxim that the mission of the intellect is to make things more real rather than less real—the very opposite method of the overrated 'critical thinking'.

The previous section covered various radical attempts to reduce entities to their *relations* with other entities, though different possible degrees of zealotry in this project became visible. But along with saying that an entity is nothing more than its relations, there is a different sort of radicalism that holds objects to be nothing more than bundles of specific qualities. On this point Whitehead cites David Hume, the most famous mascot for such doctrines: 'But my senses convey to me only *the impressions of colored points*, disposed in a certain manner. If the eye is sensible of any thing further, I desire it may be pointed out to me'.[56] And elsewhere: 'I would fain ask those philosophers, who [base] so much of their reasonings on the distinction of

---

56. Whitehead, *Process and Reality*, p. 117, emphasis added. Cited from David Hume, *A Treatise of Human Nature*, Oxford, Oxford University Press, 1978, Book 1, Part II, Section III.

substance and accident, and imagine we have clear ideas of each, whether the idea of *substance* be derived from the impressions of sensation or from reflection?'.[57] For Hume, our visual experience is made up of tiny colored points woven arbitrarily into larger-scale things through the force of habit.

But this is precisely the model of perception that Husserl rightly rejects. For who on earth ever experienced a visual field made up of 'impressions of colored points, disposed in a certain manner'? One can well imagine a science fiction tale in which the narrator's visual experience decomposes horrifically into autonomous dots, as in the pointillist paintings of Georges Seurat. But neither I, nor the reader, nor David Hume himself ever experienced such a nightmarish world. The very suggestion is anything but empirical: it is based on a sensationalist ideology not ratified by the experience of any living creature. As Husserl beautifully puts it, 'here is my friend Hans and I call him "Hans." He is no doubt individually determined, he is always at a particular point in space and time. If these determinations were, however, concurrently meant, the name "Hans" would change its meaning with every step my friend takes, on every occasion that I address him by name'.[58] But in fact each of us continues to call him Hans even as he changes position, facial expression, clothing, and exact spatial distance from us. It is purely arbitrary to discount our view that it is the same Hans in all these cases in favor of a mere Humean dogma that the exact qualitative configuration must be identical for the person to be the same person. In fact, this simply amounts to another 'radical' attempt to belittle whatever one's initial ideology does not admit. Just as materialists delight in tearing all layers of reality down to their supposed atomic substratum, sensationalists wish to eliminate everything but a purported superstratum of specific color-pixels. Or as Husserl objects: 'unthinkingly one credits to *contents* everything that acts place in the *object*, in their straightforward reference; its attributes, colours, forms etc., are forthwith called "contents" and actually interpreted as contents in the psychological sense, e.g. as sensations'.[59] And further, 'the concrete phenomenal thing is treated as a complex of contents, i.e. of attributes grown together in a single image'.[60] But if that were the case, how could we ever experience things such as 'three-dimensional solids?'.[61] The third dimension can never be given as a mental *content*, since contents come only in the form of two-dimensional flat surfaces, with the third dimension never receiving direct visual expression.

Simply put: we experience *objects*, not masses of sense data. In each

---

57. Whitehead, *Process and Reality*, p. 118, emphasis added. Cited from Hume, *A Treatise of Human Nature*, Book 1, Part 1, Section VI.

58. Husserl, *Logical Investigations*, p. 380.

59. Husserl, *Logical Investigations*, p. 382, translation modified slightly for reasons of clarity.

60. Husserl, *Logical Investigations*, p. 382.

61. Husserl, *Logical Investigations*, p. 382.

moment we contend with books, cats, moons, and Sri Lankan tea planta-
tions, not tiny flecks of color. When I circle an object or when it rotates freely
before me, I do not see a discrete series of closely related contents and then
make an arbitrary decision that they all belong together as a set of closely
linked specific profiles. Instead, what I experience is always *one* object undergoing accidental, transient changes that do not alter the thing itself. When
my friend Hans walks, I do in fact see my unified friend Hans undergoing
adventures in time and space while remaining the same Hans. I do not see a
chain of slightly different entities called Hans1, Hans2, Hans3, Hans4, etc.,
united by some sort of 'family resemblance' (in accordance with one overly admired 'radical' move). Instead, we simply experience a unified Hans
walking along through merely accidental changes of position. The question might now be asked: what are the criteria for when Hans has changed
enough that he is no longer Hans? And the answer is simple: *it does not matter, for we ourselves are the judges*. After all, we are not speaking here of real
objects—a realm where mistaken inferences are possible. We are speaking
solely of intentional objects, a sphere where each of us is absolute master. If
I decide that Hans is still Hans despite recent drastic change in his properties, then he is still Hans—end of story. The fact that it may be Jürgen or
Katje who is mistaken for Hans is irrelevant until we begin to speak of *real*
objects. As long as I tacitly accept that the new set of appearances are still
Hans-appearances, then they simply are. No error is possible at this level,
since intentional objects consist solely in their relation with me.

Husserl's critique is directed not only against British Empiricism, but
also against his own teacher Brentano—and implicitly against Twardowski,
who still followed his teacher on this point. Brentano and Twardowski, no less
than Locke, Berkeley, Hume, Kant, and almost everyone else, assume that
the realm of mental phenomena is always made up of specific *content*. In opposition to this, Husserl says that 'I do not see colour-sensations but coloured
things, I do not hear tone-sensations but the singer's song etc. etc'.[62] Whereas
Brentano thinks all consciousness is grounded in *presentation*, Husserl modifies this principle to say that all consciousness is grounded in *objectifying acts*.[63]
By now the difference should be clear enough. If we hold with Brentano that
my consciousness of a tree is a presentation, this means that I have tree-
content in my mind, and all of it is equally tree-content. Husserl's position
is slightly but decisively different. For him, not all aspects of my intention of
the tree are the same. On the one hand there is an enduring eidetic nucleus
that the tree-perception must have in order to be what it is; this is the tree
as a unified intentional object. On the other hand there is the content of the
experience, which can shift massively from moment to moment. If we look

---

62. Husserl, *Logical Investigations*, p. 559.
63. Husserl, *Logical Investigations*, p. 648.

at the tree reflected in a pool, upside-down, through orange lenses, at midnight, or blanketed with flashing strobe-lights—all of these cases alter the *presentation* drastically, but none change the object-giving act as long as I still believe that the tree is the same old tree as before.

In short, it is impossible to reduce an intentional object to a bundle of qualities. Hume's famous radicalism on this point always lends a certain critical cockiness to his admirers. They love to dismiss unified things as old-fashioned piety in comparison with the tough-minded, experience-centered theory of tiny color-patches. They adore the reduction of enduring entities to a series of closely related images united after the fact by mere family resemblance. It is fun to be a self-proclaimed radical, bursting the bubbles of gullible dupes; indeed, there are those who hold that the tedious spectacle of disabusing naïve people of their folly is the very epitome of mental life. Unfortunately, no color-dots are given in experience, and to proclaim the Dot Theory to be empirical is a travesty of what fidelity to experience ought to mean. Nor do we see a series of discrete Hans-like shapes and then decide that they are sufficiently similar that it must be the same person. None of this is empirical, since it merely serves a dogmatic reductionism that prefers to eliminate whatever it cannot handle.

Thus, along with the difference between a real object and its relations, we must now recognize a second polarity: the difference between an intentional object and its accidents. In both cases we have an enduring core object unaffected by transient changes, not reliant on the ways in which it is announced. The difference is that whereas a real object is always *more* than the specific qualities that we ascribe to it, an intentional object is always *less*. A real tree withdraws into the dusk of its being, and is never fully expressed by any of its distinct features. By contrast, an intentional tree is always before us as soon as we see a tree, or think we see a tree. It is merely flooded over or encrusted with excessive detail: too much irrelevant sunlight over that enduring tree-unity, too much personal mood not pertinent to the tree, too much specificity of angle and distance. We now have two irreducible tensions that cannot be explained away by false radicalism: real objects and intentional objects are both different from their specific presentations.

Sensual Objects are Not Bundles of Essential Qualities

What real and sensual objects have in common is that both are enduring nuclei that withstand numerous changes in their precise presentations. In other words, real and sensual objects do undergo adventures of changing qualifications. But although the tree can be seen in countless different perceptual configurations, it does not seem to have adventures with respect to its own *eidos*, which must always remain the same for as long as the thing remains the same. (We are speaking here of Husserl's eidos, not Plato's.) The tree can be seen from ten or fifty meters, at sunrise or at dusk, but in all such cases the eidos must be the same for the tree to remain the same sensual object. Husserl contends that any of our specific intentions of sensual objects can be subjected to this sort of eidetic reduction, 'which leads from the psychological phenomenon to the pure "essence," or [....] from factual ("empirical") to "essential" universality [...]'.[64] We strip away the inessential noise and confetti encrusted on the nucleus of the thing and thereby try to gain an eidetic intuition of whatever tree, mailbox, or blackbird we experience. If I suddenly realize that an apparent tree is actually an ugly light-pole disguised as a palm, as happened near my home several hours ago, then I now intend a new object with a different *eidos*. The previous palm-object underwent adventures of accidental change only as long as I took it for a palm. Once I saw that it was a streetlight in disguise, the previous palm-object was simply eliminated. Since objects cannot endure the loss of their eidos, it might easily seem as if the intentional/sensual object and its eidetic features are identical. Yet this turns out *not* to be the case, and we are confronted with a new, third form of non-radical tension: the strife between a sensual object and its essential qualities.

We can begin by asking about the nature of any sensual object that we encounter, whether it be a tree, mailbox, dog, or skeleton. A sensual object does remain unified despite its various swirling profiles. But it is not just an empty container of unity, since this would entail that all sensual objects are the same once we subtract their accidents. A snake and a river would be identical if not for their accidental surface profiles, which is clearly absurd. The problem is familiar to classical philosophy, as in Leibniz's point in *Monadaology* §8 that 'monads must have qualities, otherwise they would not even be beings'.[65] But Husserl deals with this duality of unity and particularity at the sensual level rather than Leibniz's level of *real* monads. Husserl says, for instance, that the object is snatched up in 'a single "ray of meaning"'.[66] Hence the ray is both 'single' (it is unified) and also a ray 'of meaning' (it has a particular character to it). When the sensual palm tree stays the same from every angle and distance, it remains the same in *palm-fashion* rather than in dog-fashion. The sensual object results from 'the fundamental operation of nominalization, the transformation of many-rayed synthesis into a single-rayed synthesis'. The difference between these two is that 'single-rayed acts are not articulate, the many-rayed acts are articulate'.[67] In other

---

64. Edmund Husserl, *Ideas: General Introduction to Pure Phenomenology*, trans. W.R.B. Gibson, London, Allen & Unwin, 1931, p. 44.

65. G. W. Leibniz, 'Monadology', in *Philosophical Essays*, trans. Roger Ariew and Daniel Garber, Indianapolis, Hackett, 1989, p. 214.

66. Husserl, *Logical Investigations*, p. 622.

67. Husserl, *Logical Investigations*, p. 640, emphasis removed from the first of the two passages.

words, the sensual object is a unit of definite character but not openly articulated according to its eidetic features. The palm tree is there before us, however much or little attention we might be paying it. This sensual tree is not an intellectual content, because it remains there before us even if we descend into the most deplorable stupor. Neither is it a perceptive content, for we have seen that this can change wildly from moment to moment without our perceiving a different tree. Finally, it is not an emotional content, since the unified tree can endure fluctuations of mood up to and including outright psychosis. Nonetheless, the wonderful Ortega (one of the intellectual heroes of my student years) is onto something important when he refers to such sensual objects as 'feelings':

> Keeping this name ['feeling'] for states of pleasure and displeasure, joy and sorrow, is an enormous error that psychology has only recently acknowledged. Every objective image, on entering or leaving our consciousness, produces a subjective reaction, just as a bird that lights on or leaves a branch starts it trembling, or turning on and off an electric current instantly produces a new current.[68]

To summarize, the feeling-thing or sensual object is both one and particular. It is a specific yet unarticulated unity—a sort of smooth eidetic paste, but with vastly different flavors of paste in the cases of tree, dog, and star.

Now, the very fact that the unified thing is inarticulate shows why the sensual object is not the same as its eidos. It is true that the sensual object is covered with noise, but stripping away this noise only gives us the sensual object, not the eidos. This eidos requires a higher level of articulation, which requires that we go beyond the inarticulate sensual object itself. Another term for the eidos of an object is its *meaning*, in a much broader sense than the linguistic one; we are speaking here of our dealings with unified objects, and this obviously requires neither speech nor writing. But a few of Husserl's examples drawn from language are helpful. In some cases, such as 'London' in English and 'Londres' in French, we find both the same meaning and the same object.[69] But other examples make clear how different the two poles are. For instance, the same object can be named by two different meanings: 'the victor at Jena' and 'the vanquished at Waterloo' both refer to Napoleon; the same triangle can be called both 'that equilateral triangle' and 'that equiangular triangle'[70] (Am I the only reader who finds the triangle example astoundingly funny? Husserl's wit is underrated.) Conversely, there are many cases when the *same* meaning refers to two *different* objects—as when 'horse' refers equally well to Bucephalus (the mount of Alexander the Great)

---

68. José Ortega y Gasset, 'An Essay in Esthetics By Way of a Preface', in *Phenomenology and Art*, trans. Philip Silver, New York, W.W. Norton, 1975, pp. 144-5.

69. Husserl, *Logical Investigations*, p. 287.

70. Husserl, *Logical Investigations*, p. 287.

and to an average cart horse.[71] Normally our sensual acts are focused on the object, not on its meaning, its articulated eidos. In Husserl's own words: 'If we perform [an intentional] act and live in it, as it were, we naturally refer to its object and not to its meaning. If, e.g., we make a statement, we judge about the thing it concerns, and not about the statement's meaning, about the judgment in the logical sense. This latter first becomes objective to us in a reflex act of thought [...]'.[72]

We can see, then, that the unified sensual object is a single ray of 'feeling' (in Ortega's broad sense) that is not articulated into its constituent eidetic moments. But what is remarkable is that such articulation cannot occur by means of sensual intuition at all. Even though Husserl holds that a thing can become present in a fulfilling intuition, this fulfillment has nothing to do with normal sensual intuition. For there is no proper angle or distance from which to view the eidos of a palm tree, Napoleon, or Bucephalus. Some vantage points on objects may be more optimal than others, but even these viewpoints can only give us accidental surface profiles of an object, never its eidos. In short, a sensual intuition is *always* accidental. Husserl notes that 'Bismarck' is a unified meaning regardless of 'whether I imagine the great man in a felt hat or coat, or in a cuirassier's uniform, or whatever pictorial representation I may adopt'.[73] If I state out loud that a blackbird is flying in the garden:

> a listener may understand my words, and my sentence as a whole, without looking into the garden: confident in my veracity, he may bring forth the same judgment without the precept [of the flying blackbird]. Possibly too he is helped by an imaginative re-enactment, but perhaps this too is absent, or occurs in so mutilated, so inadequate a form, as to be no fit counterpart of what appears perceptually, at least not in respect of the features 'expressed' in my statement.[74]

In even clearer terms, 'we must [...] locate no part of the meaning in the percept itself'.[75] The eidos of the mailbox does not appear as soon as we stare directly at the it. The eidos or meaning is tacitly present inasmuch as the mailbox is something that occupies our attention. But it is not articulated.

We already knew from the previous section that the sensual object is a unity over against the swirling accidents that accompany it. The current section has added the following additional points: (1) The eidos is not the same

---

71. Husserl, *Logical Investigations*, p. 288.

72. Husserl, *Logical Investigations*, p. 332

73. Husserl, *Logical Investigations*, p. 328.

74. Husserl, *Logical Investigations*, pp. 680-1. At the risk of beating to death the point about Husserl's wit, is there not something staggeringly comical about the idea of 'a mutilated or inadequate imaginative re-enactment of a blackbird'? Personally, I find the notion hilarious.

75. Husserl, *Logical Investigations*, p. 685.

as the sensual object, since different aspects of the eidos can be articulated by different statements, whereas the object itself is always unified in the
manner of a rigidly designating proper name. (2) Most surprisingly, the eidos
of a sensual object is *withdrawn* from view, just as real objects are withdrawn
from view. To articulate the eidos of an object is to hint at something *really*
belonging to it and *really* withdrawn from access, not to call our attention to
some adequate visual incarnation of the essence. Any fulfillment that occurs
will be purely intellectual, and never complete.

Husserl does not recognize this second point since he holds that adequate, evident intuition of things is possible. For him there is no hidden
realm of real objects, deeper than intentional objects. But here it is necessary
to depart from Husserl's own views. If we speak of the eidos of a sensual object as having *moments*, these moments are directly accessible neither through
the senses nor even through the mind. We are able to hint at the moments of
the eidos through various linguistic or non-linguistic means, but can never
quite reach them. No articulation of the eidos of a mailbox ever gets it *quite*
right. And here we have one of those paradoxical inversions that are often
a symptom of truth. The usual assumption by those who believe in real objects is that we have access to a thing's *qualities* but not to the thing itself. In
the case of sensual objects, precisely the reverse turns out to be the case: we
have immediate access to the sensual *object* from the very moment we intend
it, since that is all it takes for a sensual object to exist. Yet we have no direct
access to the genuine *moments* of a sensual object, even though we constantly
bathe in its *accidents*. And this is the third non-radical polarity of object-oriented philosophy: the sensual object vs. its eidetic moments.

A new piece of terminology seems in order for this rather surprising de-
velopment (which occurred to me only in the summer of 2008). We said that
the accidental surface profiles of a mailbox are *encrusted* on the mailbox as a
unified sensual thing. But in the case of an object's genuine eidetic moments
it turns out not to be a matter of encrustation, since these moments are by no
means accessible on the surface. Instead, we could say that the moments of
a sensual object are *submerged* from view. Although new terms in philosophy
always risk sounding precious, forced, or ludicrous, the difference between
encrustation and submergence is a key distinction between two ways for
qualities to exist. Now, it may seem odd that a merely sensual object could
submerge a *real* eidos, but the evidence leads us to conclude that this must be
so: like an imaginary tree putting down real roots, or a ghost ship ejecting
real cargo into the sea. But it should have seemed equally odd that a real object could emanate sensual qualities for a perceiver, though this scenario is
a more familiar one. These two diagonal lines, cutting from sensual to real
and from real to sensual, must be a clue as to how things are able to communicate despite the withdrawal of objects from each other. They hint at a
solution to the problem of vicarious causation.

Real Objects are Not Bundles of Essential Qualities

But we now come to a fourth non-radical polarity in objects. For just as a sensual object differs from its real qualities (intentional object vs. its eidos), the same holds true for real objects that exist apart from our access to them. This issue is of no concern to Husserl, since he does not even recognize what I have called a 'real object' lying outside the intentional realm; it was Heidegger's tool-analysis that brought these real objects into phenomenology for the first time. If a real object withdraws from any access, such a notion is clearly anathema to Husserl, since he thinks that nothing can withdraw beyond the possibility *in principle* of being adequately known, however difficult this may be in practice. For this reason I turn briefly to the Spanish Basque philosopher Xavier Zubíri (1898-1983), disciple of Heidegger and Ortega and a formidable thinker in his own right. My own insistence on the subterranean reality of objects apart from any perception of them owes a good deal to his masterwork *On Essence*.[76] Since I have discussed Zubíri extensively in *Tool-Being*,[77] a briefer summary will suffice here.

From the outset of *On Essence*, Zubíri stakes out a deeper terrain than the sensual realm—a land that can be safely described as belonging to so-called 'realism'. When we ask about essence, Zubíri says, 'we are asking, in the first place, for the essence considered, *not as the term of our way of confronting real things*, but rather as a moment of those things themselves'.[78] In other words, we are not dealing with Husserlian phenomena or intentional objects. Instead, Zubíri begins to trace a path through the essence of what I have called *real* objects. 'In a wide sense, the "what" of anything comprises all its notes, properties, characteristics (it matters little which term we employ). These notes are not free-floating or detached, but constitute a unity [...]'.[79] This unity is crucial, for 'if they lacked this unity and if each one stood by itself, we would not have "one" thing but a number of things. If the unity were merely additive or external, we would have a conglomerate of things, but not, in any strict sense, "one thing"'.[80]

But to speak of *all* of a thing's notes, properties, characteristics has a very different meaning depending on what is included in the 'all'. And here Zubíri takes us through three increasingly deeper concepts of the whole of a thing's characteristics, two of them already found in Husserl. For in the first and widest sense, 'the "what" means all those things which the thing in

---

76. Xavier Zubíri, *On Essence*, trans. A. Robert Caponigri, Washington, Catholic University of America Press, 1980.

77. Graham Harman, *Tool-Being: Heidegger and the Metaphysics of Objects*, Chicago, Open Court, 2002, §22-§23.

78. Zubíri, *On Essence*, p. 47, emphasis added.

79. Zubíri, *On Essence*, p. 51.

80. Zubíri, *On Essence*, pp. 51-2

question, as a matter of fact, is, with the totality of notes which it possesses *hic et nunc*, including this very *hic* and this very *nunc*'.[81] Here we are in the realm of things determined in utter specificity, as with Latour and Whitehead. It is not just the sunflower, but rather the sunflower viewed in four o'clock shadow from ten meters in deepest sadness, and so forth. Such overly determinate experience has a definite quiddity that can be described in as much detail as we wish. But this is not what Zubíri is looking for.

This leads him to a second version of the whole of a thing's traits, which is closer to what Husserl did with the term 'essence'. Here, the object 'presents notes which rapidly take on a function which is characteristic or distinctive of it, differently from other notes which it possesses, so to say, indistinctly in a real, though indifferent, manner'. More precisely, 'it is an apprehension of the thing *as being "the same,"* despite the fact that these indifferent notes may vary'.[82] In this second version of essence the angle and distance of the sunflower, or the mood in which it is viewed, are subtracted from the picture. Instead, we have the sunflower as an enduring sensual object that undergoes adventures of changing determinations. Although this is close enough to what Husserl desires, it remains quite far from what Zubíri hopes to attain.

The third sense of essence, which Zubíri himself endorses, has to do with the thing itself rather than the thing as conceived by us. Here it is no longer a question of setting human criteria by which to demarcate entities from one another, but a question of the essence of real things themselves. Zubíri seeks the notes 'which, taken in and by themselves, not only characterize a thing more or less so that it may not be confused with other things, but rather, that they can in no sense fail or that they can in no sense be absent from a real thing without this latter, in a strict sense, ceasing to be what it is'.[83] To return to our previous melancholic example, we speak of something deeper than both the overly determined sunflower *and* the sunflower as an enduring unit of human experience. Instead, we are speaking of the *real* flower and those traits it must have in order to keep on being what it is. And here we finally reach what Zubíri is seeking: 'the unitary conjunction of all these notes is what in the strict sense I shall call essence'.[84] As he puts it in a wonderful further passage that I have never been able to forget: 'it is a unity such that, with respect to it, *the notes are nothing but moments* in which, so to phrase it, the unity in question *exhaustively deploys itself*'.[85]

We already have before us the basic features of Zubíri's model of essence, portrayed in such massive detail in his hundreds of further pages. He seeks the essence of real objects, not just of things that appear to us (intentional

81. Zubíri, *On Essence*, p. 52.
82. Zubíri, *On Essence*, p. 52, emphasis added.
83. Zubíri, *On Essence*, p. 53.
84. Zubíri, *On Essence*, p. 53.
85. Zubíri, *On Essence*, p. 53, emphasis added.

objects). This essence is a unity, and moreover it is a unity that 'exhaustively deploys itself' in notes that count as its 'moments'. Just as Husserl's sensual object is a unity over against its accidents, Zubíri's real object is a unity over against its moments. The interplay here between the unity and plurality of the thing is called 'essence'. And the essence is incarnated in the very reality of the individual thing; it is not a universal perfect form lying outside the thing and shared by many individuals: 'the essence does not repose on itself; it reposes on the real thing according to that mode of reposing on it which is "to be it." Consequently, it follows that the essence is in itself something completely made factive. *There are no essences which are real and physically immutable and absolute*'.[86] In other words, destroy the real object and you have destroyed the essence at the same time, which is not what happens for Plato. In Zubíri's case, the object in its own right is exhaustively deployed in its essence, without remainder. In this essential unity, 'each note is turned to the others "from itself" [...] it is "this" note in "this" given system which is intrinsically turned to the others'.[87] Simply put, the moments are not abstract qualities able to float around outside their specific incarnations (as with Whitehead's rather Platonic 'eternal objects', happily absent from Latour). Instead, they are more like what analytic philosophy calls 'tropes': individualized qualities that cannot be stripped from the entity to which they belong and shared elsewhere. And yet for Zubíri there are multiple notes to any unified entity: a 'richness' in the thing to go along with its 'solidity', or a specific 'talitative' character that accompanies its 'transcendental' unity. But this oneness is not a *mere* unity, as if every real thing shared the same transcendental dimension of oneness. Instead, as the final sentence of Zubíri's book puts it, 'the essence is structural principle of the [individual] substantivity'.[88] In short, having seen that the sensual object had real moments, we now see even more easily (because less paradoxically) that the real object has real moments as well.

We have now shifted standpoint from Latour's utterly concrete onefold actor to a completely polarized model of fourfold objects. Instead of having all objects on the same plane of reality, we have two kinds of object: real and sensual. And instead of a thing being the same as its qualities, we now have a duel that plays out in both kinds of objects: the unified systematic thing and its plurality of features. This necessarily gives us a quadruple model of the world. Stated differently, there are two kinds of objects and two kinds of traits. We have the real sunflower (assuming it exists) and the sensual translation of it that appears to humans or other entities. We have the real moments that the sunflower needs in order to be what it is, and the accidental specific qualities through which the sensual sunflower is incarnated in the experience

86. Zubíri, *On Essence*, p. 65, emphasis added.

87. Zubíri, *On Essence*, p. 274.

88. Zubíri, *On Essence*, p. 457.

of perceivers. We have also brushed up against the different sorts of relations that can occur between these poles, but will mostly leave these until later.

Elsewhere I have described the similarity between this model and Heidegger's celebrated yet neglected *Geviert* or 'fourfold'. In *Tool-Being* I wrote as follows: 'Zubíri's quadruple structure [the one just outlined] and Heidegger's have precisely the same structure. They are identical'.[89] But this statement was insufficiently precise. Along with whatever violence the disciples of Heidgger and Zubíri might claim I am doing to their heroes (and I am always delighted to fight them), there is a more obvious issue here— namely, Heidegger's fourfold model is different in 1949 (when it becomes explicit) from in 1919 (when it was toyed with vaguely in a sketchy early form). The one that most resembles the fourfold arising from my Husserl/Zubíri hybrid model is not the famous 1949 fourfold, but the earlier one from 1919. For it was only there that the young Heidegger was speaking of the tension within *individual* entities, whether in the mode of revealed ('occurrence') or hidden ('event'). By contrast, the 1949 fourfold pays no heed to the tension within individual beings (as Husserl and Zubíri do), but only to that between the world *as a whole* and individual things. 'Earth' and 'mortals' do not represent individual things for the later Heidegger, but the totality of all. 'Gods' and 'sky' are the only quadrants of the fourfold where we find individual particularity. Otherwise the models are structurally similar, though Heidegger's 1949 model is damaged by his false appeal to a global unity at both the veiled and unveiled levels.

The Interior of Objects

It might now seem that there is a tension between two aspects of this book. In the first place I attacked correlationism and demanded that the relations between any two objects be placed on the same footing as that between human and world. But now I have insisted that there is not a total democracy of objects or 'flat ontology' of the type defended by Latour, but rather *two* types of objects—(a) real and (b) intentional or sensual. To speak of intentional objects makes it seem as if this book were invoking a privileged realm of human phenomenology, inapplicable to such cases as cotton's interaction with fire or the collision of hailstones with wood. But surprisingly enough, this turns out to be a mere prejudice. Brentano was right to speak of intentional objects as having 'intentional inexistence', an existence on the interior of something else. He was simply wrong to say that this inner space is the inside of the human mind.

In one sense the intentional relation is one, but in another sense it is two. For in a first sense, when staring at a mailbox I remain perfectly distinct from it—intentionality is two. By no means do the mailbox or I fuse

---

89. Harman, *Tool-Being*, p. 266.

together into a single continuum or heap of molten slag. I am one thing and the mailbox is another, which is precisely why I am able to intend it. There is also a fascinating asymmetry in this situation. For the mailbox is merely a sensual or intentional object, one that will vaporize as soon as I cease paying attention to it; at best, it is a translation or distortion of some real object that withdraws from any sensual rendition. But by contrast, the 'I myself' that encounters this mailbox is a perfectly *real* object. It is I myself who expend energy taking the mailbox seriously as an object of attention, not some image of me. And here we have an important principle that assists in developing the theme of vicarious causation. All direct contact is between objects of *different* types—just as fertility requires both male and female, and just as magnets make contact only when opposite poles meet. We can call this the *Principle of Asymmetry*. Latour's flat ontology of actors leaves no room for asymmetry, and this is why Joliot will fail to touch politics or neutrons every bit as much as they fail to touch one another, leading to the problem of infinite mediators. What Joliot *is* able to bridge are the sensual caricatures of politics and neutrons.

To take a brief detour, we now have a model of the mediation between objects that carries at least three separate implications (as well as a pair of corollaries to the second of them):

1. For as we have seen, two *real* objects withdraw from one another into secluded depths, and for that very reason they cannot make contact with one another. Meanwhile, the various *sensual* objects that co-exist in a single intentional act (intentional trees, mountains, leopards) merely sit around in a contiguous state, touching one another only in the sense that the perceiver perceives them both simultaneously. After all, sensual objects consist only in being encountered, not in encountering. If I expend my energy in taking them seriously, they themselves have no such energy to expend; they are purely passive figments for an encounter of my own. Hence they are incapable of direct interaction of any sort, and belong to the same perceptual moment only through the mediation of me the perceiver. Real objects can touch only through the medium of an intentional object, and intentional objects can touch only through the medium of a real one. This is the Principle of Asymmetry. One fascinating but slightly perverse consequence of this principle is that there *cannot* be anything like a mind/body problem: two mental images can never touch, and two real objects can never touch, but contact between opposite forms of objects *always* can.

2. It follows from Asymmetry that any case of direct contact must consist of two terms, no more. For given that any permutation of three or more objects must contain at least two of the same type (whether real

or sensual) all direct contact between more than two terms becomes impossible. It follows that when contact *seems* to be made of more than two, something else must be happening. Perhaps the initial object is built from a pair, like Lennon and McCartney as the pre-existent core of the Beatles. Or perhaps an already existing object draws multiple new objects into its orbit simultaneously and separately (as when several nations join the European Union on the same day). The general demand that any contact has only two terms can be called the *Binary Contact Principle*, with the abiding proviso that such terminology is disposable and can easily be replaced or abandoned if it sounds absurd in practice.

a. As a corollary, it will always be the case that one object will be the dominant 'real' object and the other a merely sensual image. However, in many cases it will happen that each term of the pair has an active relation to the passive caricature of the other—like two mutually reinforcing objects giving the appearance of one, with the real tree encountering an image of me as well. In fact, *reinforced object* may be a good technical term to use for such cases. (Perhaps Lennon/McCartney is a classic example of a reinforced object, since neither of these figures could easily be called a mere puppet or simulacrum deployed by the other.)

b. As an added corollary, we must reject the popular view that there is no single cause for an event but rather a multitude of environmental factors. This view is defended by John Stuart Mill and lucidly upheld by the entertaining W. Teed Rockwell.[90] While agreeing that environmental factors are always present and relevant, I deny that they deserve the name of 'cause'. Of the various contextual factors that surround me right now, not all are having an effect on me. Of those that are, they have an effect only insofar as they are part of an object that affects me. There is no 'context' except as inscribed in individual objects (as also supported by Whitehead's 'ontological principle' that everything that happens has its reasons in the constitution of some actual entity). For this reason, triggering incidents cannot be viewed as interchangeable flukes that might easily have been replaced with some other initiator; instead, they suffuse the entire causal event with their personal style. Bismarck's dismissive (and correct) prediction that the next war would come from 'some damn fool thing in the Balkans' is amusing, but does no justice to Gavrilo Princip's act of pulling

---

90. W. Teed Rockwell, *Neither Brain Nor Ghost: A Nondualist Alternative to the Mind-Brain Identity Theory*, Cambridge, MIT Press, 2005, ch. 4.

the trigger. We must restore dignity to individual causes and resist the seductive dogma of total context. Here I will resist the
easy pun on Princip's name and speak instead of *Gavrilo's Corollary*.
Mill's view regards individual causes as merely 'damn fool things
in the Balkans', but this cannot be endorsed.

3. But not only is it the case that sensual objects lead a merely contiguous existence without making direct contact: more than this, they do
   not even make such contact with their own sensual qualities. For both
   the enduring intentional object 'tree' and its highly specific surface-
   profiles lead a merely sensual existence. They vanish instantly if I die,
   sleep, or turn my attention elsewhere. Here again, both are purely passive targets of awareness, without experience in their own right. They
   need the real perceiver to mediate and bind them just as two sensual
   objects require this service. The fact that one is an object and another
   is a quality is insufficient asymmetry for contact to occur. Two sensual
   realities cannot make direct contact, because both consist entirely in
   their reality for some real entity. For lack of a better name, let's call this
   the *Foreign Glue Principle*, since the bond between a sensual object and
   its qualities must be outsourced from the sensual realm. But this term
   is somewhat ridiculous, and is meant only as a placeholder for some
   more euphonious phrase that I or another might invent.

We have seen that sensual realities cannot make direct contact but require a
real mediator, whether we speak of two sensual objects or of sensual objects
and sensual qualities. But this raises the specter of something even more bizarre at the level of *real* objects. For it seems to follow that real objects would
have equal difficulty making contact with their own real qualities, given that
both are real. After all, real entities are fundamentally incapable of direct,
untranslated contact with one another. But due to the principle of asymmetry, a real object would need a *sensual* object to mediate between the real object and its own qualities—as though only some *external* thing enabled a thing
to link with its own qualities, just as the perceiver performs this service for
sensual objects. Much else follows once asymmetry is accepted as a principle.
An entire book of philosophy could be constructed from such deductions.

But we must now return to the duality of intentionality as both one and
two. In 'On Vicarious Causation'[91] I showed how the relation between the
real me and the intentional tree can be treated as a unified real object insofar as it has an integral reality that no interpretation ever exhausts. This is
true, but irrelevant to the main point, and hence the article is misleading on
this question. I would no longer say that the intentional relation between me
and the sensual tree is what contains the two parts, and it is strange that I

---

91. Graham Harman, 'On Vicarious Causation', *Collapse*, vol. II, Oxford, 2007, pp.
181-6.

ever said so in the first place. For my interaction with the tree is a direct *contact*, not a vicarious *relation*, and can never become the latter. The relation at issue is that between the real me and the *real* tree. After all, my perception of a tree is not an object in its own right, but only becomes one through retrospective analysis in a psychological or phenomenological act. And thus it is not my *intentional* relationship with the tree that contains the two pieces of the relation (which is contact, not relation). Instead, this honor goes to the relation between the real me and the real tree, however this may occur. Due to Asymmetry such relation can never be direct, but only by means of some sensual mediator.

But what is truly of interest is that *any relation forms a new object*. Assuming that the real tree and I are able to enter into some sort of genuine relation, we form a new integral reality that is something over and above both of us, and also something deeper than any external view that might be taken on that reality. And that is what 'object' really means, despite the usual prejudice that objects must be physical entities or at least relatively durable. Instead of saying that the sensual tree has 'intentional inexistence' in human consciousness, we should say that both the sensual tree and the real me 'inexist' on the interior of the object composed of the real me and the real tree.[92] In this way, the contact between real and sensual objects always takes place on the interior of a more comprehensive real object. And if Dante and the tree combine to form a new object with a new interior, notice too that both Dante and the tree are themselves objects formed of component-objects of their own. Thus, we have a chain of objects descending without limit, each of them with a molten internal space where new encounters can arise.

Panpsychism

It will be noticed that the model just sketched does not require a human being or even an animal to be the real object confronting sensual caricatures on the interior of a larger real object. The model allows any real entity, from sand to bacteria to the Exxon Corporation, to have such an intentional life. If an object encounters anything then this cannot be another real object, due to the mutual withdrawal of objects that we have described. It can only be some sort of sensual reality. I also hold that the split between sensual objects and their swirling accidental qualities can be found even at the inanimate level. For the remaining option is that this split would be the special production of human or animal intelligence. Yet this is not the case, because

---

92. In the case under discussion this involves a real me and a sensual tree, but there might be a parallel relation and hence parallel object in which the real tree confronts a sensualized version of me. There may also be cases where the things encounter me without my encountering them at all: in Nietzschean terms, an abyss that stares back at me without my ever staring into it. For reasons of space I omit this additional issue here, though it is briefly discussed in Harman, 'On Vicarious Causation'.

the split within the phenomenal realm is something already found there, not something produced by us or anything else. Just as numerous gradual changes can occur in the human perception of a tree without the tree itself seeming to alter, inanimate objects must also confront a world quantized into chunks capable of accidental variation that can be sensed without being important. Though it may take a highly developed nervous system to gain an explicit sense of the difference, and thought it may take Edmund Husserl to turn it into a well-defined philosophy, this does not entail that the difference is not present even in the most primitive recesses of the world.

This step immediately raises the dreaded spectre of 'panpsychism', the doctrine that everything thinks. Before addressing this concern, let me first deny the criticism that my model is guilty of anthropomorphizing the world by retrojecting purely human mental traits into the non-human world. The illegitimacy of this critique is easy to show. When we consider those psychic traits that may be uniquely human or perhaps animal, we might list thinking, language, memory, emotion, visual experience, planning for the future, or the ability to dream. In no case have I ascribed such capacities to inanimate objects. What I have done, instead, is to reduce human cognition to its barest ontological feature—the translation or distortion of a withdrawn reality that it addresses. And it should be easy to see that even inanimate causal impact show exactly the same feature. Hence we can speak of a sparse, bedrock form of relationality that holds good for all real entities in the cosmos, and from which all the special plant, animal, and human mental features must develop as if from some primal kernel. To my guests I offer black coffee, without the milk and saccharine of human ornamental features. Rather than anthropomorphizing the inanimate realm, I am morphing the human realm into a variant of the inanimate.

As for the term 'panpsychism' itself, I have recently been warming to it. In *Guerrilla Metaphysics*[93] I was negative toward the term. My concern matched that of most critics—that panpsychists are quick to retroject specifically human cognitive traits into the primal form of relation that lies in the most primitive psyche. While accepting this critical worry, I merely denied that it applied to my own model, but feared that most out-of-the-closet panpsychists were guilty of it. But now I have lost most of this worry as well. For that danger now strikes me as greatly outweighed by the truly perilous risk of preserving the dominance of the human-world rift. As a result, my tactical sympathies have shifted toward the panpsychist insight that human cognition is just a more complicated variant of relations already found amidst atoms and stones. The rather different concern that some panpsychists might be too sloppy in exporting special human features to a more primitive level than they deserve now strikes me as a technical worry, easily

---

93. Graham Harman, *Guerrilla Metaphysics: Phenomenology and the Carpentry of Things*, Chicago, Open Court, 2005, pp. 83-4.

policed on a case-by-case basis. Moreover, it has always been the case that I feel greater *temperamental* sympathy for panpsychists than for their opponents. As long as we insist on a highly primitive form of relationality as the basis of panpsychism, I am more than willing to pay dues to the movement. For so-called inanimate objects do not encounter disembodied qualities alone, but encounter other objects. And it does not encounter them in their naked purity any more than humans do. Instead, it encounters a unified object swirling with accidents, which can change within certain limits without changing the overall object. This will occur differently for every sort of entity, and it may be possible to shed more light on each of these cosmic layers of psyche than is usually believed. I would even propose a new philosophical discipline called 'speculative psychology' dedicated to ferreting out the specific psychic reality of earthworms, dust, armies, chalk, and stone.

But there is one important restriction to my alliance with the panpsychists. It refers to the prefix 'pan-' (meaning 'all', in Greek), which seems to go too far. For in the first place, not all entities can have psychic life, but only *real objects*. For instance, it would seem pointless to claim that *qualities* have mental life, whether we mean a universal green or a particular instance of this hue. Nor are *intentional* objects capable of mental life of any sort, since they exist only as passive figments encountered by something real. Thus, the supposed 'pan' of panpsychism is already restricted to one of the four basic entities acknowledged by the object-oriented model. But the restriction goes even further than this, since even *real* objects need not have psyche. By this I do not mean that there is some arbitrary cutoff point between the vegetable and mineral realms where psyche ceases to exist. No—all real objects are *capable* of psyche, insofar as all are capable of relation; for real objects have psyche not insofar as they *exist*, but only insofar as they relate. And what I deny is that all entities are always in some sort of relation. It is only in Latour's model that an actor is not real if it does not transform, modify, perturb, or create something else. In the model presented in this book, an object is real by virtue of its autonomous reality, or its possession of genuine qualities. It certainly needs to have component pieces that relate in order for this to occur, but if it is a real object then it will not be identical with such pieces. It will be something 'over and above' those components. And it is quite possible that there are numerous objects that do unify component-objects in such a way that they have reality, but are simply never activated by further relations to achieve an outward effect. We would have to look carefully at specific cases to see whether certain objects deserve this designation— 'untapped markets', 'unknown masterpieces', 'the McCain 2008 victory coalition'. It may be hard to pinpoint individual cases that clearly meet the criteria for non-relating objects, but there is no reason other than prejudice to suppose that no such thing exists.

What we are speaking about are entities with numerous component relations below but none above. Several analogies will help make this more vivid. The first analogy is that all living organisms have a long unbroken chain of ancestors, though not all of them have offspring. The obvious flaw in this analogy is that creatures either reproduce or not, whereas objects can drift back and forth between being in relation or not being in relation at different times. A better analogy is to compare non-relating objects to drops of water at the turbulent surface of the ocean, with countless other drops of water beneath but only empty sky above. But the best metaphor for entities that are real despite entering into no outer relations is perhaps 'sleeping' or 'dormant' entities. To sleep is to withdraw to some extent from all outward associations. Although humans surely never achieve a perfect state of sleep, we can see that the act of human sleep has a metaphysical significance beyond its clear physiological one.

In passing, we must also reject those hasty traditional analogies that refer to death as a long and peaceful sleep. For in metaphysical terms, death and sleep could hardly be more different. If we put aside any considerations of afterlife (which is a merely physical death anyway) and identify death with cessation of existence, then death means that a specific unique object no longer exists in the world. Death shatters the bond between a creature's component objects to such an extreme that its essence is shattered, as opposed to internal survivable changes such as the death of component cells. By contrast, sleep preserves the creature perfectly intact—but free for now of relation, ready for another day. The highly refreshing character of good sleep has the metaphysical significance of freeing us from the various trivial encrustations of relation in which we become enmeshed. It restores us for a time to the inner sanctum of our essence, subtracting all surface ornament. Reversing the usual association of higher organisms with greater wakefulness, it might be the case that higher entities are higher precisely through their greater capacity to sleep: ascending from insects through dolphins, humans, sages, angels, or God. If someone took the gamble of an object-oriented theology, the omniscient God of monotheism might be abandoned in favor of something resembling Cthulhu, the sleeping monstrosity of H.P. Lovecraft:[94]

> *Ph'nglui mglw'nafh Cthulhu R'lyeh wgah'nagl fhtagn.*

In his house at R'lyeh dead Cthulhu waits dreaming.

But this would require that we take the word 'dead' as a metaphor for sleep. To sleep is not to be dead, as we have seen.

D. TIME, SPACE, ESSENCE, AND EIDOS

The model of the world proposed here retains Latour's flat ontology in one sense while rejecting it in another. All natural and artificial objects are

---

94. H.P. Lovecraft, *Tales*, New York, Library of America, 2005, pp. 179, 181.

equally objects, and in this respect the Dutch East India Company cannot be eliminated in favor of quarks and electrons or multi-dimensional strings. An object is real not by virtue of being tiny and fundamental, but by virtue of having an intrinsic reality that is not reducible to its subcomponents or exhausted by its functional effects on other things. Yet there is another sense in which certain objects (such as the aforementioned 'Monster X') are not real, but purely sensual. Such intentional objects have no interior of their own, but exist purely *on the interior* of some other object. This holds not only for wild fictional monsters, but even for the sensual versions of things we would be more inclined to call 'real'—for instance, an oak tree or carbon atom insofar as they are encountered. All of these objects are such hopeless caricatures of their genuine referents that they disappear if we fall asleep, stop paying attention, or die. This gives us a kind of dualism despite the leveling of all natural and artificial things: objects either have an interior (real objects) or exist on the interior of something else (sensual), but not both.

Yet this is not a 'two-world theory' of the usual kind, in which a supposed real world inhabits one plane of reality and human images another. If we speak of the real hammer that withdraws from all relation, this hammer is still the relational product of pieces that are still more deeply withdrawn; these hammer-pieces in turn are relational compounds of other withdrawn real objects, and thus presumably to infinity. The world is composed of countless layers of withdrawn real things, each with a molten core where one of its real pieces confronts the sensual image of another piece, thereby forming a bridge between one layer of reality and the next. It would be necessary to provide a full-blown 'nuclear metaphysics' detailing the mechanics of what unfolds in the molten core of objects, but the ambition of these closing pages lies elsewhere. For now the important thing is to remember that we must avoid both the naturalist and idealist philosophies, each of them representing one extreme of the modernism criticized by Latour. Everything is either eliminated in favor of tiny components, or this tiny little micro-realm is abolished in favor of an immanent sphere of accessibility to humans or to actors in general. What should be defended instead is a polarized ontology made up solely of objects and their interiors.

The model is of a quadruple character, like any of the historical ontologies structured around two basic oppositions. In the present case, the first opposition is the distinction between real and sensual objects, drawn from a specific reading of Heidegger. The second opposition can be found in a further strife, whether between real objects and their qualities (e.g., in Leibniz or Zubíri) or sensual objects and their qualities (e.g., in Husserl). When it comes to the 'vertical' relation between real objects and their accessibility to others, the real object is always something *more* than the translated distortion through which it is encountered. That is why the real object is said to withdraw from all access, in a manner to which Heidegger alerts us better than anyone else. But the situation is different with the 'horizontal' relations be-tween the two kinds of object and their respective qualities. Here, the object is always *less* than the features through which it is known. For on the sensual level the tree has a core or eidos that cares nothing for the specific angle or degree of shadow through which it is grasped at any moment. And on the real level, the object is not fully green or smooth or brittle, but unites these traits in a specific and limited fashion, so that any quality is an exaggera-tion of sorts even with respect to real objects. In fact, we might say that both the real and sensual objects are completely unified, with all of their qualities compressed together in bulk: 'thistreeness', for instance. This unified quality becomes pluralized only by leaking off elsewhere into a different quadrant of reality. This can easily be seen from the intentional realm, where a tree is a vaguely grasped unity that becomes plural only through its specific appear-ance (accidents) or through an intellectual grasp of its most crucial features (eidos). Otherwise, a sensual tree or wolf *per se* remain inarticulate blocks or vague feeling-things for the one who encounters them.

As described earlier, the four poles of the universe are real objects, real qualities, sensual objects, and sensual qualities. This turns out to be fairly close to what Heidegger meant by his 'fourfold'—though in its forgotten 1919 version rather than the explicit 1949 version, which removes the quadruple structure from individual things and remodels them as an interplay between thing and *world* at each level. And yet, there is something in Heidegger's *Geviert* even more interesting than the four poles: namely, the lines that con-nect each of the quadrants, which Heidegger views as a sort of 'mirroring' relation. I prefer to think of these lines as *tensions* between any two quad-rants, rather than mirror-like reflections. Now, any set of four terms normal-ly leads to six permutations: there are six ways to match up four heavyweight fighters, or four dogs when there are only two leashes for a walk in the park, or four of anything else. But *tension* in this model has a very specific mean-ing, and refers to the ambiguous interplay of objects and qualities, since ob-jects are both attached and not attached to their qualities. For this reason the four poles in the model are more like two men and two women in the eyes of the village matchmaker. (And in fact, Heidegger sometimes uses the term 'wedding' as a synonym for 'mirroring'.) Here there are only *four* pos-sible marriages, at least in traditional societies. They are as follows: sensual object/sensual quality, real object/sensual quality, real object/real quality, sensual object/real quality.

And here we have a fascinating model to play with, like the periodic ta-ble of elements, or the Bohr model of the atom, or the four forces of nature: strong, weak, gravity, electromagnetism. In object-oriented philosophy we have a different set of four fundamental forces, and to describe their me-chanics in detail will need a lengthier treatise. Among other things, this 'nu-clear metaphysics' would need to determine whether *every* tension between two of the terms is mediated by one of the other two terms. We have seen that this happens in the case of a real object (the perceiver) mediating between sensual objects and sensual qualities. I also surmised, without proving, that an intentional object may serve in turn to mediate between a real object and its real qualities. The latter question is new to me, and remains unclear. But even more unclear is whether the other two tensions require a mediator: those between real objects and sensual qualities, and sensual objects and real qualities. Such questions must be left to a different book. My goal for the moment is more limited, though just as interesting. Namely, I want to show that this fourfold model is not just a flashy gimmick relevant only to private musings on the post-Heideggerian landscape. Instead, it sheds immediate possible light on one particular set of important cosmic structures.

Most people of a philosophical bent probably recall private philosophical topics of early childhood. Among the most popular themes for early reflection are time and space, whose profound and paradoxical features are hard to forget at any age. This most often takes the form of wondering whether we can travel in time, whether time itself might reverse and flow backwards, whether space might have additional hidden dimensions, and so forth. In later years, one also learns that they can be treated mathematically as a combined four-dimensional space-time, as proposed (with great success) by Hermann Minkowski. My own childhood question was different. What I always wondered was why just these two terms—time and space—were always treated as *peerless* structures of the cosmos. It never seemed obvious to me that nothing else deserved to be mentioned in the same breath as these dual monarchs. For if both time and space could be derived from a more primitive root, then the result might be a slightly expanded peer group of basic dimensions of reality. In recent years, my greatest intellectual excitement came from realizing that the fourfold object-oriented model allows us to do precisely this. For it turns out that time and space can be described as two forms of the tensions between object and quality. Better yet, this directly entails that time and space are joined by two unexpected colleagues at the root of the world.

We have seen that in the sensual realm, unified intentional objects endure even when viewed from countless different angles and distances and in ever-shifting moods. The intentional/sensual object is not the mythical 'bundle of qualities', but a unit able to sustain an infinite number of specific 'adumbrations', to use Husserl's term. Let's call this *Tension Number 1*, between a sensual object and its equally sensual qualities. Now notice that this is exactly what we mean by the experience of *time*. Tension Number 1 is time. There would be no sense of time if we could not experience streets or plastic bottles under subtly shifting conditions from one instant to the next. The feeling that time is flowing along is in fact a sense of the swirling play of accidents on the surface of slightly deeper intentional objects. We can postpone any consideration of how this relates to other possible concepts of time found in history, the natural sciences, or elsewhere. To engage in such debate it will first be useful to establish a foothold in this object-oriented model of time as the tension between an intentional object and its shifting, accidental manifestations. Philosophy is not the handmaid of the natural sciences, and should not feel obliged to report to the Head of Laboratories for permission to speculate beyond the bounds of present-day scientific orthodoxy. On the contrary, the two greatest scientists of the last century (Einstein and Bohr) took especial inspiration from metaphysics, and would not advise us to limp along scraping up crumbs from their descendants. We should look for inspiration and points of interface from the sciences, but it is not the case that either they or we must dominate the conversation.

We have also seen that real objects withdraw behind whatever sensual qualities they manifest to view. Try as we might, we cannot adequately translate the subterranean execution of things into any discursive list of tangible properties; such attempts always fall somewhat short of the thing itself. My favorite passage in Plato comes on the first page of the *Meno*, when Socrates says: 'If I do not know what something is, how could I know what qualities it possesses?'.[95] This sentence contains the entire paradox of philosophy: though things can obviously be known only by way of listing their qualities, Socrates is right that the thing itself must be known quite apart from those qualities. We can call this *Tension Number 2*, between a real object and the sensual qualities through which it is accessible. Put differently, it is the tension between a real object and its *relations*, since relating to a thing only gives us a specific range of tangible qualities rather than the thing itself. Now notice that this is exactly what we mean by the concept of *space*. Leibniz is famous for claiming that space is not an absolute empty container, but only a site of relations between things. But although Leibniz remains my favorite philosopher throughout the ages, his suggestion can be no more than a half-truth. Space is not the site of relation, but of both relation *and* non-relation. We have a strong pre-philosophical grasp of this teaching: space is a medium in which I *can* fly to Bangkok or Dubai, but also one in which I am not currently in those places. Space is both nearness and distance. Things make contact along specific surfaces but are not exhausted by this contact, and recede partially into private depths. Tension Number 2 is space.

Let's turn now to the concealed underworld of real objects, or genuine tool-beings. The real object is a unified thing, but not an empty unity. It possesses a multitude of qualities that it unifies in a highly specific way, as indicated in the views of Leibniz and Zubíri cited earlier. We can give this the label of *Tension Number 3*, between real objects and their equally real qualities. The classical name for this duality is *essence*. Tension Number 3 is essence.

---

95. Plato, 'Meno', trans. G.M.A. Grube anf revised by John M. Cooper, Indianapolis, Hackett, 2002, p. 60.

Notice that this is the only one of the four that unfolds entirely at the real level without a sensual component. By analogy, we could call it a kind of time experienced by no one.

There remains a fourth and final case, an apparently odd scenario in which the sensual object exists in a duel with real qualities. According to the now familiar pattern, we must call it *Tension Number 4*. Once time, space, and essence came together in this model, it took some months even to realize that such a fourth situation is possible even though Husserl's phenomenology already points directly toward it. For if on the one hand a sensual tree is an enduring unit apart from its shifting crust of accidents, it is also a unit quite apart from the roster of its essential features unlocked by the phenomenologist. The tree has an *eidos*: Tension Number 4 is eidos, in Husserl's sense rather than Plato's. Whatever the eidetic features of the tree may be, they have no sensual component whatsoever. This gives us the unusual situation of a sensual object having real qualities, just as relationality gave us sensual qualities for a real object: the shared paradox of the two diagonal lines of our quadruple structure.

By viewing time and space as the byproducts of a tension between objects and qualities, we generated a schema with two missing terms. As is so often the case in intellectual history, this indicated additional places worth searching for new information. It came about that time, space, essence and eidos all belong on the same footing, rather than the first two standing alone as a pampered king and queen, in the usual manner. Let the model soak in your mind for a few weeks, and you may find as I do that it brings a new metaphysical weight to everyday experience. While common sense continues to view time and space as real neutral continuua in which events unfold, to rethink them as products of the inadequate relations objects have with their own properties carries powerful intuitive consequences for everyday life. Time no longer seems to roll forward uniformly with incidents transpiring on an empty three-dimensional grid. Instead, we feel secluded in a honeycomb of objects locked in a permanent of state radioactive decay—losing and absorbing qualities from the outside like neutrons.

But everyone knows that tensions can be paradoxically stable. The mere fact that there is tension between objects and their qualities may make various changes possible, but is not yet sufficient to trigger them. If a beachball or chunk of granite are in tension with their own qualities, there is no reason why this tension should not persist indefinitely, without seismic changes of any sort. Instead of tension, what we need is a rupture in the bond between the thing and its qualities so that these qualities can be exchanged from one object to the next, like photons in the Bohr atom. While this notion might give the impression of science fiction, it is in fact a highly classical motif. Witness for instance its key role in the *Disputationes Metaphysicae*[96] of Francisco Suárez, the very icon of rigorous Aristotelo-Scholastic philosophy. For Suárez substantial forms do not interact directly, but only by means of *accidents*, which become detached from their home substances and travel elsewhere in the world to wreak havoc. One example would be heat leaving the substance of fire and setting up shop in iron or water for a time. In other cases a much higher power takes control, as when the accidents of wine are transferred to the absent blood of Christ during the Eucharist, or semen is detached from the substantial form of the father and wielded directly by God to generate a new soul *ex nihilo* in the mother's womb. The question for a later date is whether each of the four tensions in the model each have their own way of breaking down under pressure and thereby triggering change.

It is unfortunate that there is not more time to discuss Suárez, one of the great masters of metaphysics, wrongly derided as an arid late-growth Scholastic. But I would say in passing that his theory matches up nicely with the four basic features of causation in object-oriented philosophy. First, substantial forms (or objects) do not make direct contact with each other. They can only be linked indirectly, or to use my new favorite English word—*vicariously*, by way of some vicar or deputy. Causation can only be *vicarious*. For him, the vicar is always an *accident* of some substance. Second, Suárez insists that causality stems not from the accidents of the patient, but from those of the agent,[97] which implies that causation comes not when accident meets accident, but only when accident meets substantial form. Causation must be *asymmetrical*. Third, although this asymmetry is present at all times, this is insufficient to make anything happen. Fire is always making some sort of contact with the accidents of neighboring entities, yet this causes something to happen only when it uses those accidents to find some way to affect the object underneath. This happens relatively rarely, and much contact leads nowhere. In short, causation does not instantly occur as soon as two objects are in proximity. One is shielded from the other by accidents that obstruct or hinder. But this means that causation is *buffered*. And fourth, we must generalize the actual *split* between a substantial form and its accidents that Suárez confines to restricted cases. He thinks this happens only when accidents travel physically far from their source, as with heat from the sun; or when they shift to a foreign medium, such as heat migrating from its homeland in fire into exile in water or iron; or when detached from their substance and controlled by God, as with Sacramental wine. In cases where this does not happen things will always remain in control of their own accidents, each quality staying forever in its own orbit. For this to happen, accidents must be transferred from one substance to another while still retaining the trace

96. Francisco Suárez, *On Efficient Causality: Metaphysical Disputations 17, 18, and 19*, trans. Alfred J. Freddoso, New Haven, Yale University Press, 1994.

97. Francisco Suárez, *On Efficient Causality: Metaphysical Disputations 17, 18, and 19*, p. 66.

of their previous substance. This is the event that I have often called allure. Causation is *alluring.*

All of this can be restated without reference to a historical figure, for those who might find the reference distracting. Causation is *vicarious* insofar as two real or two sensual objects cannot touch. *Asymmetry* merely addresses the other side of that story by pointing to a place where objects *do* in fact touch—a place where real objects meet sensual ones. Causation is *buffered* insofar as we meet an object that is not yet split from its own qualities, and *alluring* insofar as that split does eventually occur. If left untended these repeated quadruple structures might start to pile up like some New Age debris field. But handled skillfully, they cast repeated new light on novel various aspects of the quartet of basic structures at the core of the world.

E. MORE METAPHYSICS

The words 'ontology' and 'metaphysics' have no fixed meaning, but are redefined by every era (and sometimes every author) as conditions dictate. In the Heideggerian tradition in which I was raised, metaphysics serves as a pejorative term for philosophies that reduce reality to its explicit presence and ignore the being that withdraws behind all present-at-hand configurations. By contrast, I have chosen to embrace the word 'metaphysics'. This decision implies a passage beyond the prison of the human-world or Dasein-Sein correlate in favor of a reflection upon reality itself. But this seems to violate the strictures of Kant's Copernican Revolution, which celebrates this prison as the very condition of intellectual rigour. It also suggests a revival of speculation on some of the metaphysical themes that Kant held to be permanently suspended. This topic is of great relevance to a book on Latour. For despite Latour's vehement rejection of Kant (much stronger than my own mixed attitude) we still find less cosmological speculation in Latour than in his great ancestor Whitehead. Let's use 'ontology' to refer to a general theory of the principles governing all objects and their interactions. And let's use 'metaphysics' for a philosophical theory giving positive information about distinct objects of especial concern—such as the specific features of human consciousness as opposed to relation more generally, the finitude or infinity of the universe, the existence or non-existence of a soul and a necessary being, and other such topics. With these definitions in mind, actor-network theory would have to be called ontology rather than metaphysics—for its successful flattening of entities onto a single plane is largely free of any gambler's speculation on the metaphysical questions just enumerated.

Latour is not alone in this agnostic caution, which dominates the post-Kantian landscape. Even the fourfold model of interactions between objects defended in this book has not ventured far into truly metaphysical terrain. But if we want to reverse the impact of the Copernican earthquake, we must also attempt to retrieve at least some of the lost speculations that were evicted from philosophy in 1781 as hopelessly dogmatic. Moreover, despite my admiration for Whitehead's boldness in simply turning back the clock to the seventeenth century, we should not do this in the name of a philosophy that would be pre-Kantian. After all, it is true that *dogmatic* metaphysics was dealt a mortal blow by Kant's epochal philosophy. Yet it is mistaken to infer that realism *per se* is dogmatic while the transcendental standpoint is not. Dogmatism is a matter of holding that human knowledge can adequately *model* reality-in-itself, not that *there is* such a reality. Failure to observe this distinction leads to a widespread conflation of onto-theology with simple realism among Derrideans and many others. Indeed, we might even say that the critique of ontotheology requires realism, since otherwise whatever is present will be a perfectly adequate representative of reality, and we merely have a dogma built of surface-effects and plays of signification.

Immanuel Kant is justly recognized as one of the greatest philosophers ever to have lived. If asked by telephone survey to rank the giants of our craft, I would probably put him in third place, trailing only Aristotle/Plato or Plato/Aristotle according to my mood at the time. Kant's clarity and seriousness, along with his remarkable breadth of interests, have seldom been paralleled even among thinkers of the highest rank. Although I have opposed Kant for placing the human-world relation on a pedestal above all others, my defense of the withdrawal of objects beyond all access clearly has something in common with his things-in-themselves. Indeed, I have been accused of being both too Kantian and too anti-Kantian, at different times and in different respects. And as mentioned earlier in the case of the double assault on Latour ('social constructionist!'—'reactionary realist!') such ambivalent attacks are often a sign that critics are on the wrong track altogether. Though I normally portray Kant as someone to be overcome, this has been a purely tactical choice; my aim was to focus on the evils of human-centered 'philosophies of access' (for which Meillassoux's 'correlationism' can serve as a more euphonious substitute). But I could just as easily have chosen to defend Kant as the champion of the *Ding an sich* against rejections of any reality external to thought. A different history of philosophy is possible in which Kant might have been the ancestor of object-oriented philosophy. For whereas Fichte and his heirs focused on the amputation of things-in-themselves as useless vestigial stumps, post-Kantian thinkers in a parallel universe might criticize Kant instead for not *globalizing* the transcendence of things beyond the merely human sphere. That is to say, they might well have injected a phenomenal/noumenal distinction into inanimate relations themselves, just as I propose to do. This step would already be sufficient to yield an object-oriented philosophy. All it would have taken was an early heir with a more Leibnizian inclination than Fichte himself.

But if there is another aspect of Kant that I truly regret, it is his suspension of traditional metaphysics in the 'Transcendental Dialectic' of the *Critique of Pure Reason*. The three terms *paralogism, antinomy,* and *ideal* mark the impossibility of human knowledge about classical metaphysical problems, even if Kant rightly notes that humans cannot stop asking these questions whose answers are forever withheld. Though the pillar of Kant's Copernican Revolution is the primacy of the human/world relation above all others, the suspension of traditional metaphysical questions as 'dogmatic' is one of its chief consequences. But this gives cause for suspicion. Even more than other fields of knowledge, philosophy seems to be periodic in character. If certain doctrines are forever abandoned as primitive artifacts (such as the now quaint notion that each of the planetary spheres is a neo-Platonic emanation) it also happens that abandoned doctrines return from the dead. Any new theory is likely to sell its predecessors short, and for this reason we should always pay special attention to whatever philosophical doctrines *are not* currently in fashion, or even those that now seem unthinkable, since these may be the philosopher's greatest chamber of forgotten treasures. Realism is greatly out of fashion in continental circles in our time, and for this very reason it can be expected to have many fresh lessons to teach us. The same is true of speculation on weighty metaphysical issues. Kant apparently decimates these themes in his Transcendental Dialectic. But it does not seem likely to me that, a millennium from now, historians of philosophy will be saying the following: 'After Kant, no serious philosophical attention was ever paid again to whether time and space are finite or infinite. Kant settled the issue permanently'. For his suspension of traditional metaphysical questions derives from his placing the human-world correlate at the center of philosophy, and it is improbable that this surprisingly feeble doctrine will maintain its suffocating dominance in the centuries to come. Far more likely is that Kant put an end to a certain *manner* of dealing with metaphysical problems, while the problems themselves remain, preparing even now to throw a counterpunch.

The difference between Kant and the object-oriented model can already be seen in the following passages from the *Prolegomena to Any Future Metaphysics*: 'For the specific nature of our understanding consists in thinking everything discursively, i.e., by concepts, and so by mere predicates [...]'.[98] And furthermore, given that 'all illusion consists in holding the subjective ground of our judgments to be objective [...,]' we must avoid 'the aberrations into which reason falls when it mistakes its destination, and transcendently refers to the object in itself that which only concerns reason's own subject and its guidance in all immanent use'.[99] On these points he is the heir of Hume, in two distinct senses that this book has already opposed. For in the

---

98. Immanuel Kant, *Prolegomena to Any Future Metaphysics*, trans. Paul Carus and revised by James W. Ellington, Indianapolis, Hackett, 1977, p. 70.

99. Kant, *Prolegomena to Any Future Metaphysics*, p. 65.

latter passage, Kant restricts us to speaking about the *immanent* realm of the understanding. And in the former, he holds that the understanding encounters nothing but bundles of *predicates*. Kant's term 'discursive' performs both labors at once, leaving us stranded in a kingdom of palpable qualities for which underlying objects are expelled from consideration. These are generally viewed as scrupulously minimalist claims, tethered admirably to the evidence of experience. By contrast, I hold that they are unjustifiably 'radical' claims about the nature of reality, reducing the world to the single *radix* of human access. Philosophy *can* go beyond distinct predicates and beyond immanence. In this book I have employed Husserl to reject the bundle of predicates and Heidegger to reject the quarantine amidst immanence. If my arguments on those points is persuasive, then Kant's suspension of traditional metaphysical problems immediately fails. For it is not the case that 'the object is only an idea invented for the purpose of bringing the cognition of the understanding as near as possible to the completeness indicated by that idea'.[100] Here I will not repeat a detailed defense of the role of objects in philosophy, but will only say briefly why I think Kant's restrictions are invalid.

The ideal, or theological idea, is best left for another occasion. The paralogism, or psychological idea, aims to show that the permanence of substance is unknowable even in the case of one's inner self. But the truly interesting question is not so much permanence as the sheer *endurance* of a substance through various shifting accidents, though Kant rejects even this. Of even more colorful interest are the four antinomies, or cosmological ideas. Latour's theory of black boxes already led us to suspect that the Second Antinomy was wrong.

The reason for Kant's rejection of dogmatic metaphysics can be seen most clearly in his reason for refusing traditional substance. 'People have long since observed that in all substances the subject proper, that which remains after all the accidents (as predicates) are abstracted, hence the substantial itself, remains unknown, and various complaints have been made concerning these limits to our insight'.[101] Kant does not join their lament, of course, but sees these limits as an insurmountable feature of reality: since we can only think 'discursively', we cannot make any sense of a subject that would exist in itself without predicates. He continues:

> Pure reason requires us to seek for every predicate of a thing its own subject, and for this subject, which is itself necessarily nothing but a predicate, its subject, and so on indefinitely (or as far as we can reach). But hence it follows that we must not hold anything at which we can arrive to be an ultimate subject, and that substance itself can never be thought by our understanding, however deep we may penetrate, even if all nature were unveiled to us.[102]

100. Kant, *Prolegomena to Any Future Metaphysics*, p. 68.
101. Kant, *Prolegomena to Any Future Metaphysics*, p. 69.
102. Kant, *Prolegomena to Any Future Metaphysics*, pp. 69-70.

But notice that Kant mixes two distinct claims here. First, he states that substance would have to be something different from the predicates we ascribe to it, and this he regards as impossible. Second, he asserts that substance would have to be something *ultimate*. And this he also rejects as impossible: insofar as any layer of things that we reach can only be described via predicates, we never reach a truly substantial layer.

Both claims are refused by the object-oriented model. In the first case, phenomenology exposes as false the view that objects of sense are just a bundle of distinct predicates. To observe a tree is not to piece together a set of independent free-floating features; rather, such features radiate from the tree as a whole. The green and leafiness of the tree are impregnated with the style of the tree, which they would lose if encountered elsewhere. On this particular point it is Husserl who is original, while Kant merely follows the dictates of Hume—whose theory of arbitrarily bundled qualia corresponds to no experience at all. In this sense Husserl was more of an empiricist than Hume ever was. And in the second case, there is no reason to restrict substances to *ultimates* in the sense demanded by Kant and many philosophers of a naturalist bent. The fact that hammers and even neutrons are not ultimate particles of physics does not entail that they are not objects. Heidegger shows that the hammer has a reality independent from current uses or perceptions of it, and this is enough to make it an object. The fact that hammers (like neutrons) need to be made of pieces, and hence are not ultimate, does not strip those pieces of their emergent autonomy. This can be seen from the various criteria for emergence cited earlier from DeLanda. Among other considerations, the hammer has hammer-qualities not found in its pieces. Moreover, these hammer-qualities are not just functional effects on the environment, since the hammer has other untapped hammer-qualities than those currently registered by neighboring things. In addition, within certain limits, the hammer can withstand numerous changes in its pieces without losing its individual hammerness.

Substances need only be autonomous, not ultimate. And though Kant denies that we can think anything in isolation from predicates, this is a symptom of his correlationist dogma, which is every bit as dogmatic as the dogmatic metaphysics he rejects. When the hammer surprises us with its breakdown, the exact character of this surprise can admittedly be described by various predicates. But note that 'surprise' is only the phenomenal *result* of the previously concealed hammer. The veiled, underground hammer cannot be identified with the surprises it generates, since these merely allude to its existence. (Allusion and allure are legitimate forms of knowledge, but irreducible to specific predicates.) If we now focus explicitly on the broken hammer rather than on our previous project of building a house, we do not thereby capture the object that disrupted our previous labors. Only the dogma that all knowledge is discursive knowledge via predicates could support the belief that subterranean things are reducible to the tangible disruptions they cause in the phenomenal world. For it is perfectly easy to deduce the existence of real objects from the inadequacy of the current expression of things. And as for *sensual* objects, their existence need not even be deduced. These can be experienced directly and immediately, provided one is willing to jettison Hume's thoroughly unempirical dogma of bundles of qualities.

But not only do objects not *need* to be ultimates—they *cannot* be ultimates, as mentioned during the discussion of Latour's black boxes. This leads us into direct conflict with Kant's Second Antinomy: 'Thesis: Everything in the world is constructed out of the simple. Antithesis: There is nothing simple, but everything is composite'.[103] Given Kant's prejudice that there is no knowledge other than the discursive kind in which things are exhausted by their accessible predicates, it does indeed follow that parts and wholes 'are mere representations; and the parts exist merely in their representation, consequently in the division [...] and the division reaches only so far as such experience reaches'.[104] A thing has parts or fails to have them only in experience, and thus to assert either side of the antinomy is to make a claim about things-in-themselves using evidence that belongs only to appearance. But this fails for the same reason that Kant's rejection of substance failed. For what it really means for something to have parts is that its components are not exhausted by their relations; the parts have some sort of autonomous life. When I use a hammer, this is a relation made up of me and the hammer. By reducing the hammer to its discursive appearance through predicates, Kant denies it autonomous life outside its relation to me. Ironically, this means that he takes sides in an Antinomy that was meant as evidence of his neutrality on such questions. Namely, Kant effectively claims that experience has no parts. The experience of the hammer is said to be purely immanent, and hence nothing can be said about the various components that exist outside the relation. This is the ontological meaning of both skepticism and empiricism, which for our purposes are barely distinguishable. Whereas for occasionalism the world is populated with autonomous substances that cannot interact without God's assistance, for empiricism the world is filled with interactions that cannot establish the autonomy of their pieces. I have already remarked that this is a deeper division than Kant's more famous epistemological rift between rationalism and empiricism. Rather than mediating between two traditions as he claims, Kant takes continental philosophy on a deliberate swerve into the skeptical lane, where it remains even now.

To be more specific, the irony is this: Kant *does* claim the existence of an ultimate, though it is human experience rather than a physical microparticle that serves as his ultimate layer. It is upside-down reductionism, or

---

103. Kant, *Prolegomena to Any Future Metaphysics*, p. 74.
104. Kant, *Prolegomena to Any Future Metaphysics*, p. 77.

naturalism in reverse; all reality takes its measure from the conditions of human experience. It is little use claiming that Kant or Hume concedes that there *might* be something outside the human-world correlate, since their skepticism amounts to a dogmatic claim that direct access is the stuff of all the reality we encounter. To say that 'there *might* be something outside the correlate; I never denied it' is no more philosophically effective than if I say there *might* be unicorns or forty extra spatial dimensions. Unless things-in-themselves play some genuine role in a philosophy, they may as well not be there. For the same reason, the view called 'agnosticism' is really no different from atheism, and merely takes a cynical distance from its own claims. If a sociologist focuses only on human societies, this comes as little surprise. But if a philosopher remains adrift in measurements of human access to the world, it turns this access into the root of the universe even when concessions are made that something may lie beyond it.

But objects cannot be simple (Second Antinomy) for the same reason that we should not expect them to be ultimate (Paralogism). Instead there are black boxes, and black boxes can always be opened. Let's concede Kant's irrefutable point that to encounter something always means to encounter it; we cannot encounter the unencountered. But my treatment of Heidegger's tool-analysis showed that to encounter a black box means to relate to it, and that relation is always a kind of distortion or caricature of its object. This relation has two terms: the black box and me. We should both be viewed as pieces of the relation, neither of us exhausted by this encounter with the other. Hence any black box we encounter can be opened *by definition*, since we have artificially closed it merely by dealing with it. Whatever value 'point particles' may have for mathematical physics, they are of no use to metaphysics. For even a point particle has various properties, and the 'bundle of properties' is just as incoherent a model for real objects as 'bundle of predicates' is for sensual ones. Behind any registration of effects on the environment, the thing and its environment exist in autonomy from one another, as pieces of the total relation. The descent of black boxes into the depths must be infinite.

In short, the critique of presence-at-hand is enough to set us free from the Second Antinomy. Human experience is the dogmatic simple and ultimate of Kant's ontology, and once experience is undercut by the objects that recede from its grasp, the possibility of any relational whole without parts immediately disappears. This is implicit, but *only* implicit, in both Latour and Heidegger. For Latour tends to treat it simply as a maxim of method: black boxes can be opened *as far as we wish*. He never asserts that the process is actually infinite, though I insist that it must be. Heidegger by contrast does make withdrawal into an absolute principle of philosophy, yet unlike Latour he remains fettered to a two-storey model of the world, with being on the ground floor and Dasein's awareness on the top floor. Thus, infinite descent into tinier boxes can have no place in his theory. Whereas Kant essentially claims the existence of a partless human experience, this is rendered impossible by Heidegger's hammer. In this way the Second Antinomy is outflanked as soon as the correlationist dogma is outflanked. I will leave the other three Antinomies for a different occasion.

The subtitle of this book is *Bruno Latour and Metaphysics*. These two topics have never been publicly linked to the extent attempted here. Let's close this book with a quick reminder of what Latour achieves for metaphysics—a brisk shot of espresso at the end of a multi-course meal. First, Latour replaces traditional substance with *actors*. This has the advantage of dumping the superstition that substances must be both natural and permanent. Latour's actors include artificial plutonium no less than natural argon, and transient festivals no less than immortal souls. This theory also has the disadvantage (in my opinion) of relationizing objects in a manner that leaves them with nothing apart from their effects on others. Second, despite turning actors into bundles of relations, Latour is admirably aware of how difficult it is for those relations to occur at all. Like the occasionalists before him, Latour sees entities as basically cut off in their current relations, unable to enter new ones without a third actor mediating on their behalf. Instead of appealing on high to an almighty God whose workings lie beyond philosophical scrutiny, Latour gives us the first *secular occasionalism* ever known. Though I have made several criticisms of his position in the latter half of this book, they are made solely for the purpose of modification or debugging: in the name of Secular Occasionalism 2.0. Thanks to Latour, an object-oriented philosophy has become possible.

bibliography

Bibliography

WORKS BY BRUNO LATOUR

For a complete list of abbreviations used in this text see page vii.

Aramis or the Love of Technology, trans. Catherine Porter, Cambridge, Harvard University Press, 1996.

La Fabrique du Droit. Une ethnographie du Conseil d'Etat, Paris, Découverte, 2002.

Laboratory Life. The Construction of Scientific Facts, with Steve Woolgar, Princeton, Princeton University Press, 1986.

'Can We Get Our Materialism Back, Please?', *Isis*, no. 98, 2007, pp. 138-142.

'From Realpolitik to Dingpolitik, or How to Make Things Public', in Bruno Latour and Peter Weibel (eds.), *Making Things Public: Atmospheres of Democracy*, Cambridge, MIT Press, 2005.

We Have Never Been Modern, trans. Catherine Porter, Cambridge, Harvard University Press, 1993.

Personal Communication, Electronic mail to Graham Harman of 11 November, 2005.

Personal Communication, Electronic mail to Graham Harman of 14 January, 2006.

'On the Partial Existence of Existing and Nonexisting Objects', in Lorraine Daston (ed.), *Biographies of Scientific Objects*, Chicago, University of Chicago Press, 2006.

Pandora's Hope: Essays on the Reality of Science Studies, Cambridge, Harvard University Press, 1999.

The Pasteurization of France, trans. Alan Sheridan and John Law, Cambridge, Harvard University Press, 1988.

Politics of Nature: How to Bring the Sciences Into Democracy, trans. Catherine Porter, Cambridge, Harvard University Press, 2004.

Reassembling the Social: An Introduction to Actor-Network-Theory, Oxford, Oxford University Press, 2005.

Science in Action. How to Follow Scientists and Engineers Through Society, Cambridge, Harvard University Press, 1987.

Paris ville invisible, Paris, Editions la Découverte, 1998. Available in English at http://www.bruno-latour.fr/virtual/index.html#

OTHER WORKS

Aristotle, *Metaphysics*, trans. Joe Sachs, Santa Fe, Green Lion Pres, 1999.

Badiou, Alain, *Being and Event*, trans. Oliver Feltham, London, Continuum, 2006.

Bhaskar, Roy, *A Realist Theory of Science*, London, Continuum, 2006.

Bloor, David, 'Anti-Latour', *Studies in the History of the Philosophy of Science*, vol. 30, no. 1, March 1999, pp. 81-112.

Brassier, Ray, *Nihil Unbound: Enlightenment and Extinction*, London Palgrave, 2007.

Brassier, Ray, Personal Communiction, electronic mail to Graham Harman of 12 August, 2008.

Brassier, Ray, Iain Grant, Graham Harman, and Quentin Meillassoux, 'Speculative Realism', *Collapse*, vol. III , Falmouth, Urbanomic, 2007.

Braver, Lee, *A Thing of This World: A History of Continental Anti-Realism*, Evanston, Northwestern University Press, 2007.

Brentano, Franz, *Psychology from an Empirical Standpoint*, trans. A. Rancurello, D. Terrell, and L. McAlister, New York, Routledge, 1995.

Brentano, Franz, *Theory of Categories*, trans. Roderick M. Chisholm and Norbert Guterman, The Hague, Martinus Nijhoff, 1981.

Bruno, Giordano, *Cause, Principle, and Unity and Essays on Magic*, trans. Robert de Lucca, Cambridge, Cambridge University Press, 1998.

Chalmers, David, *The Conscious Mind*, Oxford, Oxford University Press, 1996.

DeLanda, Manuel, *Intensive Science and Virtual Philosophy*, London, Continuum, 2002.

DeLanda, Manuel, *A New Philosophy of Society: Assemblage Theory and Social Complexity*, London, Continuum, 2006.

Derrida, Jacques, 'White Mythology', in *Margins of Philosophy*, trans. Alan Bass, Chicago, University of Chicago Press, 1985.

Edrélyi, Peter, 'Remembering the Harman Review', blog post at http://www.anthem-group.net/tag/the-harman-review/

Erdélyi, Peter, 'ANT, the Fourfold, and the Thing in Common: A Multi-Case Study of Organising, Strategising and ICTs ine-Tailing SMEs in the UK', unpublished thesis proposal, Department of Management, London School of Economics.

Fodor, Jerry 'Water's Water Everywhere', *London Review of Books*, 21 October, 2004.

Harman, Graham, *Tool-Being: Heidegger and the Metaphysics of Objects*, Chicago, Open Court, 2002.

Harman, Graham, *Guerrilla Metaphysics: Phenomenology and the Carpentry of Things*, Chicago, Open Court, 2005.

Harman, Graham, *Heidegger Explained: From Phenomenon to Thing*, Chicago, Open Court, 2007.

Harman, Graham, 'On Vicarious Causation', *Collapse*, vol. II, Oxford, 2007.

Harman, Graham, 'Quentin Meillassoux: A New French Philosopher', *Philosophy Today*, vol. 51, no.1, Spring 2007, pp. 104-117.

Heidegger, Martin, *Being and Time*, trans. John Macquarrie and Edward Robinson, New York, Harper and Row, 1962.

Heidegger, Martin, 'Einblick in das was ist', in *Bremer und Freiburger Vorträge*, Frankfurt, Vittorio Klostermann, 1994.

Höfler, Alois and Alexius Meinong, *Logic*, Vienna, 1890.

Hume, David, *An Enquiry Concerning Human Understanding*, Indianapolis, Hackett, 1993.

Hume, David, *A Treatise of Human Nature*, Oxford, Oxford University Press, 1978.

Husserl, Edmund, *Ideas: General Introduction to Pure Phenomenology*, trans. W.R.B. Gibson, London, Allen and Unwin, 1931.

Husserl, Edmund, 'Intentional Objects', in *Early Writings in the Philosophy of Logic and Mathematics*, trans. Dallas Willard, Dordrecht, Kluwer, 1993.

Husserl, Edmund, *Logical Investigations*, 2 Vols., trans. J.N. Findlay, London, Routledge and Kegan Paul, 1970.

Ingarden, Roman, 'Dzialalnosc naukowa Twardowskiego', in *Kazimierz Twardowski: Nauczyciel—Uczony—Obywatel*, Lvov, 1938.

Kant, Immanuel, *Critique of Pure Reason*, trans. Norman Kemp Smith, London, Palgrave Macmillan, 2003.

Kant, Immanuel, *Prolegomena to Any Future Metaphysics*, trans. Paul Carus and revised by James W. Ellington, Indianapolis, Hackett, 1977.

Kripke, Saul, *Naming and Necessity*, Cambridge, Harvard University Press, 1996.

Kuhn, Thomas, *The Structure of Scientific Revolutions*, Chicago, University of Chicago Press, 1970.

Leibniz, G. W., 'Monadology', in *Philosophical Essays*, trans. Roger Ariew and Daniel Garber, Indianapolis, Hackett, 1989.

Leibniz, G. W. and Samuel Clarke, *Correspondence*, Indianapolis, Hackett, 2000.

Levinas, Emmanuel, *Existence and Existents*, trans. Alphonso Lingis, The Hague, Martinus Nijhoff, 1988.

Lovecraft, H.P., *Tales*, New York, Library of America, 2005.

McLuhan, Marshall and Eric, *Laws of Media: The New Science*, Toronto, University of Toronto Press, 1988.

Meillassoux, Quentin, *Après la finitude*, Paris, Editions du Seuil, 2006.

Meillassoux, Quentin, *After Finitude*, trans. Ray Brassier, London, Continuum, 2008.

Meillassoux, Quentin, Personal Communication, electronic mail to Graham Harman of 21 February, 2007. trans. Graham Harman.

Meillassoux, Quentin, Personal Communication, electronic mail to Graham Harman 16 September, 2007. trans. Graham Harman.

Merleau-Ponty, Maurice, *Phenomenology of Perception*, trans. Christopher Smith, London, Routledge, 2002.

Nancy, Jean-Luc, 'Corpus', trans. Claudette Sartiliot, in *The Birth to Presence*, trans. B. Holmes et. al., Stanford, Stanford University Press, 1993.

Ortega y Gasset, José, 'An Essay in Esthetics By Way of a Preface', in *Phenomenology and Art*, trans. Philip Silver, New York, W. W. Norton, 1975.

Plato, 'Gorgias', trans. W. D. Woodhead, in *The Collected Dialogues of Plato*, Edith Hamilton and Huntington Cairns (eds.), Princeton, Princeton University Press, 1961.

Plato, 'Meno', trans. G. M. A. Grube and revised by John M. Cooper, Indianapolis, Hackett, 2002.

Rhodes, Richard, *The Making of the Atomic Bomb*, New York, Touchstone, 1986.

Rockwell, W. Teed, *Neither Brain Nor Ghost: A Nondualist Alternative to the Mind-Brain Identity Theory*, Cambridge, MIT Press, 2005.

Rorty, Richard, *Truth and Progress: Philosophical Papers, Volume 3*, Cambridge, Cambridge University Press, 1998.

Russell, Bertrand, *The Analysis of Matter*, London, Kegan Paul, 1927.

Schnelle, T., *Ludwik Fleck—Leben und Denken*, Freiburg i.B., Hochschulverlag, 1982.

Smith, Barry, *Austrian Philosophy: The Legacy of Franz Brentano*, Chicago, Open Court, 1994.

Sokal, Alan and Jean-Luc Bricmont, *Fashionable Nonsense*, New York, Picador, 1998.

Spinoza, Baruch, *Ethics*, trans. Samuel Shirley, Indianapolis, Hackett, 1992.

Stengers, Isabelle, *Cosmopolitics*, 2 vols., Paris, Editions La Découverte, 1997.

Stove, David, *The Plato Cult and Other Philosophical Follies*, Oxford, Blackwell, 1991.

Strauss, Leo, *What is Political Philosophy?*, Chicago, University of Chicago Press, 1988.

Strawson, Galen 'Realistic Monism', *Journal of Consciousness Studies*, vol. 13, nos. 10-11, 2006, pp. 3-31.

Suárez, Francisco, *On Efficient Causality: Metaphysical Disputations 17, 18, and 19*, trans. Alfred J. Freddoso, New Haven, Yale University Press, 1994.

Toscano, Alberto, *The Theatre of Production*, London, Palgrave, 2006.

Twardowski, Kasimir, *On the Content and Object of Presentations*, trans. by Reinhard Grossmann, The Hague, Martinus Nijhoff, 1977.

Watson, James, *The Double Helix*, New York, Norton, 1983.

Whitehead, Alfred North, *Process and Reality*, New York, Free Press, 1978.

Žižek, Slavoj and Glyn Daly, *Conversations with Žižek*, Cambridge, Polity, 2003.

Zubíri, Xavier, *On Essence*, trans. A. Robert Caponigri, Washington, Catholic University of America Press, 1980.

Index

LaVergne, TN USA
01 September 2010
195455LV00004B/183/P